OBJECTIVE	
DOMAIN 5.0 DESIGN SELECTION	
5.1 Given a scenario, predict the performance of a given frequency and power (active/passive) as it relates to: read distance, write distance, tag response time, storage capacity	5
5.2 Summarize how hardware selection affects performance (may use scenarios)	5
5.2.1 Antenna type	
5.2.2 Equipment mounting and protection	
5.2.3 Cable length/loss	
5.2.4 Interference considerations	
5.2.5 Tag type (e.g., active, passive, frequency)	
DOMAIN 6.0 INSTALLATION	
6.1 Given a scenario, describe hardware installation using industry standard practices	7
6.1.1 Identify grounding considerations (e.g., lightning, ground loops, ESD)	
6.1.2 Test installed equipment and connections (pre-install and post-install)	
6.2 Given a scenario, interpret a site diagram created by an RFID architect describing interrogation zone locations, cable drops, device- mounting locations	7
DOMAIN 7.0 SITE ANALYSIS (I.E., BEFORE, DURING AND AFTER INSTALLATION)	
7.1 Given a scenario, demonstrate how to read blueprints (e.g., whole infrastructure)	3
7.2 Determine sources of interference	3
7.2.1 Using analysis equipment such as a spectrum analyzer, determine if there is any ambient noise in the frequency range that may conflict with the RFID system to be installed	
7.3 Given a scenario, analyze environmental conditions end-to-end	3
DOMAIN 8.0 RF PHYSICS	
8.1 Identify RF propagation/communication techniques	1
8.2 Describe antenna field performance/characteristics as it relates to reflective and absorptive materials (may use scenarios)	1
8.3 Given a scenario, calculate radiated power output from an antenna based on antenna gains, cable type, cable length, interrogator transmit power (include formulas in scenario)	1

Sybex®
An Imprint of
WILEY

OBJECTIVE	CHAPTER
2.2 Identify reasons for tag failure	8
2.2.1 Failed tag management	
2.2.2 ESD issues	
2.3 Given a scenario, contrast actual tag data to expected tag data	8
DOMAIN 3.0 STANDARDS AND REGULATIONS	
3.1 Given a scenario, map user requirements to standards	9
3.1.1 Regulations, standards that impact the design of a particular RFID solution	
3.2 Identify the differences between air interface protocols and tag data formats	9
3.3 Recognize regulatory requirements globally and by region (keep at high level, not specific requirements—may use scenarios)	9
3.4 Recognize safety regulations/issues regarding human exposure	9
DOMAIN 4.0 TAG KNOWLEDGE	
4.1 Classify tag types	4
4.1.1 Select the RFID tag best suited for a specific use case;	
4.1.1.1 Pros and cons of tag types;	
4.1.1.2 Tag performance;	
4.1.1.2.1 Tag antenna to region/frequency	
4.1.2 Identify inductively coupled tags vs. back-scatter	
4.1.3 Identify the differences between active and passive	
4.2 Given a scenario, select the optimal locations for an RFID tag to be placed on an item	4
4.2.1 Evaluate media and adhesive selection for tags	
4.2.2 Tag orientation and location; 4.2.2.1 Tag stacking (shadowing)	
4.2.3 Package contents	
4.2.4 Packaging; 4.2.4.1 Items; 4.2.4.2 Tags; 4.2.4.3 Labels; 4.2.4.4 Inserts	
4.2.5 Liquids	
4.2.6 Metal	
4.2.7 Polarization	

NOTE Exam objectives are subject to change at any time without prior notice and at Microsoft's sole discretion. Please visit Microsoft's Training & Certification website (`www.microsoft.com/trainingandservices`) for the most current listing of exam objectives.

Sybex® An Imprint of WILEY

CompTIA RFID+ Study Guide

RFID+ Exam Objectives

OBJECTIVE	CHAPTER
DOMAIN 1.0 INTERROGATION ZONE BASICS	
1.1 Describe interrogator functionality	2
1.1.1 I/O capability	
1.1.2 Hand-held interrogators	
1.1.3 Vehicle- mount interrogator	
1.1.4 LAN/Serial communications	
1.1.5 Firmware upgrades	
1.1.6 Software operation (GUIs)	
1.2 Describe configuration of interrogation zones	2
1.2.1 Explain interrogator- to- interrogator interference	
1.2.2 Optimization	
1.2.3 System performance and tuning	
1.2.4 Travel speed and direction	
1.2.5 Bi-static / mono-static antennas	
1.3 Define anticollision protocols (e.g., number of tags in the field/response time)	2
1.4 Given a scenario, solve dense interrogator environment issues (domestic /international)	2
1.4.1 Understand how a dense interrogator installation is going to affect network traffic	
1.4.2 Installation of multiple interrogators, (e.g., dock doors, synchronization of multiple interrogators, antenna footprints)	
DOMAIN 2.0 TESTING AND TROUBLESHOOTING	
2.1 Given a scenario, troubleshoot RF interrogation zones (e.g., root-cause analysis)	8
2.1.1 Analyze less- than- required read rate; 2.1.1.1 Identify improperly tagged items	
2.1.2 Diagnose hardware; 2.1.2.1 Recognize need for firmware upgrades	
2.1.3 Equipment replacement procedures (e.g., antenna, cable, interrogator)	

Sybex®
An Imprint of
WILEY

OBJECTIVE	CHAPTER
DOMAIN 9.0 RFID PERIPHERALS	
9.1 Describe the installation and configuration of an RFID printer (may use scenarios)	6
9.2 Describe ancillary devices/concepts	6
9.2.1 RFID printer encoder	
9.2.2 Automated label applicator	
9.2.3 Feedback systems (e.g., lights, horns)	
9.2.4 RTLS	

NOTE Exam objectives are subject to change at any time without prior notice and at Microsoft's sole discretion. Please visit Microsoft's Training & Certification website (`www.microsoft.com/trainingandservices`) for the most current listing of exam objectives.

Sybex®
An Imprint of
WILEY

CompTIA RFID+™ Study Guide

CompTIA
RFID+™
Study Guide

Patrick J. Sweeney II

Wiley Publishing, Inc.

Acquisitions Editor: Jeff Kellum
Development Editor: Toni Zuccarini Ackley
Contributor: Eva Zeisel
Technical Editor: Bruce Wilkinson
Production Editor: Sarah Groff-Palermo
Copy Editor: Sharon Wilkey
Production Manager: Tim Tate
Vice President and Executive Group Publisher: Richard Swadley
Vice President and Executive Publisher: Joseph B. Wikert
Vice President and Publisher: Neil Edde
Media Development Supervisor: Laura Atkinson
Media Development Specialist: Kate Jenkins
Media Quality Assurance: Steve Kudirka
Book Designer: Judy Fung
Compositor: Jeffrey Wilson, Happenstance Type-O-Rama
Proofreader: Rachel Gunn
Indexer: Ted Laux
Anniversary Logo Design: Richard Pacifico
Cover Designer: Ryan Sneed

Published simultaneously in Canada

ISBN-13: 978-0-470-04232-8
ISBN-10: 0-470-04232-X

Library of Congress Cataloging-in-Publication Data is available from the publisher.

10 9 8 7 6 5 4 3 2 1

Sybex®
An Imprint of
WILEY

To Our Valued Readers:

Thank you for looking to Sybex for your RFID+ exam prep needs. We at Sybex are proud of our reputation for providing certification candidates with the practical knowledge and skills needed to succeed in the highly competitive IT marketplace. Certification candidates have come to rely on Sybex for accurate and accessible instruction on today's crucial technologies and business skills.

Just as CompTIA is committed to establishing measurable standards for certifying RFID professionals by means of the RFID+ certification, Sybex is committed to providing those individuals with the knowledge needed to meet those standards.

The authors and editors have worked hard to ensure that this edition of the *CompTIA RFID+ Study Guide* you hold in your hands is comprehensive, in-depth, and pedagogically sound. We're confident that this book will exceed the demanding standards of the certification marketplace and help you, the RFID certification candidate, succeed in your endeavors. As always, your feedback is important to us. If you believe you've identified an error in the book, please send a detailed e-mail to support@wiley.com. And if you have general comments or suggestions, feel free to drop me a line directly at nedde@wiley.com. At Sybex we're continually striving to meet the needs of individuals preparing for certification exams.

Good luck in pursuit of your RFID certification!

Neil Edde
Vice President & Publisher
Sybex, an Imprint of Wiley

This book is dedicated to all the men and women in our armed services who put their lives on the line so we can enjoy freedoms so many take for granted, and so many others in this world will never know.

Acknowledgments

Special thanks to Dr. Daniel Engels, Chetan Karani and all the crew at ODIN Technologies for their help and support. And once again thank you to my beautiful wife Christen who lived with me during the hectic process of writing a book and running a hyper-growth company. And thank God for giving me the talent to do all this.

About the Authors

Patrick J. Sweeney II is the president and CEO of ODIN Technologies (www.ODINtechnologies.com) and one of the foremost authorities on RFID. He holds patents specific to the design and testing of RFID systems and is the author of *RFID For Dummies*. He is responsible for the largest RFID deployment in the world for the U.S. Department of Defense's Defense Distribution Centers. He speaks frequently on the subject of RFID and entrepreneurship and is often quoted in magazines and industry trade publications. He lives in Middleburg, Virginia, with his wife, three children and three dogs, one of which has an RFID chip implanted in him.

Eva Zeisel is one of the foremost authorities on training and education in RFID. She was an instrumental figure in helping to set standards and drive quality in the RFID certification process. This is the second book on training she has co-written.

Contents At A Glance

Contents

Introduction

If you're preparing to take the CompTIA RFID+ exam, you'll undoubtedly want to find as much information as you can concerning radio frequency identification (RFID). The more information you have at your disposal and the more hands-on experience you gain, the better off you'll be when attempting the exam. This Study Guide was written with that in mind. I have attempted to dispense as much information as I can about RFID. My goal was to provide enough information that you'll be prepared for the test but not so much that you'll be overloaded with information outside the scope of the exam.

This book presents the material at an intermediate technical level. Experience with and understanding of various components of RFID systems, design, installation and troubleshooting of RFID systems as well as related subjects such as RF physics or standards related to this technology will help you get a full understanding of the challenges facing you as an RFID professional.

I've included review questions at the end of each chapter to give you a taste of what it's like to take the exam. If you're already working in the RFID field, I recommend that you check out these questions first to gauge your level of expertise. You can then use the book mainly to fill in the gaps in your current knowledge. This Study Guide will help you round out your knowledge base before tackling the exam.

NOTE

In addition, I have included an assessment test directly after this Introduction. This will also help you gauge your level of knowledge.

If you can answer 80 percent or more of the review questions correctly for a given chapter, you can probably feel safe moving on to the next chapter. If you're unable to answer that many correctly, reread the chapter and try the questions again. Your score should improve.

WARNING

Don't just study the questions and answers! The questions on the actual exam will be different from the practice questions included in this book and on the CD. The exam is designed to test your knowledge of a concept or objective, so use this book to learn the objective *behind* the question.

Before You Begin

Before you begin studying for the exam, it's imperative that you understand a few things about the RFID+ certification. RFID+ is a certification-for-life from CompTIA granted to those who obtain a passing score on a single exam.

When you're studying for any exam, the first step in preparation should always be to find out as much as possible about the test; the more you know up front, the better you can plan your study. The current exam number, and the one this book is written to, is RF0-001; it consists of 81 questions. You have 90 minutes to take the exam, and the passing score is 630 on a scale from 100 to 900. Both Pearson VUE and Thomson Prometric testing centers administer the exam throughout the United States and several other countries.

The exam is multiple choice, sometimes with short, terse questions followed by four possible answers, sometimes with lengthy scenarios and relatively complex solutions. This is an entry-level exam of knowledge-level topics and it expects you to know a great deal about RFID topics from an overview perspective but also their implementation. In many books, the glossary is filler added to the back of the text; this book's glossary should be considered necessary reading.

You should also know that CompTIA is notorious for including vague questions on all its exams. You might see a question for which two of the possible four answers are correct—but you can only choose one. Use your knowledge, logic, and intuition to choose the best answer, and then move on. Sometimes the questions are worded in ways that would make English majors cringe—a typo here, an incorrect verb there. Don't let this frustrate you; answer the question and go to the next. Although I haven't intentionally added typos or other grammatical errors, the questions throughout this book make every attempt to re-create the structure and appearance of the real exam questions. CompTIA offers a page on study tips for the exam at `http://certification.comptia.org/rfid/default.aspx`, and it is worth skimming.

NOTE

In addition, CompTIA frequently includes "item seeding," which is the practice of including unscored questions on exams. The reason they do that is to gather psychometric data, which is then used when developing new versions of the exam. Before you take the exam, you are told that your exam may include unscored questions. In addition, if you come across a question that does not appear to map to any of the exam objectives—or for that matter, is not covered in this exam—it is likely a seeded question.

Why Become RFID+ Certified?

There are a number of reasons for obtaining an RFID+ certification:

Provides Proof of Professional Achievement Specialized certifications are the best way to stand out from the crowd. In this age of technology certifications, you'll find hundreds of thousands of IT professionals who have one or many professional accomplishments. To set yourself apart from the crowd, you need a little bit more.

Increases Your Marketability Almost anyone can bluff their way through an interview. After you're RFID certified, you'll have the credentials to prove your competency. And certification can't be taken from you when you change jobs—you can take that certification with you to any position you accept.

Provides Opportunity for Advancement Individuals who prove themselves to be competent and dedicated are the ones who will most likely be promoted. Becoming certified is a great way to prove your skill level and show your employer that you're committed to improving your skill set. Look around you at those who are certified: they are probably the people who receive good pay raises and promotions.

Fulfills Training Requirements Many companies have set training requirements for their staff so that they stay up-to-date on the latest technologies. Having a certification program provides RFID professionals with another certification path to follow when they have exhausted some of the other industry-standard certifications.

Raises Customer Confidence As companies discover the CompTIA advantage, they will undoubtedly require qualified staff to achieve these certifications. Many companies outsource their work to consulting firms with experience working with RFID. Firms that have certified staff have a definite advantage over firms that don't.

How to Become an RFID+ Certified Professional

As this book goes to press, there are two RFID+ exam providers: Thomson Prometric and Pearson VUE. The following table contains all the necessary contact information and exam-specific details for registering. Exam pricing may vary by country or by CompTIA membership.

Vendor	Website	Phone Number	Exam Code
Thomson Prometric	`www.2test.com`	U.S. and Canada: 800-977-3926	SY0-101
Pearson VUE	`www.vue.com/comptia`	U.S. and Canada: 877-551-PLUS (7587)	SY0-101

When you schedule the exam, you'll receive instructions regarding appointment and cancellation procedures, ID requirements, and information about the testing center location. In addition, you'll receive a registration and payment confirmation letter. Exams can be scheduled up to six weeks out or as late as the next day (or, in some cases, even the same day).

NOTE

Exam prices and codes may vary based on the country in which the exam is administered. For detailed pricing and exam registration procedures, please refer to CompTIA's website, `www.comptia.com`.

After you've successfully passed your RFID+ exam, CompTIA will award you a certification that is good for life. Within four to six weeks of passing the exam, you'll receive your official CompTIA RFID+ certificate and ID card. (If you don't receive these within eight weeks of taking the test, contact CompTIA directly by using the information found in your registration packet.)

Who Should Buy This Book?

If you want to acquire a solid foundation in RFID technologies and your goal is to prepare for the exam, this book is for you. You'll find clear explanations of the concepts you need to grasp and plenty of help to achieve the high level of professional competency you need to succeed in your chosen field.

If you want to become certified as an RFID+ holder, this book is definitely what you need. However, if you just want to attempt to pass the exam without really understanding RFID, this Study Guide isn't for you. It's written for people who want to acquire hands-on skills and in-depth knowledge.

NOTE In addition to reading the book, you might consider downloading and reading the white papers on RFID that are scattered throughout the Internet.

How to Use This Book and the CD

I've included several testing features in the book and on the CD-ROM. These tools will help you retain vital exam content as well as prepare to sit for the actual exam:

Before You Begin At the beginning of the book (right after this Introduction) is an assessment test that you can use to check your readiness for the exam. Take this test before you start reading the book; it will help you determine the areas you may need to brush up on. The answers to the assessment test appear on a separate page after the last question of the test. Each answer includes an explanation and a note telling you the chapter in which the material appears.

Chapter Review Questions To test your knowledge as you progress through the book, there are review questions at the end of each chapter. As you finish each chapter, answer the review questions and then check your answers—the correct answers appear on the page following the last review question. You can go back to reread the section that covers each question you got wrong to ensure that you answer correctly the next time you're tested on the material.

Electronic Flashcards You'll find 150 flashcard questions on the CD for on-the-go review. These are short questions and answers, just like the flashcards you probably used to study in school. You can answer them on your PC or download them onto a PDA device for quick and convenient reviewing.

Test Engine The CD also contains the Sybex Test Engine. Using this custom test engine, you can identify weak areas up front and then develop a solid studying strategy. Our thorough `readme` file will walk you through the quick, easy installation process.

In addition to taking the assessment test and the chapter review questions in the test engine, you'll find two sample exams. Take these practice exams just as if you were taking the actual exam (without any reference material). After you've finished the first exam, move on to the next one to solidify your test-taking skills. If you get more than 90 percent of the answers correct, you're ready to take the certification exam.

Full Text of the Book in PDF The CD-ROM contains this book in PDF (Adobe Acrobat) format so you can easily read it on any computer. If you have to travel but still need to study for the exam, and you have a laptop with a CD-ROM drive, you can carry this entire book with you.

Exam Objectives

CompTIA goes to great lengths to ensure that its certification programs accurately reflect the IT industry's best practices. The company does this by establishing Cornerstone committees for each of its exam programs. Each committee comprises a small group of IT professionals, training providers, and publishers who are responsible for establishing the exam's baseline competency level and who determine the appropriate target audience level. After these factors are determined, CompTIA shares this information with a group of hand-selected Subject Matter Experts (SMEs). These folks are the true brainpower behind the certification program. In the case of this exam, they are IT-seasoned pros from the likes of DHL, *RFID Journal*, and ODIN Technologies, to name just a few. They review the committee's findings, refine them, and shape them into the objectives you see before you. CompTIA calls this process a Job Task Analysis (JTA). Finally, CompTIA conducts a survey to ensure that the objectives and weightings truly reflect the job requirements. Only then can the SMEs go to work writing the hundreds of questions needed for the exam. And, in many cases, they have to go back to the drawing board for further refinements before the exam is ready to go live in its final state. So, rest assured—the content you're about to learn will serve you long after you take the exam.

NOTE

Exam objectives are subject to change at any time without prior notice and at CompTIA's sole discretion. Please visit the certification page of CompTIA's website at `www.comptia.org` for the most current listing of exam objectives.

CompTIA also publishes relative weightings for each of the exam's objectives. The following table lists the five RFID+ objective domains and the extent to which they are represented on the exam.

As you use this Study Guide, you'll find that I have administered just the right dosage of objective knowledge to you by tailoring my coverage to mirror the percentages that CompTIA uses.

Domain	Percent
Interrogation Zone Basics	13%
Testing and Troubleshooting	13%
Standards and Regulations	12%
Tag Knowledge	11%
Design Selection	11%
Installation	11%
Site Analysis (i.e., before, during, and after Installation)	11%
RF Physics	11%

RFID Peripherals	7%
Total	100%

Domain 1.0 Interrogation Zone Basics

1.1 Describe interrogator functionality

1.1.1 I/O capability

1.1.2 Handheld interrogators

1.1.3 Vehicle-mount interrogator

1.1.4 LAN/serial communications

1.1.5 Firmware upgrades

1.1.6 Software operation (GUIs)

1.2 Describe configuration of interrogation zones

1.2.1 Explain interrogator-to-interrogator interference

1.2.2 Optimization

1.2.3 System performance and tuning

1.2.4 Travel speed and direction

1.2.5 Bi-static/mono-static antennas

1.3 Define anticollision protocols (e.g., number of tags in the field/response time)

1.4 Given a scenario, solve dense interrogator environment issues (domestic/international)

1.4.1 Understand how a dense interrogator installation is going to affect network traffic

1.4.2 Installation of multiple interrogators, (e.g., dock doors, synchronization of multiple interrogators, antenna footprints)

Domain 2.0 Testing and Troubleshooting

2.1 Given a scenario, troubleshoot RF interrogation zones (e.g., root-cause analysis)

2.1.1 Analyze less-than-required read rate

2.1.1.1 Identify improperly tagged items

2.1.2 Diagnose hardware

2.1.2.1 Recognize need for firmware upgrades

2.1.3 Equipment replacement procedures (e.g., antenna, cable, interrogator)

2.2 Identify reasons for tag failure

2.2.1 Failed tag management

2.2.2 ESD issues

2.3 Given a scenario, contrast actual tag data to expected tag data

Domain 3.0 Standards and Regulations

3.1 Given a scenario, map user requirements to standards

3.1.1 Regulations, standards that impact the design of a particular RFID solution

3.2 Identify the differences between air interface protocols and tag data formats

3.3 Recognize regulatory requirements globally and by region (keep at high level, not specific requirements—may use scenarios)

3.4 Recognize safety regulations/issues regarding human exposure

Domain 4.0 Tag Knowledge

4.1 Classify tag types

4.1.1 Select the RFID tag best suited for a specific use case

4.1.1.1 Pros and cons of tag types

4.1.1.2 Tag performance

4.1.1.2.1 Tag antenna to region/frequency

4.1.2 Identify inductively coupled tags vs. backscatter

4.1.3 Identify the differences between active and passive

4.2 Given a scenario, select the optimal locations for an RFID tag to be placed on an item

4.2.1 Evaluate media and adhesive selection for tags

4.2.2 Tag orientation and location

4.2.2.1 Tag stacking (shadowing)

4.2.3 Package contents

4.2.4 Packaging

4.2.4.1 Items

4.2.4.2 Tags

4.2.4.3 Labels

4.2.4.4 Inserts

4.2.5 Liquids

4.2.6 Metal

4.2.7 Polarization

Domain 5.0 Design Selection

5.1 Given a scenario, predict the performance of a given frequency and power (active/passive) as it relates to read distance, write distance, tag response time, storage capacity

5.2 Summarize how hardware selection affects performance (may use scenarios)

5.2.1 Antenna type

5.2.2 Equipment mounting and protection

5.2.3 Cable length/loss

5.2.4 Interference considerations

5.2.5 Tag type (e.g., active, passive, frequency)

Domain 6.0 Installation

6.1 Given a scenario, describe hardware installation using industry standard practices

6.1.1 Identify grounding considerations (e.g., lightning, ground loops, ESD)

6.1.2 Test installed equipment and connections (preinstall and postinstall)

6.2 Given a scenario, interpret a site diagram created by an RFID architect describing interrogation zone locations, cable drops, device-mounting locations

Domain 7.0 Site Analysis (i.e., before, during and after Installation)

7.1 Given a scenario, demonstrate how to read blueprints (e.g., whole infrastructure)

7.2 Determine sources of interference

7.2.1 Use analysis equipment such as a spectrum analyzer to determine if there is any ambient noise in the frequency range that may conflict with the RFID system to be installed

7.3 Given a scenario, analyze environmental conditions end-to-end

Domain 8.0 RF Physics

8.1 Identify RF propagation/communication techniques

8.2 Describe antenna field performance/characteristics as they relate to reflective and absorptive materials (may use scenarios)

8.3 Given a scenario, calculate radiated power output from an antenna based on antenna gains, cable type, cable length, interrogator transmit power (include formulas in scenario)

Domain 9.0 RFID Peripherals

9.1 Describe the installation and configuration of an RFID printer (may use scenarios)

9.2 Describe ancillary devices/concepts

9.2.1 RFID printer encoder

9.2.2 Automated label applicator

9.2.3 Feedback systems (e.g., lights, horns)

9.2.4 RTLS

Tips for Taking the RFID+ Exam

Here are some general tips for taking your exam successfully:

- Bring two forms of ID with you. One must be a photo ID, such as a driver's license. The other can be a major credit card or a passport. Both forms must include a signature.
- Arrive early at the exam center so you can relax and review your study materials, particularly tables and lists of exam-related information.
- Read the questions carefully. Don't be tempted to jump to an early conclusion. Make sure you know exactly what the question is asking.
- Don't leave any unanswered questions. Unanswered questions are scored against you.
- There will be questions with multiple correct responses. When there is more than one correct answer, a message at the bottom of the screen will prompt you to either "Choose two" or "Choose all that apply." Be sure to read the messages displayed to know how many correct answers you must choose.
- When answering multiple-choice questions that you're not sure about, use a process of elimination to get rid of the obviously incorrect answers first. Doing so will improve your odds if you need to make an educated guess.
- On form-based tests (nonadaptive), because the hard questions will eat up the most time, save them for last. You can move forward and backward through the exam.
- For the latest pricing on the exams and updates to the registration procedures, visit CompTIA's website at `www.comptia.org`.

Assessment Test

1. What are the two primary types of energy fields used in RFID communication? (Select two options.)
   - **A.** The electric field
   - **B.** The magnetic field
   - **C.** The playing fields
   - **D.** The circularly polarized field
2. High-frequency (HF) RFID is best suited for which of the following applications? (Select two options.)
   - **A.** Animal tracking
   - **B.** Container tracking
   - **C.** Item-level pharmaceutical
   - **D.** Toll booth
3. The magnetic field created by an electric current flowing through a straight wire ____________________.
   - **A.** flows from the end of the wire in the direction of the electric current (the north pole), out into space, and back into the other end of the wire (the south pole)
   - **B.** flows from the end of the wire in the opposite direction of the electric current (the north pole), out into space, and back into the other end of the wire (the south pole)
   - **C.** flows around the wire in concentric circles in a direction following the right-hand rule
   - **D.** flows around the wire in concentric circles in a direction following the left-hand rule
4. What kind of interface do interrogators not usually provide?
   - **A.** USB
   - **B.** Serial RS-232
   - **C.** Ethernet RJ-45
   - **D.** RS-485
5. What are the parts of the interrogator? (Select three options.)
   - **A.** Transmitter
   - **B.** Receiver
   - **C.** Light stack
   - **D.** Processor
   - **E.** RFID portal

6. What is the listen-before-talk technique used for?

   A. When frequency hopping, the interrogator has to listen for whether the channel it intends to use is available.

   B. Active tags use this technique when communicating with an interrogator.

   C. It is used only when writing to the tags.

   D. It is used in conjunction with sessions.

7. Which commands are supported by Generation 2 interrogators? (Select two options.)

   A. Kill command

   B. Select command

   C. Secure command

   D. Unkill command

8. What is ambient environmental noise (AEN)?

   A. Soft music usually played in the background during test sessions

   B. Other electronic transmissions that are taking place in a facility and that may interfere with an RFID network

   C. The static electricity caused by routing power cords too close to each other in an RFID rack

   D. The type of signal from a poorly tuned antenna

9. What is the primary purpose of using blueprints when designing an RFID network deployment?

   A. To see how old the building is

   B. To determine the overall square footage of the facility

   C. To determine location of the RFID portals and associated electrical and local area network (LAN) connections

   D. None of the above

10. What is the proper test equipment for an adequate site survey?

    A. Packet sniffer

    B. Oscilloscope

    C. E-field probe

    D. Spectrum analyzer and signal generator

11. What type of chip-attachment method is the most suitable for handling very small chips?

    A. Flip-chip method

    B. Strap-attachment method

    C. Self-adhesive method

    D. A and B

12. Which type of tag has the longest read ranges?
   - A. Active tags
   - B. Passive UHF tags
   - C. Semi-passive tags
   - D. Passive microwave tags
13. What is the maximum expected read rate of Gen 2 tags in the United States?
   - A. 150 tags per second
   - B. 1,500 tags per second
   - C. 150 kilobits per second
   - D. 1,500 kilobits per second
14. What is the difference between an ultra-high-frequency (UHF) tag and a high-frequency (HF) tag?
   - A. UHF has two chips, and HF has only one.
   - B. UHF uses the strap-attachment method, and HF uses the flip-chip.
   - C. UHF usually uses a dipole antenna (conductive material attached to the chip), and HF uses multiple loops of antenna material attached to the chip.
   - D. A, B
15. A tag has concentric rings of conductive ink attached to a single chip and is read about six inches from the reader, what type of tag is it most likely?
   - A. A SAW tag
   - B. A UHF dual dipole tag
   - C. A CHS pipe tag
   - D. An HF inductively coupled tag
16. When testing for ambient environmental noise (EAN) how long should you run the spectrum analyzer for the most effective results?
   - A. 24 hours
   - B. 12 hours
   - C. 6 hours
   - D. 1 hour
17. The differential time of arrival is related to which of the following?
   - A. Diverters
   - B. Real-time location system
   - C. Smart label applicators
   - D. Advanced shipping notice

18. Light stacks are used mainly for what?
    - A. For signaling that the interrogation was triggered
    - B. In conjunction with label applicators, signaling that the label was placed on a product
    - C. In conjunction with RFID printers, signaling that the label was printed
    - D. For providing feedback about valid or invalid tags at the verification point
19. Why does a printer have to know the location of the RFID inlay within a label?
    - A. So that it does not print over the inlay.
    - B. Inlay position indicates the type of tag.
    - C. So that it knows how long it will take to print one label.
    - D. In order to encode the tag properly and avoid damage to the chip.
20. What do you need to make sure of when installing an interrogator? (Select two options.)
    - A. That it is protected from dust and environmental conditions
    - B. That you attach the interrogator to a wall with nails used for concrete
    - C. That you always use a protective enclosure such as NEMA
    - D. That it has enough space around for cables, access, and ventilation
21. What do you need to do in order not to delay the installation?
    - A. Do not worry about people logistics, as long as the equipment is on-site.
    - B. Do not worry about the equipment, as long as your installers are on-site.
    - C. Establish communication channels, make sure that everyone has travel plans and will be on-site and ready to go, and have the equipment tested and ready to be put in.
    - D. Establish chain of command, and make sure that everyone has accommodations and will bring the equipment needed for installation when coming on-site.
22. What is the first step you should take to troubleshoot an RFID network?
    - A. Check the manual for the reader.
    - B. Set up a signal generator with a frequency equal to the center frequency of the interrogator and attach the reader's antenna to the signal generator.
    - C. Reboot the reader.
    - D. Flash the firmware.
23. Which type of cable connecting an antenna to a reader would exhibit the lowest loss?
    - A. LMR-240
    - B. LMR-400
    - C. Declonian
    - D. B and C

24. What primary role does middleware play on an RFID reader?
    A. Filters and smooths data
    B. Determines which protocols are read
    C. Monitors performance of each reader
    D. Provides operational awareness

25. What is the main purpose of tag data protocols?
    A. Standardize tag data formatting
    B. Standardize tag anticollision procedures
    C. Specify frequency allocations for tag operation
    D. Standardize the tag construction

26. What does the ISO/IEC 14443 specify?
    A. Air interface protocol for UHF tags
    B. Guidelines for animal identification
    C. Guidelines for proximity cards
    D. Guidelines for freight containers

27. What is the most important concern when installing an RFID system?
    A. Equipment protection
    B. Personnel safety
    C. Protection of safety devices
    D. Protection of hearing

Answers to Assessment Test

1. A, B. Electromagnetic waves form the basis for near-field and far-field communication using RFID. An electromagnetic field is made up of both an electric field and a magnetic field. For more information, see Chapter 1.

2. A, C. HF has a shorter range than UHF, microwave, or active tags, so it is best suited for close-range applications, particularly if metal or liquids are involved. For more information, see Chapter 1.

3. C. The current flowing through a straight wire does not create a magnetic north pole and south pole. The current creates a magnetic field that forms concentric circles around the wire. The right-hand rule is used to determine the direction of the magnetic field. For more information, see Chapter 1.

4. D. RS-485 is not usually provided by the interrogators. The most common interfaces are serial, Ethernet, USB, and I/O control. For more information, see Chapter 2.

5. A, B, D. An interrogator includes a transmitter, a receiver, and a processor. It does not include a light stack, which is usually connected to the interrogator as an I/O device through an I/O port. An RFID portal is the implemented structure, including the interrogator, antennas, mounts, and possible I/O devices. For more information, see Chapter 2.

6. A. A listen-before-talk (LBT) technique can be used during frequency hopping. The reader has to listen for whether any other reader transmits on the chosen channel; only after it determines that the channel is available can it start using this channel for communication. If the channel is being used by another reader, the listening reader has to switch to another channel in order to transmit. For more information, see Chapter 2.

7. A, B. The Select and Kill commands are supported by Generation 2 interrogators. The commands Secure and Unkill do not exist (yet). For more information, see Chapter 2.

8. B. The site survey and full Faraday cycle analysis are performed to determine whether there are any other systems in place that may interfere with the performance of an RFID network. Some of these systems include barcode scanners, alarm sensors, communication systems, and air traffic control radar. For more information, see Chapter 3.

9. C. The blueprints are your canvas to lay out the RFID network based on business process flows identified in the project planning phase. You cannot install an RFID reader without adequate power and some sort of connectivity. The blueprints will tell you what is in place already, and where you will need to install portal racks, receptacles, or LAN connections. For more information, see Chapter 3.

10. D. The spectrum analyzer is the most widely used testing tool in RFID, because it allows understanding and viewing of invisible waves in the local atmosphere. The signal generator adds to the functionality by allowing you to specifically replicate transmission of a reader and then test its behavior. For more information, see Chapter 3.

11. B. The most suitable method for handling very small chips is the strap-attachment method. A chip is placed on a conductive and the strap is then attached to an antenna. The strap provides a larger surface to connect to the antenna than the chip by itself. For more information, see Chapter 4.

12. A. Active tags have the longest read ranges because of their ability to broadcast a signal to the environment. They carry a battery to power the chip's circuitry as well as its transmitter and other components. For more information, see Chapter 4.

13. B. Theoretical read rates for Gen 2 tags are around 1,500 tags per second in the United States and 600 tags per second in Europe because of regulatory restrictions. For more information, see Chapter 4.

14. C. An HF tag is easily recognized by the multiple loops of antenna that circle around the chip, usually for five or six turns. This is so it can couple with the near field. The UHF tag has a single antenna, usually on either side of the chip. For more information, see Chapter 5.

15. D. If there is inductive coupling, a loop of some conductive metal like copper or silver or conductive ink needs to be looped several times to successful get power to the chip. This is the easiest way to tell an HF tag from a UHF tag. For more information, see Chapter 4.

16. A. The spectrum analyzer should be run for an entire business cycle, this is part of a full Faraday cycle analysis which looks at the environmental changes over all shifts of a business. There may be night-time security systems, adjacent radar facilities, communications gear, all which change their state at different times of the day. A 24-hour investigation is the only way to accurately detect those interferers. For more information, see Chapter 3.

17. B. The differential time of arrival is one of the principles used in real-time location systems. This principle is based on the difference in time it takes the signal to travel from the tag to each of the access points (RFID readers). For more information, see Chapter 6.

18. D. Light stacks are used mainly at the verification points to provide feedback as to whether a tag placed on a product functions correctly. For more information, see Chapter 6.

19. D. Knowing the location of the RFID inlay embedded in a label is important for proper reading, encoding, and verification. A best practice is also to avoid printing over the RFID chip because that can damage it. For more information, see Chapter 6.

20. D. When you are mounting an interrogator, you have to make sure that it has enough space for proper connections to antennas, network, and power, as well as for ventilation and possible troubleshooting. It also has to be protected from various environmental conditions including dust, rain, snow, heat, and others. For more information, see Chapter 7.

21. C. To prevent delays in installation, you must follow a project plan and not forget to establish communication channels. Do not underestimate people logistics or equipment logistics, including hardware certification and preassembly. For more information, see Chapter 7.

22. C. Sometimes readers will overload their processing capability and freeze, much like a laptop. The simplest first step after you've checked to see whether the power is on is to reboot the reader and see whether that fixes the problem. For more information, see Chapter 8.

23. B. LMR is most frequently used for RFID networks. The higher the number after "LMR," the better the insulation. So LMR-400 will have the least loss and should be used for the longer runs. For more information, see Chapter 8.

24. A. Middleware is at its basic level a very simple tool for filtering and smoothing data being captured by each RFID reader. As the name implies, it sits between the reader and the application—in the middle—and needs to be specifically written for each reader. It usually sends out data in an XML format to applications such as SAP, Oracle, and other business applications. For more information, see Chapter 8.

25. A. Tag data protocols specify the size and structure of the tag memory; tag data formatting and length; and the means of storing, accessing, and transferring information. For more information, see Chapter 9.

26. C. ISO/IEC 14443 provides guidelines for RF power, signal interface, transmission protocol, and physical characteristics of proximity cards. Guidelines for animal identifications are set by ISO 11784, ISO 11785, and ISO 14223. The air interface protocol for UHF tags is defined in ISO/IEC 18000-6, and the guidelines for freight containers in ISO 10374. For more information, see Chapter 9.

27. B. The most important concern when installing any system should be personnel safety. When you are installing a system, make sure that you appropriately connect and safeguard the electrical equipment so that it cannot harm anyone or cause any trip, fall, or injury hazards. You cannot block any safety devices or exit doors. For more information, see Chapter 9.

CompTIA
RFID+™
Study Guide

Chapter 1

The Physics of RFID

RFID+ EXAM OBJECTIVES COVERED IN THIS CHAPTER:

- ✓ 8.1 Identify RF propagation/communication techniques
- ✓ 8.2 Describe antenna field performance/characteristics as they relate to reflective and absorptive materials (may use scenarios)
- ✓ 8.3 Given a scenario, calculate radiated power output from an antenna based on antenna gains, cable type, cable length, interrogator transmit power (include formulas in scenario)

If your only memory of high-school physics is of your wrapping some copper wire around a hunk of metal and seeing if you could make it stick to your friend's braces, you might have missed the lovely nuances of the science while simultaneously ensuring continued income for the local orthodontist. Physics is the foundation and basis for everything that happens in radio frequency identification (RFID). All too often people (usually in marketing) try to blame physics for the failures of RFID systems, when in actuality knowledge of physics can be the biggest asset in deploying RFID.

This chapter may make you feel like you are going back to high-school or college physics, but I assure you there will be no goofy experiments, only sage advice that will help you to deploy faster and more-accurate RFID systems and to troubleshoot the real sticklers you might one day encounter.

The physics of RFID revolve mostly around the behavior of the magnetic fields and electromagnetic waves generated by an RFID system. Because physics dictates how these fields and waves are generated, behave, and react, the RFID+ exam has a significant number of questions that will test your base knowledge of the physics of RFID. To get you ready for that part of the exam and to help you begin deploying real-world systems, this chapter will cover the following:

- The types of waveforms surrounding radio frequency (RF)
- The characteristics of those waves
- How to measure things that can't be seen
- The basics regarding some of the equations of RF

Electromagnetic Radiation

Electromagnetic radiation in the frequency ranges used by RFID systems cannot be seen, heard, tasted, smelled, or touched, so you might be a little skeptical that electromagnetic radiation exists. For those unbelievers among you, you are invited to turn on your car radio or use your mobile phone to talk with someone on the other side of the world to experience the wonders of electromagnetic radiation. RFID, of course, uses electromagnetic radiation for communication and, in the case of passive RFID systems, for transferring power to the tags.

Because we cannot experience electromagnetic radiation directly, we must understand the physics of electromagnetic radiation to gain insight into how electromagnetic radiation works and how to make it work effectively for our RFID systems. Through study and the intuition that knowledge brings, we will be able to understand why various environments and environmental fixtures create better, or worse, RFID communication reliability. And, we will be able to correct any deficiencies that may be found.

In my book *RFID for Dummies* (Wiley Publishing, 2005), I spent a lot of time explaining the detailed physics of RFID. The reason is simple: if you can picture the invisible, solutions to complex problems become that much easier. In preparation for the CompTIA exam, I'll give you information about some of the physics surrounding RFID and help you get a clear picture in your mind of what is happening when you plug a reader into a socket and start making waves.

Near Field

You are probably familiar with the many modern conveniences that utilize electromagnetic radiation, but have you ever wondered why the particular radiation used by these devices—radios and cell phones, for example—are called "electromagnetic"? The simple answer is that the radiation consists of both an electric field and a magnetic field.

Crushing Cars with RFID

Quite a few movies contain a scene in which the bad guy tries to kill the hero in an agonizingly slow death by using a scrap yard and a car crusher. Well, the big crane with the magnet attached to it is doing some of what an RFID reader does. It is using electricity to charge a piece of metal with a magnetic signal. In this case, it's strong enough to pick up a car.

We are all familiar with magnets and the magnetostatic, or static magnetic, fields that they generate. Magnetic fields flow from the north pole of the magnet, out into space, and back into the south pole of the magnet. The magnetic field describes a volume of space near the magnet, where a change in energy attributable to the magnet can be detected. Magnetic fields are strongest close to the magnet and diminish in strength as one moves away from the magnet. Magnetic fields generated by magnets are static power storage fields. They do not vary over time. This stasis lets your refrigerator magnet firmly hold your child's artwork on the refrigerator without it falling off periodically.

Magnetic fields do interact with moving electric charges. The magnetic field will change the direction of motion of a charged particle, but it cannot change its speed. Thus, a current-carrying wire experiences a force upon it when it is placed within a magnetic field. Time-varying magnetic fields, possibly caused by physically moving a magnet closer to a wire, will perform work upon a charge, thereby creating an electric current within a wire. We will examine this interrelation between dynamic electric and magnetic fields when we investigate Maxwell's equations later in this chapter.

Magnets are not the only sources of magnetic fields. Electric currents flowing through wires also generate magnetic fields. The strength of the magnetic field around the wire is proportional to the current carried by the wire. Just as with magnets, the magnetic fields generated by flowing currents are strongest near the wire and diminish in strength as one moves away from the wire. Unlike with magnets, the magnetic fields created by electric currents do not flow into and out of the wire carrying the electric current. Instead, they flow around the wire in concentric circles. The direction of the magnetic field generated by an electric current is easily determined by using the *right-hand rule*. If you grasp the electric current–carrying wire in your right hand with your thumb pointing in the direction of the current, then your fingers will circle the wire in the direction of the magnetic field.

The strength of the magnetic field that is created by electric currents carried in a wire can be increased by forming the wire into a loop or coil (that is, multiple overlapping loops). The magnetic field created by each loop of wire combines with the fields from the other loops to produce a concentrated magnetic field in the center of the coil. The magnetic field generated by a solenoid, a tightly constructed coil, is similar to that of a bar magnet. The magnetic field is relatively uniform and of high strength within the center of the coil. The magnetic field flows from the north pole of the coil (this can be determined by using the right-hand rule with the fingers pointing in the direction of the north pole) out into space and returns to the south pole of the coil.

Magnetic fields generated by electric currents vary as the current through the wire varies. Thus constant, or direct current (DC), electric currents generate static magnetic fields (in the steady state) just as do magnets. Alternating electric currents, which is to say time-varying currents with a constant period, or frequency, such as that used to power the lights in our homes and to communicate information across telecommunication wires, generate time-varying magnetic fields that follow the periodicity of the electric currents. Time-varying magnetic fields, in turn, generate time-varying electric currents that follow the periodicity of the magnetic fields. In this alternating fashion, the electrical energy flowing through the wire is transformed into a series of alternating magnetic fields and electric fields that are radiated into space.

By utilizing alternating electric currents, coils and many other shapes of metals become efficient radiating elements that send electromagnetic radiation into our world, which is when they become far field.

Although a coil will radiate all frequencies based on the frequency of the electric current traveling through it, it does not radiate all frequencies equally well. The coil's resonant frequency is the frequency at which it most efficiently generates magnetic fields. When viewed as an antenna, a coil is a tuned inductance (L)–capacitance (C), or simply LC, circuit. The antenna is at resonance when the inductive impedance is equal to the capacitive impedance for a particular frequency. The resonant frequency f is then $f = 1/(2\pi\sqrt{LC})$. Consequently, low frequencies such as 125 kHz require a large number of loops to achieve proper resonance, whereas high frequencies such as 13.56 MHz require few loops to achieve resonance. Large-diameter coils also require fewer loops because of the natural radio LC (RLC) within the metal wires.

Far Field

Thus far we have investigated primarily the power storage fields (that is, magnetic fields) generated by electromagnetic radiation, but we cannot ignore the power propagation fields that result from this radiation. RFID systems operating in the low-frequency (LF) and high-frequency (HF) ranges couple to the power storage fields generated by the reader's antenna. RFID systems operating at higher frequencies such as ultra-high frequency (UHF) couple to the power propagation fields (that is, the electromagnetic waves) that result from the RFID reader's radiation.

Just as you learned in high-school physics that light rays can be modeled as a sinusoidal wave traveling in a straight line, electromagnetic radiation in the power propagation field (that is, the far field) can be modeled as electromagnetic waves that travel in straight lines. Electromagnetic waves are a model of how electromagnetic radiation travels in the far field (the region beyond the near field).

An electromagnetic wave carries energy from one point to another with a velocity equal to the speed of light in a vacuum, $c = 3 \times 10^8$ meters per second (m/s). Electromagnetic waves exhibit a property called *linearity*. Linear waves do not affect the passage of other waves as they intersect. Thus, the total of two linear waves at their intersection is simply the sum of the two waves as they would exist separately.

The electromagnetic waves utilized in RFID systems are continuous harmonic transverse electromagnetic (TEM) waves. Continuous harmonic waves are typically sinusoidal in nature; thus, they are characterized by frequency, amplitude, and phase. They are also characterized by their three-dimensional shape. For RFID systems, linear waves are common, with their polarization used as the primary shape characteristic. TEM waves are characterized by having electric and magnetic fields that are transversal to the direction of the wave's propagation.

An electromagnetic wave consists of two sinusoidal signals traveling in perpendicular planes at the same frequency (f), with one signal corresponding to the electric field (**E**) and one signal corresponding to the magnetic field (**H**). The line corresponding to the intersection of the two planes defines the direction of travel of the electromagnetic wave. At every point along this line, the ratio of the amplitudes of the electric field and the magnetic field is a constant equal to the characteristic impedance of the medium the wave is traveling through.

The amplitude of an electromagnetic wave is proportional to the energy being propagated by the wave. As the electromagnetic wave travels through a medium which creates signal loss, such as air, some of the energy being propagated by the wave is absorbed by the medium. This absorption diminishes, or attenuates, the amplitude of the electromagnetic wave. Thus, the farther a wave travels away from its source, the lower is its amplitude. The attenuation factor is a characteristic of the medium through which an electromagnetic wave travels.

The polarization of the electromagnetic wave is defined by convention by the motion of the electric field (**E**). If the motion of the electric field is confined to two dimensions (that is, a plane), linear polarization results. If the motion of the electric field is allowed to be spread in three dimensions, the polarization of the wave is defined by the path the electric field takes. Circularly polarized waves have electric fields that follow a corkscrew shape as they propagate forward in time. When looked at head-on, this corkscrew collapses into a circle, hence the name.

Remember that electromagnetic waves are simply models for the power propagation fields. When we remember that the electromagnetic wave is propagating energy away from an antenna, we understand that polarization impacts propagation distance. Circularly polarized electromagnetic waves spread their energy over three-dimensional space, whereas linearly polarized electromagnetic waves spread their energy over a plane. Because the linearly polarized electromagnetic wave maintains its energy over a smaller volume at each point in space, it is able to be detected at a greater distance than a circularly polarized electromagnetic wave emitted with the same amount of energy. The total energy propagated by each wave is the same; however, the contours of the volumes through which the energy propagates differ.

Polarization of the waves becomes important in tag antenna designs and deployments. Antennas may be designed such that they efficiently capture and communicate with energy in one or a few different polarizations. If a reader antenna is linearly polarized and the tag antenna is linearly polarized, then the tag and the reader may communicate only when both antennas are oriented in the same linear direction. Circularly polarized antennas reduce the orientation requirements, but do not completely eliminate the orientation dependence for optimal performance.

Propagation and Interference of Waves

Electromagnetic waves are more than just a convenient model for electromagnetic energy propagation. They are an accurate model of how the energy propagation field behaves. As with all waves, electromagnetic waves interact with one another whenever they intersect at a point in space. Depending on the phase, amplitude, and polarization, intersecting waves may either constructively interfere or destructively interfere. This is one of the basic properties of linear waves. The observed wave at a point of intersection is the addition of all of the waves at that point. Constructive interference increases the amplitude of the detectable wave at that point. Destructive interference decreases the amplitude of the detectable wave.

Wireless communication within an indoor environment is often plagued by prolonged deep fades that degrade and possibly prohibit communication between the transmitter and the receiver. The electromagnetic waves radiated by the transmitter undergo multiple reflections and diffractions through an often highly cluttered environment. Every object in the environment both absorbs and reflects electromagnetic waves. Conductors, such as metals, reflect the electromagnetic waves at UHF frequencies with little loss to the wave's energy. Other, non-conducting materials, such as cardboard, also reflect electromagnetic energy incident upon it, although typically at much reduced energy.

Fundamental physics, through the Uniform Theory of Diffraction, tells us that at every boundary between two materials, electromagnetic waves incident upon that boundary will be both transmitted from one material to the other and reflected back into the material in which they are traveling. Conducting materials, such as metals, act similar to perfect reflectors for UHF radiation. Materials such as glass, concrete, and cardboard are effectively RF transparent for waves that are incident upon them with an angle of incidence of 90 degrees, but they become less transparent as the angle of incidence becomes more oblique.

Some materials, such as water, act as both good reflectors of electromagnetic waves and good attenuators, or absorbers, of electromagnetic energy. The partial reflection of a wave results in the energy of the wave being separated to traverse multiple paths. The result is that a partial reflection attenuates the partially transmitted wave by the amount of energy reflected at the boundary.

By passing through several materials and being reflected by several more, an electromagnetic wave traverses a path through the environment. In addition to attenuating the wave as it travels through the environment, the environment may impact the polarization of the wave. Two long parallel metal strips separated by a few inches, for example, will filter the UHF waves that are incident upon them by allowing waves that are polarized parallel to the metal strips to pass through the space between the strips while waves polarized perpendicular to the metal strips will be reflected.

When two waves that have traversed different-length paths intersect at a point, they will be out of phase with one another. The phase difference is due to differences in the time required to traverse the different paths. Most phase differences cause destructive interference and may cause the observed wave at a point to appear to have a different frequency than what was originally transmitted.

Electromagnetic waves are linear, meaning that the wave experienced at a point in space and time is the sum of the waves that intersect at that point. Because of reflections, attenuation, and different path lengths caused by objects in the environment, the waves that arrive at a point in space may have an amplitude that sums to zero or nearly zero. Passive RFID tags are not able to harvest sufficient operating power from low-amplitude, hence, low-power, locations. When these near-zero amplitude locations are surrounded by much-higher amplitude locations where passive RFID tags are able to operate, the low-amplitude location is called a null. The position of nulls may be changed or the nulls may be eliminated by changing the position of the objects in the environment or changing the frequency being radiated by the antenna. When the environment is static, standing waves may result. This phenomenon can be described as a *standing wave* or a *null*. The most common occurrence is when the two waves intersect each other exactly half a wavelength out of phase and completely cancel the signals. This creates the null spot where a tag would not be read.

Real World Scenario

Environmental Coincidences

In Chapter 3, "Site Analysis," you'll learn how to perform an analysis of the interrogation zone before actually setting up a reader. This is referred to as creating a path loss contour map (PLCM) that shows how RFID will react when put in a very specific location. Without a foundation in physics, following the PLCM procedure will leave you scratching your head if you come across a problem.

One of the ODIN technologies engineers was on-site at a client's facility performing a series of PLCMs when he found that one of the interrogation zones had a significant null (RF dead spot), and tags would not be read if a reader was set up at that location. He had to find out why. After looking around the area and moving some RF-transparent items (cardboard boxes), he uncovered ladder racks for data cables that measured 12″ × 12″ for each step. Because he was an expert in RF physics, he knew that 12″ is about 33 cm, which is almost exactly the wavelength of an RF wave at 915 MHz. The racks were acting like a sponge, sucking in the RF energy. Moving them out of the area resulted in a perfect interrogation zone location. Lots of headaches and frustration were saved by knowing the physics of RFID.

Maxwell's Equations

James Clerk Maxwell was the first to correctly assemble the complete laws of electrodynamics in his classic treatise in 1873. Modern electromagnetism theory is based on the four fundamental equations known as *Maxwell's equations.*

Before Maxwell, the laws of electrodynamics, including Gauss's Law, Ampere's Law of Magnetostatics, and Faraday's Law, were laws of electrostatics, and did not predict waves. These laws correctly described what is known as the *near field* (that is, the electrostatic field of an electric charge and the magnetostatic field of a current loop). These laws described the observable impact of electric charges and magnetic fields close to the source but failed to describe the distant impact of these forces.

In the static case, when all electric charges are permanently fixed or if they all move at a steady state, the electric field and the magnetic field are not interconnected. This allows us to study electricity and magnetism as two distinct and separate phenomena.

Up until Maxwell challenged conventional wisdom the separation of electricity and magnetism was the accepted state of the world. He corrected Ampere's Law of Magnetostatics to become Ampere's Law as corrected by Maxwell, so that consistency with the Law of Conservation of Charge now occurred. Maxwell added a term indicating that vortices of magnetic fields can be displacement current density (time-varying electric flux density) as well as conduction current density. The resulting corrected equations define the complete laws of electrodynamics and predict electromagnetic waves. Heinrich Rudolf Hertz confirmed experimentally that these waves exist.

The Complete Laws of Electrodynamics

The Complete Laws of Electrodynamics define the relationship between the electric field quantities and the magnetic field quantities. These quantities are the electric field vector (**E**), the electric flux vector (**D**) (where $\mathbf{E} = \varepsilon \mathbf{D}$ and ε is the electrical permittivity of the material), the magnetic field vector (**H**), and the magnetic flux vector (**B**) (where $\mathbf{H} = \mu \mathbf{B}$ and μ is the magnetic permeability of the material). The Complete Laws of Electrodynamics are as follows:

Faraday's Law Faraday's Law states that any magnetic field which is changing in the time dimension creates an equal change in the electromotive force. To be more specific the circulation of the electric field vector (**E**) around a closed contour is equal to minus the time rate of change of magnetic flux through a surface bounded by that contour. This only holds true if the positive direction of the surface is related to the positive direction of the contour by the right-hand rule.

Ampere's Law as Modified by Maxwell The circulation of the magnetic field vector (**H**) around a closed contour is equal to the sum of the conduction current and the displacement current passing through a surface bounded by that contour. Again, the right-hand rule is what dictates this behavior in relation to the contour and the surface.

Gauss's Law for the Electric Flux The total electric flux (defined in terms of the **D** vector) emerging from a closed surface is equal to the total conduction charge contained within the volume bounded by that surface.

Gauss's Law for the Magnetic Flux The total magnetic flux (defined in terms of the **B** vector) emerging from any closed surface is zero.

Maxwell's Equations With the aid of Gauss's and Stokes' laws of mathematics and the definitions

$$D = \varepsilon_0 E + P \text{ and } B = \mu_0 (H+M)$$

the complete laws of electrodynamics may be expressed, when the fields are spatially continuous, in the familiar differential form

$$\nabla \times E = -\frac{\partial B}{\partial t}$$

$$\nabla \times H = J + \frac{\partial D}{\partial t}$$

$$\nabla \cdot D = \rho$$

$$\nabla \cdot B = 0$$

where **J** is the current density per unit area and ρ is the electric charge density per unit volume. These equations hold in any material and at any spatial location.

Equations in Use for Plastic and Concrete

The equations I've covered in this chapter can make physics your best friend in deploying a 100% accurate RFID network. There is one other principle that is helpful to know and that's called the dielectric effect. A dielectric is any material that is resistant to passing along an electric current. Since passive RFID tags are trying to gather electricity from a reader's field the material they are affixed to will dramatically effect how they perform. For example Lexan is a clear plastic material that is RF transparent but if you place a tag on it the dielectric properties of the Lexan detunes the tag enough to degrade its performance. A tag affixed to concrete will be detuned enough to render it useless because of the dielectric properties of concrete. The big reason behinds this is twofold—first the electric charge decreases as it passes through any dielectric material and second the velocity of the wave changes and the RFID wave will behave as if it had a shorter wavelength.

Interpreting the Complete Laws

The detailed derivation and use of Maxwell's equations will allow you to understand the propagation of electromagnetic waves in astounding detail that will amaze your friends. However, being able to analytically determine the absolute theoretical path and power of an electromagnetic wave does not do you much good in a complex real-world environment where you know precious few of the variables needed to accurately solve the equations. The time it would take you to accurately solve the equations would ensure that your friends no longer talk to you. Intuition will serve you well in understanding the messy and complex real world. To this end, we examine the intuitive source and vortex interpretation of Maxwell's equations.

In the source and vortex interpretation, Maxwell's equations state that the electric field vector (**E**) can have vortices caused by changing magnetic flux; the magnetic field (**H**) can have vortices caused by conduction or displacement currents; the electric flux density (**D**) can have sources caused by conduction charge density; and the magnetic flux density vector (**B**) can have no sources.

In linear media, some of the statements about electric flux density (**D**) and magnetic flux density (**B**) can be extended to the electric field (**E**) and the magnetic field (**H**). However, when nonuniform fields and boundaries are considered, it can be shown that the electric field (**E**), the electric flux density (**D**), and the magnetic field (**H**) can have both sources and vortices, but the magnetic flux density (**B**) is alone in that it can have no sources.

Figures 1.1 and 1.2 provide archetypical illustrations of the source nature of the electrostatic field (Figure 1.1) and the vortex nature of a magnetic field (Figure 1.2), as well as illustrations of two of the most important boundary conditions that apply when an electric field (**E**) or a magnetic field (**H**) approaches a conducting surface.

FIGURE 1.1 Electric field near a conducting surface

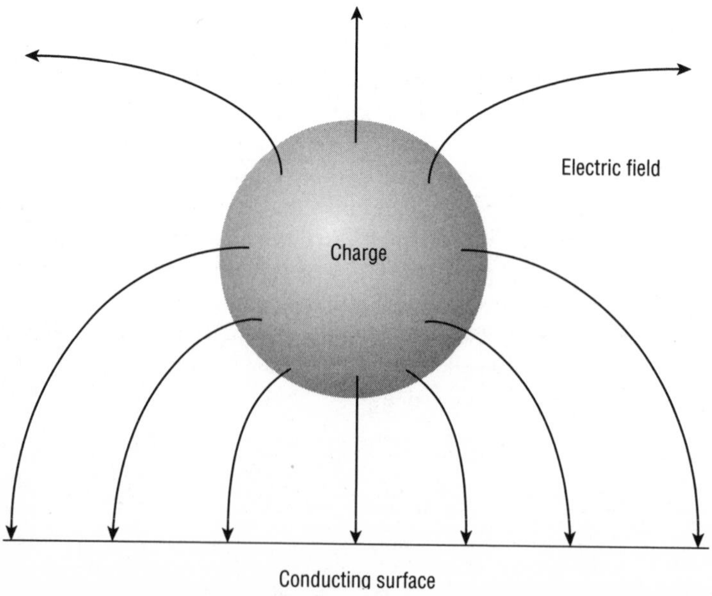

FIGURE 1.2 Oscillating magnetic field near a conducting plane

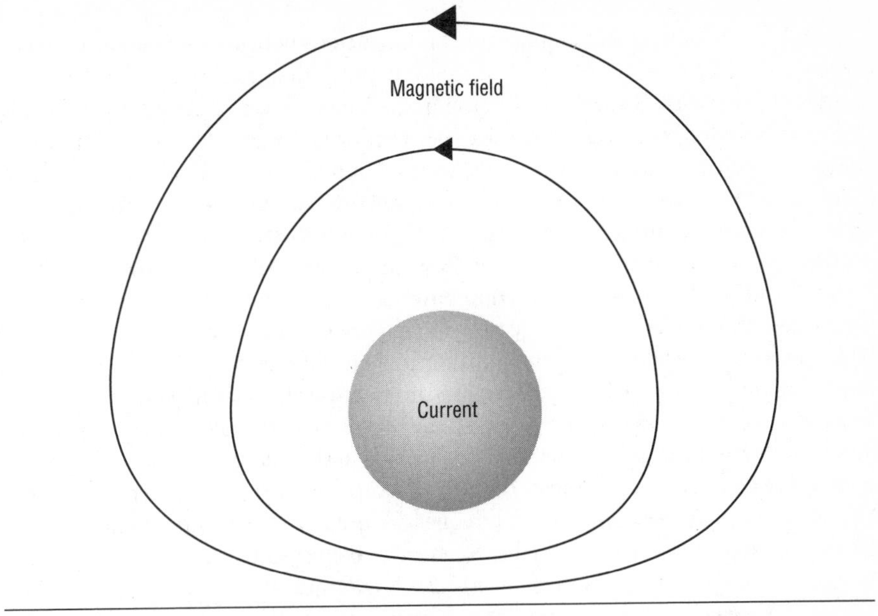

These boundary conditions tell us intuitively that bringing an electric charge close to a metal surface will result in most of the electric field from the charge coupling with the metal. In practice, this means that systems such as UHF RFID systems will have tag antennas couple to any and all close metal surfaces. This will result in a loss of efficiency of the antenna and usually a significant retuning of the antenna's center frequency unless the tag antenna is designed to operate near metal surfaces.

These boundary conditions also tell us that bringing a coil antenna near metal will inhibit the flow of the magnetic field around the coil. This, in turn, will decrease the coil's coupling efficiency to the reader's coiled antenna.

What we can deduce from the Complete Laws, without taking into account the properties of any materials involved, is that the tangential component of the electric field (**E**) is continuous across any boundary, the electric flux density (**D**) may be discontinuous across a boundary, and the tangential component of the magnetic field (**H**) may be discontinuous across a boundary.

By applying the Complete Laws to magnetic dipoles, we can identify that the distance $r = \lambda/(2\pi)$ is of significance in determining the nature of the fields surrounding the dipoles. Within this distance, known as the *near-field region*, the dominant fields are the energy storage fields (that is, the magnetic fields). Beyond this distance, known as the far-field region, the dominant fields are the electromagnetic energy propagation fields that continuously transport energy away from the dipoles. Maxwell's equations correctly describe both the energy storage field and the energy propagation field.

Permeability and Depth of Penetration

Although the physics of RFID apply to all frequencies, there are, in fact, only a few frequency ranges that RFID systems are allowed to use without requiring specific, expensive spectrum licenses. The recent 3G spectrum auction in the United States resulted in a total sale price of several billion dollars. To avoid these expensive, proprietary licenses, all commercial RFID systems are designed to work in the free-to-use but highly regulated Industrial, Scientific, and Medical (ISM) bands. These frequency bands are reserved for so-called short-range devices by national and international organizations and governments.

The rules and regulations that define what frequencies can be used by RFID systems also define the allowed bandwidth, radiation powers, transmission times, modulation modes, and other operation modes for the devices. Although the International Telecommunication Union (ITU) encourages worldwide harmonization of these rules and regulations, not all frequency ranges are usable worldwide. This is significant because tags that must operate within multiple-frequency bands are either more expensive or have a shorter maximum communication range than tags that need to operate within only a single narrow frequency band.

Why are there different frequency bands? The answer is simple: different frequencies have different propagation characteristics. All frequencies are attenuated and reflected by materials to a greater or lesser degree, with the higher frequencies being more greatly attenuated than the lower frequencies. Low frequencies, such as the 125 kHz frequency, are attenuated very little as they propagate through materials. This allows them to have significant signal-penetration capabilities through all materials including metal. When radiated and used in the far field, these frequencies can also have a significant communication range. Those of us who have traveled across the United States by car at night have experienced the propagation wonders of these low frequencies as we listened to AM radio stations (typically operating between 580 kHz and 1700 kHz) that were being broadcast 100 miles or more away from us. Try doing that with an FM radio station. (FM radio stations typically operate between 88 MHz and 108 MHz.)

Ultra-high frequencies, such as the 915 MHz frequency, are highly attenuated and reflected by most materials. This limits, for example, the depth of water through which a UHF tag may be read and the distance at which a reader may be heard. This also means that electromagnetic reflective surfaces, such as metals, act as very good mirrors for UHF energy incident upon them. Even cardboard will reflect some of the UHF energy incident upon it.

All materials, including air, attenuate magnetic fields as the fields propagate through the material. The relative ease with which a magnetic field propagates through a material is dependent on the material's *permeability*. Permeability is a material property that describes the ease with which a magnetic flux is established within the material. Permeability, μ, is the ratio of the magnetic flux density (**B**) to the magnetic field (**H**) creating the flux (often referred to as the magnetizing force), $\mu = \mathbf{B}/\mathbf{H}$. The permeability of air is 1.256×10^{-6} H/m (Hertz per meter).

The depth of penetration of a magnetic field through a material is inversely proportional to the square root of the product of the frequency and the permeability of the material. Consequently, the higher the frequency of the signal generated at the antenna, the lower the depth of penetration through a specific material. The net result is that aluminum acts as a better shield against magnetic energy than does copper or steel.

How Physics Effects the Antenna and Wave Propagation

The term *gain* seems to cause some confusion but it's really quite simple. Think of a reader as radiating a fixed reference amount of power, an antenna with a higher gain can increase that output (measured in decibels [dB]). The reader reference is usually known as 0 dBD (zero decibels referenced to a dipole). Figuring out the antenna gain in dBD is simple if you have a scientific calculator or computer. The equation is:

Antenna gain (dBD) = 10*log (Power output/Power input)

If you have looked into rules of various governing bodies you will often see the acronym ERP used, which stands for effective radiated power from an individual antenna. Effective radiated power is quite simply the power supplied to an antenna times the antenna gain in a given direction, or as the product of the antennas power and its gain relative to a half-wave dipole in a given direction:

ERP (dBm) = Power in dBm – loss in transmission line (dB) + antenna gain in dBd

Summary

In this chapter, you learned about the basic theory of electromagnetic radiation. Intuitively understanding how electromagnetic radiation behaves, both in the near field and the far field, particularly around materials commonly found in your environment, is critical to quickly and easily understanding the performance experienced by your RFID installation even before the readers are installed.

In the first section, I showed you the wonders and basic characteristics of electromagnetic radiation. You learned that electromagnetic radiation comes in two primary types of concern for RFID systems: near-field dynamic magnetic fields and electromagnetic waves. The magnetic fields are energy storage fields, whereas the electromagnetic waves are energy propagation fields.

You discovered that magnetic fields are created by fixed magnets as well as electric current traveling through a wire. The right-hand rule may be used to determine the direction of the magnetic field generated by electric currents. You learned that loops of wire increase the strength of the magnetic field within the loops, or coils. Small-diameter coils have higher magnetic field strengths within them than do larger-diameter coils when they are both tuned to the same frequency.

You also learned that dynamic, or time-varying, electric currents create dynamic, or time-varying, magnetic fields. And you learned that dynamic, time-varying magnetic fields create dynamic, time-varying electric fields by exerting force upon charges located within the magnetic field. By using time-varying currents, coiled loop reader antennas are able to induce currents within coiled loop tag antennas. When the tag is sufficiently close to the reader antenna, the induced current is sufficient to power the operation of the tag.

I discussed that electromagnetic waves result from time-varying electric currents and have numerous properties including frequency, amplitude, phase, and polarization. You also learned that they are linear, allowing for both constructive and destructive interference at a point in space without destroying the intersecting waves.

You learned that electromagnetic waves have both an electric and a magnetic component that are perpendicular to one another. Tags may couple to either or both of these components in varying degrees to harvest their operating power.

You learned that all materials attenuate the amplitude of electromagnetic waves as they propagate through them. You also learned that electromagnetic waves are reflected to greater and lesser extents at every surface boundary.

After showing you the basic characteristics of electromagnetic radiation, I discussed the Complete Laws of Electrodynamics as described by Maxwell's equations. You learned that Maxwell's equations describe the interrelationship between dynamic electric fields and dynamic magnetic fields. These fields are not interrelated in the static case.

Electric fields tend to emanate from charge sources, similar to shrapnel from hand grenades. You also saw that magnetic fields form closed loops, similar to the lines of creamer formed by a tempest in a teacup. You learned that conducting surfaces attract electric fields and that conducting surfaces inhibit the flow of magnetic fields near them.

Finally, you learned that although Maxwell's equations describe the behavior of electromagnetic waves regardless of their frequency, multiple frequencies are allowed by regulations and used by the various RFID systems because they exhibit significantly different functional characteristics across the gigahertz of frequency diversity within the radio frequency spectrum.

Exam Essentials

Explain the difference between near field and far field. The near field and the far field are two regions in electromagnetic radiation. The near field is the region near the antenna and extending approximately $\lambda/(2\pi)$ from the antenna. The near field is an energy storage field primarily characterized by the magnetic field. The far field exists beyond the near field. The far field is an energy propagation field primarily characterized by electromagnetic waves.

Explain nulls and standing waves. Just like nulls, standing waves are caused by the interference of waves, but, unlike nulls, standing waves maintain a measurable amplitude.

Explain the dielectric constant. The dielectric constant is a dimensionless quantity that characterizes the relative electrical permittivity of a material, which is to say the ability of the material to store electrical energy in an electric field. For most materials under most conditions, the dielectric constant has a constant value independent of both the magnitude and direction of the electric field.

Identify RF propagation techniques. Radio frequency energy propagates through a medium in a manner that may be modeled as an electromagnetic wave. An electromagnetic wave consists of two perpendicular components, an electric field and a magnetic field, that are both orthogonal to the direction of travel of the wave. Electromagnetic waves exhibit linearity and may be refracted, deflected, reflected, and attenuated as they propagate through an environment.

Describe antenna field performance as it relates to reflective and absorptive materials. An antenna within an unobstructed free-space environment radiates energy in a pattern specific to that antenna. For antennas commonly used in UHF RFID systems, this pattern is similar in shape to an egg. When RF reflective and RF absorptive materials are present in the environment, the antenna's radiation pattern no longer resembles the simple free-space pattern for the antenna. Reflective material redirects the antenna's radiated energy, thereby distorting the field in a manner specific to the location of the reflective material relative to the antenna. A large sheet of metal, for example, that is placed at a 45-degree angle to the antenna approximately half-way into the antenna's pattern will cause the antenna's radiation pattern to extend 90 degrees to either the left or the right (depending on which of the two 45-degree angles is chosen). In this way, the radiation pattern can be made to extend around corners. Shielding, such as a cage, can also be used to trap the energy in a confined space. This has the effect of increasing the available energy in that space. RF absorptive materials absorb the energy emitted by the antenna. In this way, they reduce the size of the radiation pattern, limiting its reach in the directions where it must pass through the absorptive materials. Highly absorptive materials can be used to completely absorb energy in certain areas where the amount of RF energy is desired to be reduced.

Key Terms

Before you take the exam, be certain you are familiar with the following terms:

gain

linearity

Maxwell's equations

near field

near-field region

null

permeability

right-hand rule

standing wave

Review Questions

1. Which type of material might you use to steer electromagnetic waves around a corner?

   A. Water

   B. Chicken wire

   C. Glass

   D. Cardboard

2. Which of the following absorbs electromagnetic wave energy at UHF frequencies? (Select three options.)

   A. Water

   B. Chicken wire

   C. Glass

   D. Cardboard

3. RFID systems that operate in which of the following frequency ranges rely on energy storage fields for communication? (Select two options.)

   A. LF

   B. HF

   C. UHF

   D. Microwave

4. Which of the following properties must be equalized in a resonant coiled antenna?

   A. C and L

   B. R and C

   C. R and L

   D. R, C, and L

5. Which law states that the net magnetic flux flowing out of any closed surface is zero?

   A. Faraday's Law

   B. Ampere's Law

   C. Gauss's Law for electric flux

   D. Gauss's Law for magnetic flux

6. Which type of reader antenna is least likely to communicate with a linearly polarized antenna that is located horizontally?

   A. Linear antenna positioned horizontally

   B. Linear antenna positioned vertically

   C. Circularly polarized antenna positioned horizontally

   D. Circularly polarized antenna positioned vertically

7. A UHF RFID tag may be read through which of the following materials? (Select three options.)
   A. Cardboard
   B. Water
   C. Sand
   D. Steel

8. The magnetic field created by an electric current flowing through a straight wire ____________________.
   A. flows from the end of the wire in the direction of the electric current (the north pole), out into space, and back into the other end of the wire (the south pole)
   B. flows from the end of the wire in the opposite direction of the electric current (the north pole), out into space, and back into the other end of the wire (the south pole)
   C. flows around the wire in concentric circles in a direction following the right-hand rule
   D. flows around the wire in concentric circles in a direction following the left-hand rule

9. The magnetic field of which commonly used RFID frequency range(s) penetrates small amounts of metal to the point that communication between tag and reader may occur?
   A. LF
   B. HF
   C. UHF
   D. None of the above

10. The far-field region begins at roughly what distance from the antenna?
   A. $\lambda 2\pi$
   B. λ/π
   C. $\lambda/(2\pi)$
   D. $(2\pi)/\lambda$

11. The electric field and the magnetic field are ____________________.
   A. not interconnected in the dynamic case
   B. dependent solely on electric charges
   C. not interconnected in the static case
   D. parallel in the propagation of an electromagnetic wave

12. The polarization of an electromagnetic wave is determined by ____________________.
   A. the direction of the electric field
   B. the direction of the magnetic field
   C. the direction of the electric flux
   D. the direction of the magnetic flux

13. The polarization of an electromagnetic wave may be which of the following? (Select all that apply.)

A. Square

B. Linear

C. Elliptical

D. Circular

14. The magnetic field created by an RFID reader operating in the HF frequency range decreases in proportion to the inverse of what power of the distance from the antenna?

A. 1

B. 2

C. 3

D. 4

15. The power density available to a tag operating in the UHF far field decreases as the inverse of what power of the distance from the antenna?

A. 1

B. 2

C. 3

D. 4

16. What are some of the reasons that a reader and a tag may not be able to communicate?

A. The tag is too far from the reader's signal to harvest sufficient operating energy.

B. The tag's multi-path communication signals destructively interfere at the reader's antenna.

C. The tag's multi-path communication signal is incorrectly polarized for the reader's antenna to detect it.

D. The tag's communication signal is significantly weaker than another signal received at the reader's antenna.

E. All of the above.

17. What common material can be used to mitigate the impact of poorly placed metal in the UHF RFID environment?

A. Sand

B. Water

C. Cardboard

D. Wood

18. The experienced permeability of what material may change throughout the year?

A. Sand

B. Water

C. Cardboard

D. Metal

19. Rectangular packages with foil along one side (such as blister packs for drugs) create a sequence of vertical metal bars when placed in a case and viewed from one side. What reader antenna polarization and orientation is best suited to read tags located on the other side of the case?

A. Linear polarized antenna positioned horizontally

B. Linear polarized antenna positioned vertically

C. Circularly polarized antenna positioned horizontally

D. Circularly polarized antenna positioned vertically

20. Which frequencies are best able to communicate through 12 cm of water? (Select two options.)

A. LF

B. HF

C. UHF

D. Microwave

Answers to Review Questions

1. B. Chicken wire acts as an efficient reflector of electromagnetic radiation in the UHF frequency spectrum. By placing it at an angle to the radiation source (the RFID antenna), the emitted signal can be directed around corners.

2. A, C, D. UHF electromagnetic waves do not pass through the metal of the chicken wire but do pass through the other materials.

3. A, B. LF and HF RFID systems communicate and operate within the near field, which is the energy storage field. UHF and microwave systems operate in the far field, which is the power propagation field.

4. A. A coiled antenna is resonant when its capacitance (C) and inductance (L) are equalized.

5. D. Gauss's Law for magnetic flux defines how magnetic fields behave. One of the properties of magnetic fields is that they form closed loops. A magnetic field flows from the north pole of a magnet out into space and back into the south pole of the magnet.

6. B. A horizontally positioned linearly polarized tag antenna is unlikely to capture any of the energy emitted by a vertically positioned linearly polarized reader antenna. The horizontally positioned linearly polarized reader antenna is most likely to communicate with the tag. The circularly polarized antenna will be able to communicate with the tag regardless of its orientation.

7. A, B, C. Only steel prevents UHF frequencies from penetrating it. UHF RFID tags may be read through small amounts of water and relatively larger amounts of cardboard and sand.

8. C. The current flowing through a straight wire does not create a magnetic north pole and south pole. The current creates a magnetic field that forms concentric circles around the wire. The right-hand rule is used to determine the direction of the magnetic field.

9. A. The magnetic fields generated by the LF frequency ranges do penetrate small thicknesses of metals. This penetration allows readers to communicate with tags located next to and even behind metal surfaces. All other frequency ranges commonly used by RFID systems do not have magnetic fields that penetrate metals to any significant extent.

10. C. The near field ends at a distance of roughly $r = \lambda/(2\pi)$ from the antenna, at which point the far field begins.

11. C. The electric and magnetic fields are disconnected in the static case. Only when the fields are time varying (that is, dynamic) do the fields become interconnected.

12. A. The convention for describing polarization is to use the direction of the electric field vector at a point in space.

13. B, C, D. The electric field of an electromagnetic wave may rotate as the wave propagates through space. The electric field may rotate either left or right. If the electric field rotates to the right with constant amplitude, the wave is said to be right circular polarized. Circular polarization is a special case of elliptical polarization, in which the amplitude increases and decreases in a regular fashion as the electric field rotates. If the electromagnetic wave does not rotate as it propagates, it is linearly polarized.

14. C. In the near field, the magnetic field produced by the antenna diminishes at a rate proportional to $1/r^3$. The power from the antenna decreases at a rate of $1/r^6$.

15. B. In the far field, the power density decreases much more slowly than in the near field. The power density in the far field decreases proportional to $1/r^2$.

16. E. Electromagnetic waves are linear, meaning that the wave experienced at a point in time and location in space is the addition of all waves intersecting then and there. Multi-path delays, absorption by materials in the environment, and reflections and polarizations that result from those reflections are all phenomena that will be experienced by the electromagnetic waves.

17. B. Water effectively absorbs UHF energy. By placing water in front of metal fixtures that are creating too much reflection, the reflected waves can be eliminated.

18. C. Cardboard absorbs moisture from the air and its local environment. As the humidity varies throughout the year, so will the moisture content of the cardboard. During times of increased humidity, the cardboard will contain more water, which will decrease its experienced permeability in those conditions.

19. B. A linear polarized antenna positioned vertically will have all of its energy propagate through the case. The vertically oriented metal foil acts as a filter to electromagnetic radiation that is not vertically oriented. Thus, a linear polarized antenna positioned horizontally will have its energy blocked by the case, and a circularly polarized antenna will have all but the vertically oriented portion of its energy filtered by the case.

20. A, B. Although UHF and microwave frequencies can communicate through water, the power levels allowed by the local regulations for use by RFID systems prevent them from communicating through large quantities of water. LF and HF frequencies are little affected by water.

Chapter 2

Interrogation Zone Basics

RFID+ EXAM OBJECTIVES COVERED IN THIS CHAPTER:

✓ **1.1 Describe interrogator functionality**

- 1.1.1 I/O capability
- 1.1.2 Handheld interrogators
- 1.1.3 Vehicle-mount interrogator
- 1.1.4 LAN/serial communications
- 1.1.5 Firmware upgrades
- 1.1.6 Software operation (GUIs)

✓ **1.2 Describe configuration of interrogation zones**

- 1.2.1 Explain interrogator-to-interrogator interference
- 1.2.2 Optimization
- 1.2.3 System performance and tuning
- 1.2.4 Travel speed and direction
- 1.2.5 Bi-static/mono-static antennas

✓ **1.3 Define anticollision protocols (e.g., number of tags in the field/response time)**

✓ **1.4 Given a scenario, solve dense interrogator environment issues (domestic/international)**

- 1.4.1 Understand how a dense interrogator installation is going to affect network traffic
- 1.4.2 Installation of multiple interrogators, (e.g., dock doors, synchronization of multiple interrogators, antenna footprints)

Interrogation zones, despite their name, are not zones for interrogating criminals—unless these criminals carry a radio frequency identification (RFID) tag. An interrogation zone, also called a read zone, is an area specially configured for reading information from or writing information to RFID tags. Interrogation zones can consist of various hardware components, but the main devices that make these zones work are RFID interrogators with antennas connected to them. The rest of the equipment is optional, but is useful for either mounting the interrogators and antennas (such as different types of portals, racks, and stands) or adding capabilities to the zone via various peripheral devices such as RFID printers/encoders, light stacks, and motion sensors.

In this chapter, you will discover the components of an RFID interrogator as well as the interrogator's functions. You will learn that interrogators are capable of reading tags and writing information to tags; they can directly manage various input/output (I/O) devices and offer a graphical user interface (GUI) for easy configuration. You will see that interrogators can be updated through firmware upgrades and you will learn when it is appropriate to upload a new firmware version.

Next, I will show you the difference between a "dumb" reader and a "smart" reader as well as the capabilities that a smart reader can provide. You will also learn about various communication methods between readers and tags and restrictions posed on the radiated power that vary by region. Then you will go through techniques of tag population management that consist of several interrogator commands including the always popular Kill command (this chapter will be very morbid).

You will also learn about the various types of interrogators, such as fixed interrogators and mobile interrogators including vehicle-mounted interrogators, handhelds, and other kinds of mobile devices, as well as their functions, installation, and suitable applications.

After you learn the basics about interrogator construction, functions, and types, you will dive into factors that affect the performance of an interrogation zone. You will learn about the dwell time necessary for successful reading and/or writing operations, as well as various aspects of antenna performance. You will identify types of antenna polarization, such as linear or circular polarization, and antenna design, where you will learn about differences between bi-static and mono-static antennas. Next, you will understand the antenna coverage as well as its imperfections, and how the field changes with power input. You will learn about antenna configurations in the form of RFID portals and tunnels as well as their function, suitable use, and customization according to your environment and applications. You will also learn about antenna tuning and proper shielding in order to prevent RF interference.

You will then identify the dense reader environment and its challenges. You will learn how to overcome these challenges by using synchronization, the listen-before-talk (LBT) technique, and frequency hopping. Because dense reader mode solves reader collisions, you will also have to find out what happens if two or more tags respond at the same time. This situation has to be handled by anticollision methods, and you will learn about the various types of these algorithms.

Finally, this chapter will give you a great overview of various factors and challenges related to interrogation zones and their components, as well as teach you about solutions to problems that can come up when designing, installing, or using the RFID interrogation zones.

Interrogator Construction

An RFID interrogator works as a transmitter as well as a receiver of radio frequency (RF) signals. A signal is broadcast and received through antennas that are connected to the interrogator. This is all you would generally need to know in order to be able to use the interrogator in your RFID system. However, for those who are always asking how things work and why, I am including a description of the interrogator's components and their function.

An interrogator consists of an RF transmitter and RF receiver (these two components are sometimes called an RF module), a control unit (basically a computer), and communication channels going to the antenna, as well as network or peripheral devices. Sometimes there is a circulator, which is necessary for function of a mono-static antenna (a single antenna used to broadcast and receive from the same antenna port).

The RF transmitter consists of the following:

- An oscillator that creates a carrier frequency, which is the frequency the reader is operating on.
- A modulator that modulates the carrier wave from the oscillator in order to include commands or data intended for the RF tag.
- An amplifier that amplifies (strengthens) the signal before it is transferred to the antenna. The antenna then broadcasts this signal to the tags in the environment.

The RF receiver includes these components:

- A demodulator, which extracts data from the received signal that comes from the tag through the interrogator's antenna.
- An amplifier, which amplifies the demodulated signal before it is sent to be processed by the control unit.

The control unit contains the following:

- A microprocessor (and controller) that controls the function of an interrogator, governs data transmissions, processes and filters the received data, sends data via a network to the middleware or back-end applications, manages various I/O devices, receives commands from middleware or other applications, and communicates with memory.
- Memory in the form of random access memory (RAM) and read-only memory (ROM) that carries an operating system such as Linux or Windows CE. Many times there is a data storage, which is equivalent to a hard drive in a computer, which captures operation logs and data transferred to and from the tag.

Interrogator Functions

Interrogator functions used to vary by manufacturer. Today, the competition is high and all manufacturers try to provide the best functionality possible within the most competitive price range. Of course, the features these units offer can slightly differ, but the basic functions are pretty much included in all of them.

Read/Write Capability

Interrogators offer read and write capabilities. Some types of interrogators, particularly older handheld units, can only read tags, not read and write to tags. Most of the interrogators support currently used air interface protocols and data standards such as electronic product code (EPC) Class 0, Class 1, Generation 2, and International Organization for Standardization (ISO) 18000-6A and B (possibly C) for ultra-high-frequency (UHF) readers, or ISO 18000-3 and ISO 15693 for high-frequency readers.

Read and write ranges vary based on the interrogator's quality, tuning, the characteristics of the interrogation antenna, tags under interrogation, and present environmental conditions (including interference, RF noise, materials, and humidity). The output power is limited by various regulations and differs around the world.

The read range is the specific distance over which the reader can successfully read data from a tag. The read range can be relatively long, but you cannot forget about the loss in a signal's strength based on a distance (loss follows the inverse square rule, as pointed out in Chapter 1, "Physics of RFID"). The tag usually needs around 30 microwatts to be powered and respond back to the reader.

The write range is the distance over which the reader can successfully write data to the tag. The write range is usually a lot shorter than the read range. The shorter distance ensures higher reliability of the write operation. The writing process is also very sensitive to outside conditions. When writing to a tag, you should try to avoid RF interference from other sources, which could interrupt the operation.

TIP

To successfully write tags on a conveyor line, you should consider an RFID tunnel to avoid interference and concentrate the wanted RF signal into one area. The tunnel allows a higher reader output without affecting other tags along the conveyor.

I/O Capability

Many interrogators today can directly operate peripheral devices and provide I/O ports to connect these units to the interrogator. Devices directly operated by an interrogator include the following:

- Light stacks
- Audible devices such as horns or beepers

- Gate triggers for opening the doors
- Conveyor diverters
- Box pushers using a hydraulic arm
- Vehicle tollgates
- Video cameras

Digital I/O devices are also being integrated as an upgrade to conventional programmable logic controllers (PLCs).

NOTE You can find more information on RFID peripherals in Chapter 6, "Peripherals."

User Interface

Interrogators can be configured either through a network by using middleware, or by using a specific reader deployment tool such as ODIN's EasyReader, or directly through the reader's GUI. Every manufacturer provides a different GUI for its reader, and different GUIs can be more or less user friendly. Most of the reader manufacturers, however, have designed the GUI for highly experienced RFID engineers, and they are meant to be used for one reader at a time.

To access the GUI, you have to connect your computer to the reader either directly by using a serial connection through RS-232, through an Ethernet connection through RJ-45 (using crossover cable) or universal serial bus (USB), or through a network. If you are not connecting through a serial cable, in most cases you will need to know the Internet Protocol (IP) address of the device.

If you do not know the IP address of the reader (and this can happen if the IP is assigned dynamically), do not fret; there is a way to find it. You can connect your computer directly to the reader by using a serial connection and establish communication by using HyperTerminal or Telnet. To do this, you will need to set up your communication port (COM) with a correct data rate in bits per second (usually 38,400), data bits (usually 8), parity (usually none), stop bits (usually 1), and flow control (usually hardware or none). After you establish communication, you will be able to retrieve the reader's IP address.

After you have the reader's IP address, you have to set up your network settings in order to communicate with the reader. Then you can input the IP address into your browser (Microsoft Internet Explorer works just fine) and it will take you to the reader's Hypertext Transfer Protocol (HTTP) interface. Sometimes, access to the reader is blocked by a password; sometimes it will let you in without it.

The user interface will give you access to the reader's settings including the active antennas (antennas that are connected to the interrogator and are not disabled by the system or by the user), air interface and data protocol used or enabled, network settings such as Dynamic Host Configuration Protocol (DHCP), IP address, subnet mask and default gateway, read/write power settings, polling frequency, filtering, and other settings as well as a capability to change these settings or upload new firmware. The settings can be reconfigured either by simply clicking on a rollout menu and selecting an option or by typing in commands and parameters by using a command line.

Most of the GUIs that ship with standard readers are meant to be used as a demonstration tool, which is suited for only one reader at a time and is not scalable or automated. The team deploying the largest RFID network in the world—for the U.S. Department of Defense—used ODIN Technologies' EasyReader, which provides a simple drag-and-drop interface to set up many readers and printers at a time. This industry best-practice software allows for very fast design, configuration, and testing of entire RFID networks. This is done by dragging and dropping virtual portals onto the floor plan of the facility to be deployed.

Dumb Reader vs. Smart Reader

Honestly, when I first heard someone referring to an RFID interrogator as a "dumb reader," I was quite offended. This device (although it has already seen several winters) was able to read data in RFID tags, but not much else. However, this capability still seems to me miraculous, and therefore I would never call this device "dumb," even though the interrogators on today's market are bursting with advanced features and functions waiting to be taken advantage of.

What can a "smart" reader do? Here is a list of some of its capabilities:

Filtering Instead of reading all available data from tags and transferring the data to the host, a reader acquires only selected data and out of these, only the requested (necessary) part goes to the host/middleware/application.

Cycle acquisition A smart reader can be set up for continuous polling for tags, or it can poll in preset time intervals, such as every second, 3 seconds, 5 seconds, up to days. This reduces the amount of data going through the system, and the tags are interrogated only when needed.

> **Real-Time** The reader transfers data as soon as it acquires them.
>
> **Batch** Data are collected and sent to the host in batches.
>
> **Triggered** Data are collected and sent to the host only when triggered by a certain event or by the user.
>
> **Pull from the Host/Push to the Host** Data are accessed and copied by the host or sent to the host.

Managing Sensors Readers can manage external sensors, such as motion sensors, through their I/O interfaces.

Triggering Interrogation Interrogation can be started based on a signal from a sensor (such as a motion sensor), based on time, or manually.

Dense Reader Mode Operations Readers are able to operate in an environment with many other readers present and are able to avoid or reduce the risk of interference. This topic will be discussed further later in this chapter.

Anticollision capabilities Readers are able to poll for the tags by using certain algorithms to prevent tag collisions (two or more tags responding at the exact same time). These algorithms also will be discussed further in this chapter.

Communication

Interrogators differ in the communication methods they use. In active RFID systems, the readers send signals to active tags and receive the signal that the active tags transmit. This signal can be a response to the interrogation signal (referred to as reader-talks-first, or RTF) or a tag can beacon its serial number to the environment (referred to as tag-talks-first, or TTF).

In passive and semi-passive RFID systems, the reader always has to send out a signal first in order to receive data from the tag (RTF). The transmitted signal sent to a passive tag powers the tag's circuitry and provides it with energy to modulate the signal and send the data back to the reader. A semi-passive tag uses a battery to run its circuitry but communicates by reflecting and modulating the reader's signal in the same way as a passive tag. Passive and semi-passive systems can use inductive coupling or passive backscatter to communicate with a tag.

RFID interrogators can operate on various frequencies. Usually, an interrogator can operate on only one frequency band (the band used in its region); however, some manufacturers are coming up with devices that can operate in a wider band to include frequencies used in different regions (such as readers that can work in the United States as well as in Europe). There are also devices that use two frequency bands, such as interrogators that work on low as well as high frequency. (These are usually made up of two readers integrated into one case.)

The operations of the interrogators are regulated by government and standardization organizations around the world. These organizations not only allocate a specific frequency that can be used for RFID communication and publish standards applying to data formats and air interfaces, but also place restrictions on the output power and transmission techniques. Table 2.1 shows the allowed output power, number of channels used for frequency hopping, and other limitations related to operating frequency for interrogators around the world. (Because these restrictions are the most variable in the UHF frequency band, I will concentrate on UHF.)

TABLE 2.1 Transmission Restrictions by Region

Continent or Country	UHF Band in MHz	Allowed Output Power (ERP)	Other
North America (U.S. and Canada)	902–928	1 W up to 4 W with gained antenna (EIRP)	Should use frequency hopping—50 channels (1 channel = 500 kHz)
South America	915 (typically accepted)	Same as U.S.	
Europe	865–865.6 865.6–867.6 867.6–868 869.4–869.65	0.1 W 2 W 0.5 W 0.5 W	(1 channel = 200 kHz) Should use listen-before-talk (LBT)
Africa	865–868 (up to 870) (north) 915 (south)	Same as Europe Same as U.S.	

TABLE 2.1 Transmission Restrictions by Region *(continued)*

Continent or Country	UHF Band in MHz	Allowed Output Power (ERP)	Other
China	917–922 (temporary)	2 W	
China (Hong Kong)	865–868 and/or 920–925	Same as Europe Same as U.S.	
India	865-867	4 W (EIRP)	
Japan	952–955 952–954	0.02 W 4 W (EIRP) (need to be registered)	Should use LBT
Korea	908.5–914	4 W (EIRP)	Should use LBT and frequency hopping
Australia	918–926	1 W (EIRP)	
New Zealand	864–868 and 921–929	1 W up to 4 W when using frequency hopping	
Singapore	866–869 and 923–925	0.5 W 0.5–2 W	Unlicensed Up to 2 W licensed
Thailand	920–925	Up to 0.5 W Up to 4 W (EIRP)	Unlicensed Licensed
Malaysia	868.1 and 919–923	Both freq. up to 0.5 W Both freq. up to 2 W	Unlicensed Licensed

Information based on the document by Asia-Pacific Telecommunity: *Draft New APT Recommendation on Spectrum for Ultra High Frequency (UHF) Radio Frequency Identification (RFID) Devices.*

Tag Population Management

Interrogators manage tags that are present in the interrogation zone via commands defined by the communication and data protocols. The following commands are based on the capabilities of EPC Generation 2 interrogators, and some of them may not be available in devices operating under other protocols. There are three primary commands:

Select This command picks out a group of tags based on certain characteristics, such as a specific manufacturer's ID or other parts of the EPC number. Because this command concentrates on only a small part of the data within the tag, it is able to quickly locate and target certain tag groups within the whole tag population.

Inventory This command isolates an individual tag from the group allocated by the Select command.

Access This command is used to address a specific tag after it is singulated by the Inventory command. After the tag is accessed, other specific commands can be issued, such as the following:

Lock This command locks the access to a tag. It is protected by an Access password. The tag can be write-locked to prevent unauthorized changing of the tag's data, as well as read-locked to prevent reading the tag's data. This command also can be used to lock specific memory banks.

Kill This command is used to permanently disable the tag. After being killed, the tag is unable to respond to interrogation. The Kill command is also password protected.

Other techniques used by Generation 2 for tag management are *sessions* and *AB symmetry*. Each tag has the ability to operate in four sessions. This is useful when tags are inventoried by more than one type of reader. Each reader or group of readers interrogates tags in a separate session, and therefore does not interfere with other readers when interrogating tags. The session number is sent to a tag during the Inventory round.

After the tag is inventoried, it changes its state from A to B or from B to A. This technique is called AB symmetry and replaces the Generation 1 method, which was putting tags to sleep after they were inventoried to avoid interference with interrogation of other tags.

Firmware Upgrades

There are several reasons for uploading a firmware upgrade or patch to your interrogator. However, you should not be upgrading just because a new version is available. With interrogators as well as other electronic devices, one old rule should be applied: "If it ain't broke, don't fix it." Therefore, you should check what features the new version offers and why it was developed, and carefully consider whether it is important to upload this version to your interrogators. Why am I even discussing this? Because a simple power interruption or installation error could leave your interrogator disabled, and you may have to reload the operating system totally before being able to use this device again.

However, there are valid reasons for upgrading the firmware—for instance, if the upgrade is released to fix bugs in the existing firmware that have been causing you problems from time to time, or if you need to add new capabilities such as the ability to support the EPC Class 1 Generation 2 protocol. (RFID printers also can be upgraded to support Generation 2 through firmware.)

New capabilities often can be put into your interrogator through firmware, but sometimes you will have to purchase a new component or a completely new unit to support certain features and perform specific operations.

Interrogator Types

Various types of interrogators exist on the commercial market. They differ not only by their function, but also by their form, design, and suitability for specific applications. The main kinds are fixed interrogators—for dock doors, conveyors, and personnel doorways—and mobile interrogators such as vehicle-mounted interrogators and handheld interrogators.

Fixed Interrogators

Fixed interrogators are intended to be mounted onto a portal or a wall. They need to be locally connected to a power source and often to a network through appropriate cables. They come in a sturdy metal case, usually in dimensions roughly the size of a laptop (about 30 × 25 × 5 cm [12 × 10 × 2 inches]), but many manufacturers are working on developing smaller units. Usually the case has openings for easy attachment via screws. Other features of fixed interrogators include the following:

- Operate in temperatures around –20°C to 50°C (–4°F to 122°F).
- Withstand a certain amount of dust or moisture, but do not expect that you can splash these devices with water.
- Carry various LEDs to indicate different conditions. (Some readers do not have this option.)
- Usually support up to four antennas and have four or eight ports for antenna connections (four ports for mono-static antennas, eight ports for bi-static antennas). You can also find a fixed interrogator with an embedded antenna.
- Provide reading and writing capabilities and usually support multiple protocols (such as EPC Class 0, 1, and Gen 2; ISO; and so forth).
- Include I/O port(s) to connect various low-voltage I/O devices such as light stacks or motion sensors.
- Provide network interfaces through a serial port (RS-232), Ethernet port (RJ-45), or USB port.
- Can communicate wirelessly. Some manufacturers include this feature in the interrogator itself; in other cases you have to connect the interrogator to a wireless bridge through an Ethernet connection. Wireless local area networks (LANs) have some limitations in bandwidth, and therefore this type of networking is not always suitable in dense reader environments, but works well when used with vehicle-mounted or other mobile readers. (The various readers differ greatly in the amount of data they send out on the network, so this should be taken into consideration when choosing a reader for yourself or your client.)
- Require access to a grounded power source.
- Are used with dock door portals, conveyor portals and tunnels, door portals for access control, and many other applications.

Mobile Interrogators

Mobile interrogators are specially designed to be "on the move," often with interfaces that support wireless communication. They do not have to rely on the plug in the wall and are usually ruggedized to withstand rough handling by personnel or a vehicle. Mobile interrogators can be vehicle mounted, handheld, or come in various forms such as small PDAs, cell phones, or plug-in units.

Vehicle-mounted interrogators have the following characteristics:

- Are specially designed to be mounted onto a vehicle such as a forklift, clamp truck, or trolley.
- Usually come in slightly smaller sizes or different shapes than fixed interrogators in order to be easily integrated or mounted onto a vehicle without obstructing its functions. They are usually plugged into an on-board computer (or connected wirelessly); sometimes they come in the form of a tablet computer with a touch screen.
- Are more robust than fixed interrogators, and withstand vibrations, shock, and sometimes even high-pressure washing.
- Provide reading and writing capabilities. Most of the time they support various protocols such as EPC Class 0, 1, and Gen 2, or ISO.
- Usually communicate through a wireless LAN. They can have the wireless capability integrated or can use a wireless bridge.
- Are usually powered by the vehicle's battery or can have their own.
- When used on a forklift, are usually mounted together with antennas between the forks and connected wirelessly to the on-board computer or to the network. Sometimes interrogators are mounted on a vehicle, and the antennas are affixed to the forks. Therefore, the cables connecting these devices have to be integrated either into the hydraulic cables used for moving the forks or in a way that the cables do not get damaged.

Handheld interrogators have these features:

- Come in the shape of a "hand gun," tablet PC, or PDA, and are relatively light and compact compared to fixed and vehicle-mounted interrogators.
- Usually have the ability to read bar codes, as well as RFID tags. Most of the handhelds used today provide writing capabilities, but sometimes you can find a handheld that is read-only.
- Support various protocols such as EPC Class 0, 1, or Gen 2, and ISO.
- Can function entirely wirelessly through a wireless LAN and be powered by an integrated rechargeable battery. This type of handheld provides great mobility but relies on the battery life.
- Can be tethered allowing the power and/or communication to run through a fixed cable. This type of handheld does not have as great mobility as the wireless kind because of the limited length of the tethered cable, but you do not have to worry about the battery life.
- Have an antenna integrated into the unit, unlike the fixed and vehicle-mounted interrogators. They can come with a linear as well as a circular antenna.
- Are often used for exception processing because of their mobility.

NOTE When you are looking at purchasing handheld interrogators, be aware that some manufacturers base their pricing on the basic handheld barcode reading unit plus the price of an RFID module.

Other forms of mobile interrogators include the following:

- RFID modules integrated into cell phones (for example Nokia's NFC phone)
- RFID modules in the form of a Personal Computer Memory Card International Association (PCMCIA) card that can be inserted into a laptop or a PC
- RFID modules intended for OEM manufacturers

Interrogation Zone Performance

To achieve the best possible performance of your interrogation zone, you have to consider many aspects related to interrogation zone configuration, the number of tags in the zone, tag performance and velocity, external challenges such as environmental conditions as well as RF noise and interference, and many other issues. I will take you through some of these and together we will figure out a way to overcome these challenges and ensure that your RFID interrogation zone works.

Dwell Time

To ensure that the tags are read by the interrogation zone, you have to consider the time that the tags are present in the zone. This is called *dwell time*, or *time in beam*. The dwell time depends on how fast the tags are moving through the interrogation zone, the data-transfer rate between the tags and the interrogator, and/or whether the tags are being read or written to. Generally, the longer the dwell time, the more successful the reading and writing operations will be. However, a long dwell time can be impractical, especially when you need to achieve a certain system performance and your conveyors are set for 300 to 600 feet per minute or your forklifts drive through the RFID portals at speeds around 5 kilometers per hour.

If you cannot change the speed of the tags traveling through the interrogation zone, you will have to change the zone parameters. You can increase the possible time in beam by configuring the antennas so that they will cover more space with their RF signal. You can do this either by positioning the antennas at an angle, so that the tag goes through the widest possible part of the beam (see Figure 2.1), or by sequencing the antenna transmissions following the direction of the tag's movement (see Figure 2.2).

Antenna Performance

Interrogators use several types of antennas, and each type has slight performance differences. Antennas vary based on their polarization (linear and circular) and by their function (monostatic and bi-static).

FIGURE 2.1 Time in beam

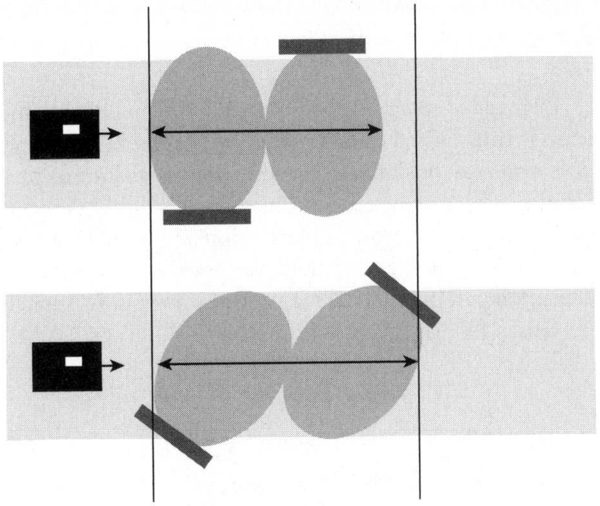

FIGURE 2.2 Antenna sequencing

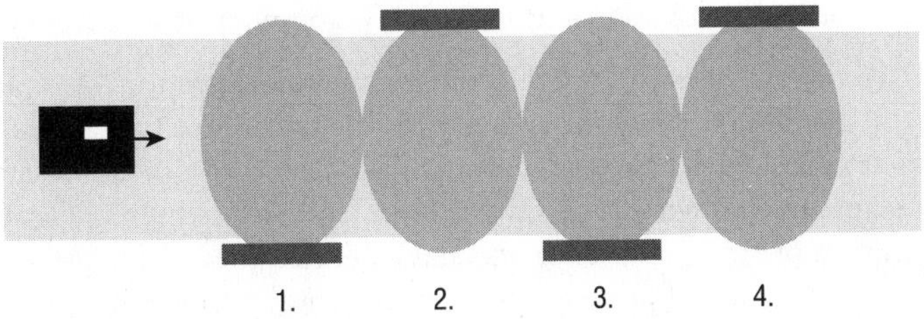

Antenna Polarization

Antennas can have either linear or circular polarization:

Circularly Polarized Antennas These produce a rotating RF field because they can receive signals from both vertical and horizontal planes and in between. These signals are a bit out of phase, which causes a certain loss of signal strength (50 percent on horizontal or vertical axes, less in between). However, because of the circulating field, often resembling a spiral, the antenna is not orientation sensitive and is suitable for use in applications where the tag orientation cannot be secured.

There are two types of circularly polarized antennas: right-hand circular and left-hand circular. With right-hand circular polarization, the rotation of the field is clockwise in the direction of the wave propagation. With left-hand circular polarization, the field rotates counterclockwise, again in the direction of the wave propagation.

TIP You can implement right-hand and left-hand circular antennas in your interrogation zone to increase read efficiency.

Linearly Polarized Antennas In contrast to circularly polarized antennas, with linearly polarized antennas the RF beam is transmitted in one plane, which can be horizontal or vertical. A linear antenna produces a consistent signal in one direction with lack of phase distortion; therefore, it can have better penetration of certain objects and slightly higher efficiency when reading tags. These tags have to have the same polarization as the antenna and be properly oriented for successful communication. Linear antennas are very orientation sensitive; therefore, they should be used in applications where the tag orientation is consistent, especially when using single dipole tags. This is further discussed in Chapter 4, "Tags."

Antenna Design

Antennas can vary by design; they can be bi-static or mono-static:

Mono-static Antenna A *mono-static antenna* fulfills both transmitting and receiving functions. An interrogator that supports mono-static antennas usually has a circulator that switches the transmitting and receiving functions and four ports intended for four antennas. An advantage of mono-static antennas is their smaller size as compared to bi-static antennas put into one case; however, they may be slightly less efficient due to using a circulator. Some manufacturers, however, such as Impinj, have tried to address this two-way communication challenge.

Bi-static Antenna A *bi-static antenna* uses two separate antennas: one for transmitting the RF signal to the tag and one for receiving the signal from the tag. These two antennas either can be integrated into one case, where each will have its own connector, or can be in separate cases. For the bi-static antennas to work, you always have to engage reciprocal antennas. Bi-static antennas are slightly more efficient than mono-static because they do not use a circulator and each antenna is solely dedicated to transmitting or receiving. An interrogator that supports bi-static antennas usually has eight antenna ports (four transmission ports, usually marked Tx, and four receiving ports, usually marked Rx) to accommodate four antennas.

TIP Transmitting and receiving antennas have the same construction; their function depends on the port you plug them into. If you plug a bi-static antenna into port Tx, it will be used for signal transmission; if you plug it into Rx, it will be used for signal reception.

Antenna Coverage

The antenna field consists of a main lobe, side lobes, and possibly back lobes. Now wait a second—back lobes? The RF signal can be diffracted (bent) to radiate to the back of the antenna—that's where the back lobes came from. The shape and size of all lobes depend on the antenna output power, antenna gain, and quality of antenna construction, as well as interference and reflections in the environment.

Most of the time, antennas do not have a perfect coverage within their lobes. These imperfections (sometimes called "holes") can be caused either by minor defects on the antenna reflector, by multi-path interference, or by external interference.

Multi-path interference is caused by reflections of an RF signal interfering with the antenna's field. When the reflected wave crosses the transmitted wave, it causes either null points with no signal or spots with a high signal concentration.

The antenna field is almost never perfect, and besides holes, its coverage usually varies in vertical as well as horizontal dimensions (see Figure 2.3). This is also usually caused by the antenna's construction and the unintentional imperfections in the antenna reflector as well as by outside interference or reflections. Before you install the antennas in your interrogation zone, you should test their function and make sure that you know their approximate coverage areas. You can do this with a tag on a yardstick or with a power tag, which measures the strength of an RF signal.

TIP

Do not forget that antenna coverage varies not only by the manufacturer, but also by each unit!

FIGURE 2.3 Perfect antenna coverage vs. reality

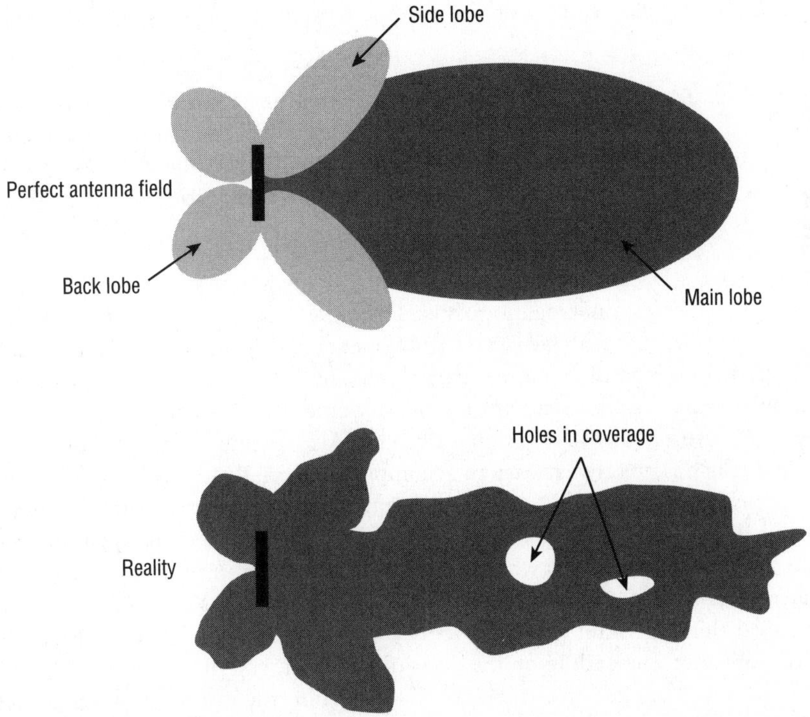

Antenna Configurations

Antennas can be installed in many ways, but are usually grouped to achieve the best coverage of a given area. Most often, antennas are housed within portals or tunnels.

RFID portals are usually implemented at dock doors, conveyors, personnel doors, and various entrance and exit doors and gates. The skeleton of a portal is usually constructed out of a sturdy material such as steel, aluminum, or thick plastic. Antennas and reader(s) are attached to this construction. There are no rules defining how the RFID portal should look. It highly depends on the application as well as the portal and hardware manufacturer. Some companies provide RFID portals already assembled and ready to be put in. This portal or stand can come with specific hardware, which is usually the case with stands provided by the reader manufacturer, as opposed to portals developed by independent integrators, for which you can choose any hardware components that you would like to integrate.

RFID stands can come either open (you can see and reach all components) or closed (the components are enclosed within the stand). The enclosure is usually done by using RF-neutral materials such as plastic, which protects the reader and antennas from damage as well as from being tampered with by unauthorized personnel.

RFID portals can carry a number of antennas; they are limited only by their size and application. The dock door portals usually include two to four antennas on each side of the door. Sometimes these antennas are accompanied by one or two antennas mounted overhead for better coverage and penetration. Overhead antennas are used with side antennas for conveyor reading, dock door pallet reading, or with stretch-wrapping machines, for instance.

TIP To modify the antenna field and change its direction and reach, it is useful to be able to rotate or move the antenna within the stand. If you are designing the stand or portal yourself, you can employ adjustable speaker holders used for home surround-sound systems or similar components to enable antenna positioning.

Usually, each RFID stand has a space for a reader. However, in many applications, you will need only one reader per interrogation zone. Therefore, all antennas at one dock door will connect to one reader that will be placed within one stand or in between the two stands. There are some restrictions regarding interrogator placement. You do not want to place the interrogator far away from certain antennas, because it would be necessary to use longer cables, which would cause a higher loss in signal strength. Also, the interrogator should stay out of harm's way, which is not always easy to accomplish, especially in a warehouse environment.

In some instances, you will use one interrogator for managing antennas belonging to neighboring dock doors. Now you are probably asking, "Why would anyone do that?" The main reason could be a problem with wiring the interrogator in order to reach antennas on both sides of the dock door. Many dock doors are sliding doors that open parallel to and closely spaced along the wall, which prevents you from installing the interrogator at the top of the door opening. Depending on the door mechanism, you may also have difficulty running the appropriate cables across the door. Using an interrogator to run antennas belonging to neighboring dock doors can provide the same results as the common "one interrogator, one dock door" approach. You will simply assign antennas to appropriate dock doors, and after the interrogator knows which antenna belongs to which dock door, it will be able to distinguish which tags were read where.

Another popular antenna configuration or a form of a portal is an RFID tunnel. Tunnels are used mainly with conveyor lines to focus the RF beam for successful reading of and writing to the tag. RFID tunnels are usually cubic enclosures made of sheet metal to prevent interference from the outside environment. On the inside, RFID tunnels contain antennas and RF-absorbent material (such as anechoic foam or ferrite) to absorb stray RF waves that could reflect and cause interference. A tunnel has front and back openings that are sometimes covered with a special curtain made of reflective material facing outside the tunnel and absorptive material facing inside the tunnel to prevent signal reflections.

TIP

To prevent reflections off the metal conveyor inside the tunnel, you can replace the existing metal rollers with rollers made of RF-neutral or absorptive material.

Antenna Tuning

To achieve the best performance from your interrogation zones, you have to tune the antenna for proper coverage. You do not want your interrogation zones to overlap and interfere with each other, but you also want to achieve the best coverage in the area that the tags will most likely travel through.

Real World Scenario

Getting out of a Jam

At an RFID installation, I had to figure out how to read tags on cases full of peanut butter that were coming down the conveyor in various orientations. Side and overhead antennas could not penetrate the peanut butter to read any tags that happened to be on the bottom of the case. I figured out that there also should be an antenna pointing to the product from the bottom of the conveyor. However, because the conveyor used metal rollers, the bottom antenna may not do much good. Fortunately, there are rollers available that are made of a special plastic that is transparent for RF waves. They do not last as long as the metal ones, but you can afford to implement them in smaller areas where they are really needed. The only problem with plastic rollers can be the generation of static electricity (see Chapter 6), which has to be solved by proper grounding. Needless to say, the plastic rollers went together on this deployment like peanut butter and jelly.

Increased power input into the antenna will also increase antenna output, which will enlarge the antenna coverage patterns and increase the reading distance. You have to make sure that you do not cross the limits set by the regulatory agencies, however. Usually, interrogators manufactured in the country where you are using them comply with local regulations; therefore, you do not have to worry about the limits. This is, of course, valid only if you use standard equipment. If you have the equipment custom designed or if you use noncertified and noncomplying components, you must make sure that your final antenna outputs do not go over the specified limit or you could be fined for each day of using noncompliant equipment.

The signal strength emitted by the antenna does not depend only on the power input into the antenna, but also on the antenna gain and cable loss. A standard antenna manufactured in the United States has a gain of 6 decibels (dB), and cable losses count in the tenths of decibels. The readers are configured in such a way that they produce power that will provide for maximum allowed antenna output with the standard gain and supplied cables. If you use an antenna with higher gain or shorter cables, you will need to turn the power down at the interrogator level.

TIP

Don't forget that with changed antenna output, the location and size of holes in the RF field may be positively or negatively affected as well.

Shielding

When you are setting up your interrogation zones and you know that some of the zones will overlap, you will have to shield each zone to prevent interference and reading of tags that belong to other zones. Do not forget that some other devices also may be affected by the RF emissions from your interrogators, such as RFID printers.

Materials most commonly used for shielding are metal mesh with holes significantly smaller than the wavelength of the frequency you are trying to shield, ferrite, or absorptive anechoic foam. You should not use metal sheets for shielding because the continuous metal surface could cause signal reflections, which could cause multi-path interference as well as interference at nearby interrogation zones.

Dense Reader Environment

The dense reader environment is defined as an environment where the number of simultaneously operating readers is larger than the number of available channels (for the United States it would be more than 50 readers in the area). You need to take into account several considerations that will affect your system.

Although *dense reader mode* is used to avoid reader-to-reader interference and increase efficiency in reading tags, it usually results in slower data-transfer rates between readers and tags. While in a single reader mode, the data rates can be up to 640 kilobits per second, but using a dense reader mode can slow them down about four times (or more).

> **Real World Scenario**
>
> **I Don't Do Windows**
>
> In a distribution center, I had to implement an RFID printer that would be used for exception processing right next to the dock door RFID portal. After the printer was in place, it kept printing out void labels. I checked its configuration and everything else that could cause this problem but could not figure out what was wrong. I finally realized that the printer could not validate the RFID tags because of interference from the nearby interrogation zone. Although the printer had metal casing that provided shielding, it also had a plastic window on the side to view the status of the media. As soon as I covered this window with an adhesive metal mesh foil to keep the view but prevent the interference–problem solved.

A dense reader environment also affects network traffic. As with any other network device, the reader will use a certain portion of the bandwidth to send the data to the host. With dense interrogator installation, you have to make sure that the network bandwidth is not already fully exhausted by various devices (such as PCs, barcode scanners, handheld readers, and RFID printers). The effect on network traffic will also vary by the type of your readers. If your readers provide filtering and data aggregation, they will send a lot less data through the network than will readers without these processing options.

Operation in dense reader mode provides a little bit more sophisticated way to avoid interference between simultaneously working readers than using shielding. Dense reader mode uses several methods to achieve these goals, such as synchronization, listen-before-talk (LBT), and frequency hopping.

Synchronization

The transmitting and receiving functions of readers in multiple-reader environments have to be synchronized to avoid interference. Without *synchronization*, the signals from other interrogation zones can interrupt the tag-reader communication or cause misreads or issues with writing to a tag. Synchronization methods include multiplexing and software synchronization.

Two types of multiplexing are currently used with RFID readers, time-division multiplexing and frequency-division multiplexing:

- *Time-division multiplexing* is based on readers sending signals on the same frequency in assigned time slots or operating for a certain time interval when other readers are turned off.
- *Frequency-division multiplexing* is based on the frequency spectrum being divided into multiple channels, and each reader can have its own channel to operate on. Some frequency bands—such as the unlicensed UHF band in the United States, which ranges from 902 to 928 MHz and can be divided into 50 to 124 channels—by law require a reader to hop off one channel onto a different one after less than half a second. If there are more readers than number of available channels, the readers have to employ frequency hopping in conjunction with the listen-before-talk and Q algorithm approaches.

Listen-Before-Talk

The *listen-before-talk (LBT)* approach is used with the frequency-division multiplexing scheme. The reader has to listen for any other reader transmitting on the chosen channel; only after it determines that the channel is available can it start using this channel for communication. If the channel is being used by another reader, the listening reader has to switch to another channel. This technique is mainly required in Europe by regulatory agencies.

Some interrogator manufacturers include a special LBT port for a single receiving antenna, which is used for listening while the reader is operating in the LBT mode.

Frequency Hopping

Frequency hopping is a method of switching channels when operating in a dense reader mode. Readers may be required to hop across multiple channels within a given frequency spectrum, mainly because of the time interval restrictions for transmitting in one channel. In the United States, the UHF band (902–928 MHz) is divided into 52 channels (500 kHz each), which are then used for frequency hopping. Readers may be required to use LBT before crossing to another channel.

Anticollision

When two tags respond simultaneously to interrogation, the event is called a collision. If a collision occurs, the reader cannot successfully transfer data within either tag. To prevent tag collisions, readers and tags employ several *anticollision* mechanisms. The main anticollision methods are *synchronous* and *asynchronous*, also called *deterministic* and *probabilistic*, respectively.

The probabilistic, or asynchronous, method is based on tags responding at randomly generated times. This method includes several specific protocols. The most well known is the *ALOHA protocol*, developed by the University of Hawaii, which was originally intended to avoid data collision in early LANs. ALOHA mode is based on a node not transmitting and receiving data packets all at once, but instead switching these functions based on time. If a collision occurs, the node transmits the data packet after a random delay.

Generation 2 tags use a slotted ALOHA-based anticollision mechanism called the Q algorithm (so named because of the University of Hawaii networking guys who came up with the protocol to be used in wireline networking). The reader sends a query with a parameter Q and a session number to a tag, and then creates a slotted time. The tag generates a random 16-bit number as a handle. When the reader inventories tags in a selected session, the tag has to generate a random number for a slot number, which has to be between 0 and 2^{Q}-1 . If this number is 0, the tag will send its handle to a reader. If the slot number is not 0, the tag waits a number of slots to send back the handle. If the reader acknowledges a single tag with a handle, it goes to an access phase and the rest of the tags have to wait for another round. If two or more tags answer, the reader has to send the same or a modified Q, and the whole process will run again.

The deterministic, or synchronous, reader protocol method is used by Generation 1 tags and is based on a reader going through the tags according to their unique ID. The most well-known synchronous method is a binary tree, or tree-walking, scheme. The reader has to know the tag IDs and then it searches the tree of all tag IDs. This method is slightly slower than the previous one because the search of all branches and sub-branches of the tree is time consuming, but the tags do not have to wait for the node to be available in order to communicate with a reader as well as hope for collision-free transmission.

Generation 2 supports two methods of backscatter encoding that tags use to send signals back to the reader. The reader assigns which method the tag should use when responding. These methods, Baseband-FM0 and Miller subcarrier, help with anticollision:

- *Baseband-FM0* encoding has been used by tags under the ISO standards but it is now supported by Generation 2 as well. This type of encoding is very fast but more susceptible to interference; therefore, it is not usually used in the dense reader mode of operation.
- *Miller subcarrier* encoding is slower but less susceptible to interference because of an advanced filtering technique that helps separate the tag responses from the signal transmitted by the reader. This method fits the tag responses between the channels used by the readers. It also guards the readers to prevent them from crossing into the tag channels.

Summary

In this chapter, you learned about the components of an RFID interrogator, which include the oscillator, transmitter, receiver, communication and antenna interfaces, and a control unit carrying the controller and processor, as well as memory.

Next, you discovered the interrogator's functions. You learned that interrogators are capable of reading tags and writing to the tags, that the read range can be longer than the write range, and that the reading operation takes less time than the writing operation.

Interrogators can directly manage various I/O devices such as light stacks or audible devices and offer a GUI for easy configuration. You saw how to access the GUI to communicate with the reader and discovered which settings can be configured through this interface.

I discussed how interrogators can be updated through firmware upgrades. It is appropriate to upload a new firmware version only when it fixes existing problems that were giving you a hard time or when it provides additional capabilities to the interrogator such as supporting new tag types or ensuring compatibility with new protocols (such as Generation 2, for instance).

You discovered the differences between a "dumb" reader and a "smart" reader as well as the capabilities the smart reader can provide. The smart readers can not only manage I/O, but also provide processing and filtering capabilities, data aggregation and transfer in real time or in batches, operation in dense reader mode, and assistance with anticollision.

You also learned about various communication methods between readers and tags including inductive coupling and passive backscatter, as well as about restrictions imposed on the radiated power that vary by region. The United States allows up to 4 watts of EIRP when hopping minimally across 50 channels in a band 26 MHz wide, whereas Europe allows up to 2 watts of ERP (which equals about 3.6 W EIRP) in a band 2 MHz wide while employing listen-before-talk.

In the tag population management section, you learned that interrogators use a set of commands including the Select command, which is used to pick out a group of tags based on a part of their EPC number; the Inventory command, which is used to singulate one tag from the group created by the Select command; and the Access command, which is used for accessing the tag and performing various data operations. Some of the subcommands of the Access command are Kill, Lock, Read, and Write.

You also learned about types of interrogators. Fixed interrogators are usually attached to an RFID portal or tunnel and usually use cables for their power as well as communication. I also discussed various kinds of mobile interrogators: vehicle-mounted interrogators are usually ruggedized and differently shaped versions of the fixed units implemented with forklifts or clamp trucks, and handhelds are portable because of their small size, integrated antenna, and wireless communication. There are other kinds of mobile devices, such as readers integrated into cell phones, PCMCIA cards, or reader modules used by OEM manufacturers.

After the interrogator construction, functions, and types, I described the factors that affect the performance of an interrogation zone. You learned that an appropriate dwell time is necessary to achieve successful reading of and/or writing to a tag.

Then I discussed the aspects of antenna performance, including types of antenna polarization, such as linear or circular polarization, and identified the differences between bi-static and mono-static antennas. Linear antennas produce more-coherent waves without phase distortion; therefore, they are a bit more efficient than circular antennas. However, they are more orientation sensitive. Circular antennas, on the other hand, are not orientation sensitive, but because of propagating in a circular manner and because of phase distortion, they are slightly less effective. In addition, bi-static antennas have two antennas with dedicated transmitting and receiving functions, whereas mono-static antennas switch these functions by using a circulator.

Next, you learned that the antenna field has imperfections, and that antenna coverage increases with increased power input. This was followed by a discussion about antenna configurations in the form of RFID portals and tunnels as well as their function, suitable use, and customization according to your environment and application. You also got some ideas about antenna tuning, and that to achieve proper shielding you should use absorptive materials such as metal mesh or anechoic foam instead of reflective materials that could cause reflections and interference.

The following section discussed the characteristics and challenges of the dense reader environment. You found out that you could overcome these challenges by using synchronization methods such as time-division or frequency-division multiplexing, the listen-before-talk technique, and frequency hopping.

You also learned that if two or more tags respond at the same time, the reader cannot communicate with either of them and, therefore, anticollision algorithms must be put in place. You have a choice between probabilistic and deterministic algorithms. Probabilistic algorithms use a slotted ALOHA protocol and its variation is used by Generation 2 tags. Deterministic algorithms use a binary-tree, or tree-walking, scheme.

In sum, you learned all the basics you need to know to understand the characteristics and functions of an interrogation zone. Your knowledge will be supplemented by the chapters that follow this one discussing system design, installation, and troubleshooting, as well as everything you need to know about RFID tags. Although this chapter touched on various regulations, they will be discussed in detail in Chapter 9, "Standards and Regulations."

Exam Essentials

Explain the function of an interrogator. An interrogator is a device that reads data from tags, writes data to tags, processes this data, and sends them to the host. Interrogators also perform filtering and aggregation of data, manage I/O devices, help with anticollision, and avoid interference by using a dense reader mode.

Define the types of interrogators. The main types are fixed interrogators and mobile interrogators. Mobile interrogators include vehicle-mounted interrogators, handheld interrogators, and other mobile interrogators (cell phone readers, readers in PCMCIA cards, and reader modules). Fixed interrogators are usually attached to an RFID portal, a tunnel, or a wall. They are connected to the power and network through cables, but can communicate wirelessly. Vehicle-mounted interrogators are usually used with forklifts, where they are either mounted with antennas between the forks or in some cases the reader itself is mounted on the vehicle. In that case, the cables have to be run through specially fitted hydraulic hoses. Handheld readers often are used for exception processing; they are usually powered by a battery and communicate wirelessly with the network. Handhelds have an integrated antenna and often a barcode scanner.

Explain the causes of interference between interrogators and solutions to this problem. Interference can be caused by more than one interrogator operating simultaneously in the area, as well as by RF noise from other RF-emitting devices (such as conveyors, fluorescent lights, microwave ovens, or wireless phones). RF interference can compromise or totally interrupt reading and writing tags. To prevent interference, you should use shielding, frequency hopping, listen-before-talk, and synchronization methods such as time-division or frequency-division synchronization, including dense reader mode.

Explain why the dwell time is important for successful reads and/or writes. Because reading and writing operations take a certain amount of time to be successful, you need to ensure that the tag stays in the interrogation zone for a sufficient amount of time. The dwell time (or time in beam) depends on how fast the tags are moving through the interrogation zone, the data-transfer rate between the tags and the interrogator, and/or whether the tags are being read or written to. Generally, the longer the dwell time, the more successful will be the reading and writing operations.

Define the differences and applications of bi-static and mono-static antennas. A mono-static antenna fulfills both transmitting and receiving functions. These functions are switched by a circulator, which is integrated into the interrogator. An advantage of mono-static antennas is their smaller size as compared to bi-static antennas put into one case; however, they are slightly less efficient because of using the circulator.

A bi-static antenna uses separate antennas for transmitting the RF signal to the tag and receiving the signal from the tag. These two antennas either can be integrated into one case or can be in separate cases. Bi-static antennas are slightly more efficient than mono-static because they are not using a circulator, and each antenna is dedicated solely to transmitting or receiving.

Explain the relationship between interrogator output power and antenna field, including the restrictions posed by regulatory agencies. Increased interrogator power output will provide increased power input into the antenna, which will increase antenna output. This will enlarge the antenna lobes and increase the reading distance. You have to make sure that you do not cross the limits set by any regulatory agencies, however, or you could be fined. In the United States, the allowed transmission power is up to 4 watts EIRP (while hopping minimally across 50 channels); in Europe it is only 2 watts ERP.

Define anticollision protocols. If a collision occurs (two or more tags respond simultaneously to the interrogator's signal), the interrogator cannot successfully communicate with either tag. The main anticollision methods are synchronous (deterministic) and asynchronous (probabilistic). The probabilistic, or asynchronous, method is based on tags responding at randomly generated times. This method includes several specific protocols. The most well-known is the ALOHA protocol. Generation 2 uses a Q algorithm that is based on the slotted ALOHA protocol. The deterministic, or synchronous, method is based on a reader going through the tags according to their unique ID. The most well-known synchronous method is a binary-tree, or tree-walking, scheme.

Understand the challenges of a dense reader environment. In a dense reader environment, the number of simultaneously operating readers is larger than the number of available channels (for the United States it would be more than 50 readers in the area). This creates a lot of RF noise and potential interference; therefore, readers have to use dense reader mode to operate well in such an environment. The dense reader mode usually results in slower data-transfer rates between readers and tags. While in a single reader mode, the data rates can be up to 640 kilobits per second; using a dense reader mode can slow them down about four times (or more). A dense reader environment also affects network traffic (by increasing it). As with any other network device, the reader will use a certain portion of the bandwidth to send the data to the host.

Key Terms

Before you take the exam, be certain you are familiar with the following terms:

AB symmetry

ALOHA protocol

anticollision

asynchronous

baseband-FM0

bi-static antenna

dense reader mode

deterministic

dwell time

frequency-division multiplexing

frequency hopping

interrogation zone

listen-before-talk (LBT)

Miller subcarrier

mono-static antenna

multi-path

probabilistic

sessions

synchronization

synchronous

time-division multiplexing

time in beam

tag collision

Review Questions

1. What materials are the best to use for shielding of adjacent interrogation zones? (Select two options.)
   A. Sheet metal
   B. Anechoic foam
   C. Metal mesh
   D. Polyurethane

2. Which anticollision algorithm uses 16-bit numbers randomly generated by tags as a handle?
   A. FM0
   B. Time-division algorithm
   C. Q algorithm
   D. Beta algorithm

3. Which statement is true about the write operation?
   A. The write operation is faster than the read operation.
   B. The write operation is more reliable in shorter distances from the reader's antenna.
   C. The write operation is less sensitive to interference than the read operation.
   D. The write operation can be performed only by Generation 2 interrogators.

4. Which technique should you use if you install 51 readers in one area?
   A. Dense reader mode
   B. Dense antenna mode
   C. Miller subcarrier
   D. Transmit power settings under 0.5 W

5. Which type of an interrogator is the most suitable for exception processing?
   A. Vehicle-mounted interrogator
   B. Fixed interrogator
   C. RFID tunnel
   D. Handheld interrogator

6. What happens to the antenna field when you increase the interrogator output power?
   A. Field increases in size; holes change size and location.
   B. Field decreases in size; holes change size and location.
   C. Field increases in size; holes stay the same and at the same location.
   D. Field decreases in size; holes stay in the same location.

7. Which devices can be directly managed by a smart reader? (Select two options.)

   A. Light stacks

   B. Horns

   C. Conveyors

   D. Vehicles

8. Where would you run the cables from the antennas to the interrogator on a forklift? The antennas are on the forks, while the interrogator is mounted near the operator's cabin.

   A. Affix them to the frame of the forks and the vehicle.

   B. Run them through the hydraulic hoses used for moving the forks.

   C. Keep them freely hanging between the forks and the rest of the vehicle.

   D. Connect the antennas wirelessly.

9. Handheld interrogators can come with which of the following? (Select two options.)

   A. A circular antenna

   B. Up to four linear antennas

   C. A light stack

   D. A barcode scanner

10. How can you ensure the success of your reading operation? (Select two options.)

    A. Avoid the interference.

    B. Use the least possible power.

    C. Speed up the conveyor.

    D. Provide sufficient dwell time.

11. Why would you use bi-static antennas over mono-static?

    A. They are smaller in size.

    B. They are more efficient.

    C. They have much longer read ranges.

    D. They are supported by all interrogators on the market.

12. Which type of antenna would you use in conjunction with a manufacturing line where the product and tag orientation are constant?

    A. A circularly polarized antenna

    B. A linearly polarized antenna

    C. A receiving antenna

    D. A transmitting antenna

13. What causes multi-path interference?

A. Tags talking to adjacent readers

B. Readers talking to adjacent tags

C. Reflected waves crossing the transmitted waves

D. Not using the anticollision mechanism

14. Which type of antenna requires a circulator in the reader?

A. Mono-static

B. Bi-static

C. Linear

D. All antennas

15. What is the Select command used for?

A. To select the tag class when configuring the interrogator

B. To select the group of tags based on part of the EPC number

C. To singulate a tag from the group of tags

D. To access a tag after it is singulated

16. What is the maximum allowed transmitted power in Europe (ERP)?

A. 0.5 W

B. 1 W

C. 2 W

D. 4 W

17. What is frequency hopping?

A. A method of transmitting in dense reader mode

B. A method of receiving in time-division scheme

C. A method of backscatter

D. A method used by the tags to avoid collisions

18. How will the installation of 50 readers affect network traffic?

A. It will not affect network traffic.

B. It will decrease network traffic.

C. It will increase network traffic.

D. It will absolutely take down the network.

19. Where is data filtering usually done? (Select two options.)

A. In middleware

B. In the application

C. At the reader level

D. At the tag level

20. What is the function of the oscillator in the interrogator?

A. It modulates the signal for transmitting.

B. It produces the carrier wave.

C. It amplifies the carrier frequency.

D. It facilitates the data transfers.

Answers to Review Questions

1. B, C. To shield adjacent interrogation zones you need to use an RF absorptive material, such as an anechoic foam or a metal mesh with openings a lot smaller than the wavelength of the used frequency. Sheet metal could cause unwanted reflections that could cause interference in both interrogation zones. Polyurethane is relatively transparent to RF waves.

2. C. The Q algorithm is based on a technique in which the reader sends a query with a parameter Q and a session number to a tag and then creates a slotted time. The tag generates a random 16-bit number as a handle. When the reader inventories tags in a selected session, the tag has to generate a random number for a slot number, which has to be between 0 and 2^{Q}-1.

3. B. The write operation requires a lot more time than the read operation, requires a stronger signal and shorter distances than the read operation, and is more sensitive to interference. It can be performed by any interrogator that has write capability, regardless of whether it is a Gen 1, a Gen 2, or an ISO compatible interrogator.

4. A. If you are installing 51 interrogators in one area, you will have to set your interrogators to work in dense reader mode to avoid interference with each other.

5. D. The most suitable interrogator for exception processing will be the handheld interrogator because it has great mobility. You can take it to a pallet or a product, and you are not restricted by power or network cables or by space.

6. A. Increasing the power output of the interrogator (which means increasing input into the antenna) increases the antenna coverage, and the holes in its field move and change their size (usually get larger).

7. A, B. Smart readers can directly manage certain low-voltage devices, such as light stacks or horns.

8. B. The cables can be run through special hydraulic hoses that are used to move the forks, if they have a space for inserting the cables. Sometimes these hoses can come with the cables already integrated. However, today the vehicle-mounted interrogators are often made in dimensions that allow them to be mounted between the forks, and therefore the cables are not being moved and stretched as the forklift works, which reduces the possibility of damage.

9. A, D. Handheld interrogators usually come with an integrated barcode scanner and one antenna. This antenna can be either circular or linear.

10. A, D. To make your reading operation successful, you should try to avoid interference or protect your interrogation zone from interference as well as provide a sufficient dwell time for the tag.

11. B. Bi-static antennas are slightly more efficient than mono-static antennas because they have dedicated antennas for transmitting and receiving functions and they do not use a circulator as mono-static antennas do.

12. B. Linearly polarized antennas are most suited for applications where the tag orientation is constant. Linear antennas are a bit more efficient than circular because they give out a coherent wave without a phase distortion.

13. C. Multi-path interference is caused by a wave that is reflected and crosses the path of a transmitted wave. The points where the waves cross can have a null or very strong signal. To avoid multi-path interference, you should use absorptive materials for shielding.

14. A. A circulator must be integrated into the reader to operate mono-static antennas. Such a reader usually has only four ports and can run up to four antennas.

15. B. The Select command picks out a group of tags based on certain characteristics, such as specific manufacturer's ID or other parts of the EPC number. Because this command concentrates on only a small part of the data within the tag, it is able to quickly locate and target certain tag groups within the whole tag population.

16. C. The allowed maximum transmitted power in Europe is 2 watts in a frequency band of 865.6–867.6 MHz.

17. A. Frequency hopping is a method of switching channels when operating in a dense reader mode. Readers may be required to hop across multiple channels within a given frequency spectrum mainly because of the time interval restrictions for transmitting in one channel.

18. C. Installation of many readers will definitely increase network traffic. Before you start such a project, you should make sure that the network is not already maxed out by other devices such as PCs, laptops, or handhelds and that you have sufficient bandwidth for your interrogators to send data through.

19. A, C. Data filtering is usually done first at the reader level, especially with smart readers. Then the data also can be filtered in the middleware so that the application gets only the data carrying some business logic.

20. B. An oscillator is a component of an interrogator that produces the carrier wave. This carrier wave is then modulated by a modulator and amplified to be transmitted through the antenna to the tag.

Chapter 3

Site Analysis

RFID+ EXAM OBJECTIVES COVERED IN THIS CHAPTER:

- ✓ **7.1 Given a scenario, demonstrate how to read blueprints (e.g., whole infrastructure)**
- ✓ **7.2 Determine sources of interference**
    - 7.2.1 Use analysis equipment such as a spectrum analyzer, determine if there is any ambient noise in the frequency range that may conflict with the RFID system to be installed
- ✓ **7.3 Given a scenario, analyze environmental conditions end-to-end**

There are two primary components that leverage the physics of radio frequency identification (RFID): the place where the network will be deployed and the items that will be tagged. In this chapter, I will discuss in detail the place where RFID is going to be deployed.

The challenge with RFID is that all radio frequency (RF) is invisible; there are more waves bouncing around a typical warehouse facility than on Hawaii's North Shore, but unless you've got X-ray vision you can't see what is going on. Add on top of this the fact that an RFID network requires supporting infrastructure such as power and Internet connectivity, and there is a lot to think about. This is all before you consider what happens with the people and the processes that need to take place every day.

All of those critical factors around the facility are what is important in a site analysis. This part of the CompTIA RFID+ exam is without a doubt one of the most critical to your success as a practitioner. You should make sure you understand the components in this chapter seven ways from Sunday to be successful and to save yourself a lot of hassle when you are out in the real world of RFID.

Business Process Flow and Mapping

RFID is truly a disruptive technology—it will disrupt not only the causative way business is carried out from now on, but also the day-to-day operations of millions of people in the next few years. As you think about how the RFID network and infrastructure may impact a typical company, consider this: by 2010, companies will have more RFID readers deployed than telephones.

As this vast technology deployment transforms the way that the manufacturing, distribution, logistics, marketing, and technical organizations do business, a practical understanding of how to deploy RFID needs to be considered. This is where business process mapping comes into play. Although many of the global system integrators (SIs) will charge hundreds of thousands of dollars to provide very specific business process engineering and consulting, a little bit of knowledge will help you make sure that you are setting up an RFID network for success. In addition, if a firm has hired one of the large SIs to do this for them, you will have an understanding of the end results.

A swim lane diagram shows how steps within a process are organized by systems, roles, locations, and business units. Swim lane diagrams should probably be called baton diagrams (as in the thing you hand off in the 440 running relay) because they really help you to understand how a team hand-off between and among people and systems happens, as with a baton in a relay.

Swim lane diagrams can be generated for the following:

- Strategic business units (SBUs)
- Resources
- Resource types
- Locations
- User-defined attributes
- Subject matter experts (SMEs)
- Enterprise entities

Most business process consultants will generate a swim lane diagram to show the *current business process*. An RFID team should either create a business process diagram similar to a swim diagram or take the one created already and overlay the RFID touch points. It is important to see where a process can be replaced by an RFID reader, and also see where a new process needs to be incorporated because of an RFID touch point. The new processes usually tend to be exception processes for an RFID tag that wasn't read or isn't supposed to be in a specific location, or for maintenance regarding software upgrades or hardware fixes. You can also add more detail to your swim lane diagram by adding inputs and outputs. If you are the person responsible for the business process diagram and mapping, you should make it easy on yourself and create three primary categories that need to be mapped:

- Facilities impact
- IT systems impact
- Business process changes

Mapping the business processes will allow you to determine the RFID touch points. After those touch points are designated, you can build revised business processes and interdependencies. After those are designed and revised as necessary, you can then figure out where you need to put in RFID interrogation zones (IZs) and what type they need to be—forklift, handheld, conveyor, or fixed portals. Before you can start installing and tuning the IZs, you need to know what is going on in the macro environment and the micro environment.

If you think of the RF field in a typical warehouse as my three-year-old thinks of Play-Doh, you'll have the right idea. If the facility does not have many sophisticated systems or isn't in the neighborhood of an airport or a military base, then it's like playing with one single can of bright pink Play-Doh. This is your RFID reader emitting clean RF waves—pink Play-Doh, bright, solid, and consistent. Of course, Play-Doh is seldom bought in single canisters. By the second day the bright pink, radiant blue, and crisp yellow Play-Doh are coming out the end of the spaghetti press looking like some sludge scraped off a 1950s drain pipe. A warehouse is the same way—you might have an alarm system, an old barcode wireless data hub, a satellite station nearby—it's like a whole host of different-colored cans of Play-Doh floating through the waves of your warehouse and making a muddy mess of the RF environment. The next steps in this chapter will do something every parent wishes he or she could—separate those different RF interferences and get back to those original crisp, clean, unadulterated cans of Play-Doh.

Blueprints, CADs, and Seeing the Big Picture

As a CEO, I'm a big-picture guy. Many people would take that to mean that I don't actually do anything useful, except dream up great ideas—like writing books. Unless you have the big picture, however, the effort that goes into the details can end up being an exercise in futility. Blueprints in an RFID network are the same way. They are your canvas to create an RFID masterpiece. But before you can create that masterpiece, you need to know how the blueprints can help you.

First and foremost you need to understand what you are looking at. A blueprint is a bird's-eye view of a floor of a building where you will be installing an RFID network. The building is drawn to scale, and the drawing shows where every door, loading dock, room, window, and other permanent components are located. Drawn to scale means that every inch on the blueprint represents a certain number of feet on the actual building. The first thing you should do when looking at a set of blueprints is to look at the scale. It's usually in one of the corners of the blueprint, maybe near the facility or architect's name and will tell you something such as 1/4 inch equals 1 foot. To make measuring on blueprints really easy, you can use a special ruler called a scale, which has increments in the most commonly used ratios on blueprints. These can be purchased in any office supply store for a couple of bucks.

Engineering drawings are the next level of detail up from a blueprint. Good engineering drawings will take the blueprint (the facilities footprint) and add in specific operational components such as conveyors, electrical information, network information, rack locations, and so on. Engineering drawings are always preferable over plain old blueprints because they save you a lot of time and effort putting in information manually.

The first step is to use the blueprints to lay out where the RFID network will be built. Sitting down at the drawing table with the end users and determining where each RFID interrogation zone is going to be located is step one in both the deployment and the site assessment. After you mark out each interrogation zone, you will look at your facility in a whole new light. You'll understand the specific areas you need to investigate from a micro perspective (more on that later in this chapter, when I talk about path loss contour maps, or PLCMs), and you'll be able to spot any interference possibilities that you can triangulate in on from the macro perspective.

Later, when measuring the signal levels in the facility, if you do encounter any random noise you can mark the exact location where you picked up the interference and the exact strength of that location. Doing this in multiple locations will also help you pinpoint the source of interference based on signal strength. If you don't have CAD drawings or actual blueprints, a simple diagram drawn to scale will help in the planning stages but should be considered a last resort.

Getting Ready to Measure

What you're going to do in the second phase of the site assessment is to try to see the invisible. The best way to do this is to perform an RF site analysis to ensure that the proposed RFID installation can operate within the planned environment at optimal performance. Sounds easy, right? Unfortunately, it's about as easy as separating those Play-Doh colors from each other, because the complexity of invisible electromagnetic waves in your working environment makes sure that it's not a simple task.

The site assessment is important to help you see the invisible—the other forms of radio frequency communication going on, intentionally or otherwise, where you want to install your reader network. The vast majority of U.S.-based RFID systems operate in the *Industrial, Scientific, and Medical (ISM) band* of 902–928 MHz, which is an unlicensed frequency in the United States. (The range is 864–870 MHz in Europe.) Other devices that use this same unlicensed band include cordless phones, long-range radios, barcode devices, alarm systems, real-time location systems, and many other gadgets looking to communicate without having to worry about expensive spectrum licenses from the Federal Communications Commission (FCC).

With all these devices vying for the same communication space, *intermodulation, or signals getting "crossed"* and *data collision* where several tags try to send their information back at once, are inevitable if more than one system is operating in that ISM band. Data collision is also messy, costly, and a real bear to clean up. But you can prevent a nasty cleanup job by performing a thorough RF site assessment. Consider the following points to plan for and execute a successful site assessment:

- Go back to your business process mapping and figure out the target locations (interrogation zones) for installing your RFID systems. These locations vary from warehouse to warehouse and need to have a power source and Ethernet connectivity for the readers. Commonly, RFID interrogation zones are placed at dock doors, stretch-wrap stations, conveyor lines, and inventory shelves. After you identify the target locations for RFID in your facility, you carry out the RF testing procedure at each one.
- What you're looking for with your site assessment is twofold: the strength of the waves that propagate through your potential interrogation zone, and the frequency those waves are operating over. Plan to perform the RF assessment at each target location one at a time so that you can get a good picture of the relative strength of signals in each area. The higher the strength and the more prevalent waves are in that band, the more difficulty you'll have implementing a successful RFID network.
- Don't make the big mistake that many people make when doing a site assessment; that is, don't simply take a snapshot of the *ambient environmental noise (AEN)* at a particular point in time (which would be like choosing golf clubs to use for an entire course by looking around the seventh green). Instead, follow a process that takes a full look at the electromagnetic world as your facility goes through its normal business operations (which is more like walking all 18 holes of the course and taking notes before you play it).

This method of capturing all the relevant data is called a *full Faraday cycle analysis*. This fancy-sounding name represents a way of gathering time-dependent spectrum analysis data across a specific band of operation at the exact locations where you'll be setting up an RFID interrogation zone. For your site assessment, this band is the 902–928 MHz (ISM) frequency band. A full Faraday cycle analysis ensures that before you begin building your RFID network, you will have all the data you need to make the right decisions regarding the type of hardware and the way it should be configured. And it will also help you understand any challenges you may face or systems you'll have to work around.

Getting the Right Test Equipment

The good news about an RFID deployment in ultra-high frequency (UHF)—at least for the United States—is the same as the bad news: the frequency band used requires no operating license or permission from any governing bodies, and the same holds true for low frequency (LF) and high frequency (HF). Although the FCC has strict rules governing operation in this FCC-allocated band (see FCC rules part 15: Industrial, Scientific and Medical Equipment, which you can find online at `http://wireless.fcc.gov`), no operating license is required if you comply with the rules. So before you deploy an RFID system, you need to become an RF detective by setting up test equipment to find out what other signals are already active in the target area and may affect the RFID performance. This is particularly important with UHF because the UHF communication and thus interference carries much farther distances than HF or LF.

You need the following equipment to correctly set up an RFID site assessment for UHF:

Spectrum Analyzer A device to measure the relative strength and specific bandwidth of communication across a given range (in our case 902–928 MHz) and serve as the data-logging mechanism in the testing setup for your site assessment.

1/4-Wave Dipole 915 MHz Antenna and Ground Plane Plate The antenna is attached to the center of a ground plane to properly load the antenna and is also attached to the spectrum analyzer by a coax cable. The antenna listens in 360 degrees to all the ambient electromagnetic signals, and then sends those signals back to the spectrum analyzer for display.

Tripod Stand The mechanism that supports the antenna in the center of the target location. A tripod should be sturdy enough to hold up the antenna and flexible enough to go from a foot or two off the ground up to five or six feet high. A high-quality camera tripod usually does the trick.

Laptop Computer The laptop is used to log time-based data captured by your RF testing setup. The computer is usually connected to the spectrum analyzer by an RS-232 or Ethernet cable. If you decided to get an older—usually cheaper—spectrum analyzer that does not have the option of connecting directly to a laptop, you can do without the laptop and use a digital camera to take pictures of the screen at various intervals to record the data. Although this is not as elegant as having the spectrum analyzer create the time-based graphs, it is equally as effective.

NOTE

The steps and methodology for assessing a facility are the same for 915 MHz, 2.45 GHz, or 13.56 MHz. The only things that will change dramatically are what the spectrum analyzer has to measure, how wide a bandwidth it needs to cover, and what the best choice of antenna is to receive those signals. Other than that, the basic principles and methodologies are the same.

Setting Up for RF Testing

As you set up your RF testing equipment, keep in mind that you want to gather data over a period of time that is representative of the normal business cycle. This is summarized by the full Faraday cycle analysis, which is described in detail later in this chapter. Make sure that normal (or close to it) operations can take place after you put the equipment for receiving signals and searching out interference in place. Although it might be easiest to test a warehouse on a Saturday morning when no one is around to get in your way, that is the worst possible time to get a true picture of the RF noise that is likely to occur. As crazy as it may be, pick the busiest time for your location and that will make the setup and deployment of your network easier by an order of magnitude.

Follow these steps to set up the test equipment:

1. Place the 1/4-wave dipole antenna on the ground plane plate and attach both to the tripod stand so that the center of the antenna is in the center of the target area, as illustrated in Figure 3.1.

   The target area is where you would like the RFID tags to be read—usually 2–3 feet above the ground for a dock door, 12 inches above a conveyor, and so on. Because you want the antenna located as close as possible to the center of the interrogation zone, the best way to mount the antenna is usually with the tripod contorted in one way or another, so make sure you purchase a tripod that is easily adjustable. You also may have to get creative and hang the antenna from above to get it in the middle of the interrogation zone.

WARNING Do not hang an antenna from its coax cable because doing so may interfere with the signal and communication and not accurately ground the antenna. Instead, use a piece of rope or other nonconductive material to hang the antenna.

FIGURE 3.1 An antenna at the center of a target area

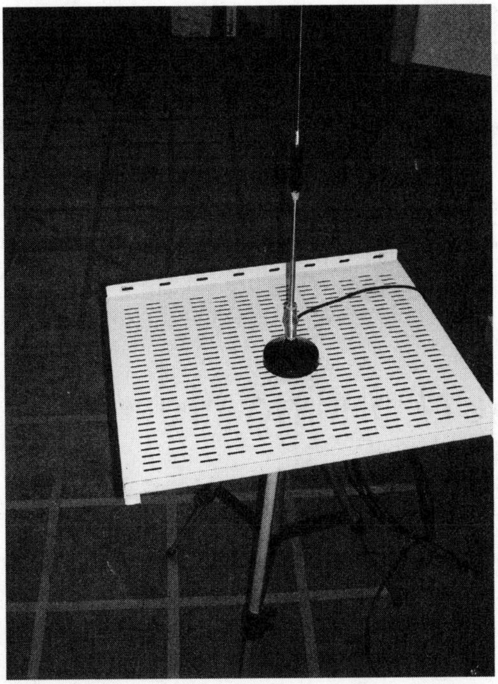

2. Connect the antenna and ground plane to the spectrum analyzer (SA) by screwing the coax cable into the input port on the SA.

> **WARNING** As with all RF equipment, you never connect an antenna to or disconnect it from a powered-up device, even if the device has fault protection. Although most of today's electronics have solid protection, connecting an antenna with the power off is a good habit to get into that may save you a few thousand dollars of fried equipment.

3. Attach the laptop computer to the spectrum analyzer by using either an RS-232 connector or an Ethernet cable. Power up the laptop.
4. Power up the spectrum analyzer and tune it to a center frequency of 915 MHz. If you are measuring in a country other than the United States, just figure out what the center frequency is in the allowable range and set it to that number. For the United States, 915 MHz is right in the middle of the 902–928 MHz range.
5. Finish setting up the spectrum analyzer by doing the following:
   - Set the span to 60 MHz. This setting ensures that the analyzer will duly note any AEN on either side of the 915 MHz center frequency. You want to know if any signals are even close because devices broadcasting at 901 MHz can cause interference.
   - Set the resolution bandwidth to 100 KHz to ensure that you are recording reasonable levels of interference.
   - Set the video bandwidth to 30 KHz to obtain a smooth plot on the SA.
   - Set the amplitude attenuation to 0 dB so that the SA will display a discernable signal-to-noise level (easy to see the interfering signals above the noise floor).
   - Turn on maximum hold so that you can capture the energy of every channel in the band you are testing.

After the antenna is in the middle of the proposed interrogation zone and attached to your correctly tuned spectrum analyzer, the virtual screen on your laptop or the video screen on the spectrum analyzer should be active. If you're seeing either one of these, you're ready to start the testing.

Measuring for AEN during Normal Operations (and Beyond)

If you are prepping for the CompTIA exam, you are likely looking to go into RFID, or want to be credible with potential clients if you are already in RFID. Deciphering the existing RF situation and making sense of the data are critical for your success. With the spectrum analyzer active, you are now collecting the first part of that critical data. If you are using a laptop to log the data,

Playing in the Frequency Band

You may hear people say they are setting up a UHF RFID system at 915 MHz frequency. This statement is only partially true. Because the FCC allows many unlicensed devices to operate at that frequency, they require that no one device broadcast for more than a certain amount of time. If only one frequency, or channel, was available and a device couldn't broadcast for more than a split second, it wouldn't be possible to put many devices on that channel. That is why devices that use unlicensed frequency spectrums (for example, 902–928 in the United States) are designed to broadcast across a *range* of channels. The process of moving through each channel is called frequency hopping (to learn more about this, see Chapters 2, 4, and 9), and most devices in this band stay on one channel for only a few hundred milliseconds or so. Therefore, to catch all the broadcasts, you need to measure not just the 915 MHz channel but the whole ISM range that goes from 902 MHz to 928 MHz. (That's 13 MHz on either side of the center frequency, or a 26 MHz span.) The reason we measure for more than twice that (a 60 MHz span) is that other licensed frequencies may be operating close enough to our ISM band and with enough power to interrupt our communications.

you should set your virtual monitor to record information every hour and actively log it. If you are using a spectrum analyzer without a laptop, you should come back and take a digital picture every two hours over the course of the normal business cycle. After taking the picture, clear the video display by resetting the video screen and begin collecting data again.

This initial measurement process is effective but represents only one data point in a facility. How large the warehouse is and how strong interfering signals are will determine what you pick up from that one location. So if you have a large warehouse, you are going to have to set up the same test procedure at several locations within the warehouse to increase the accuracy. The areas you want to make sure you are close to are the potential RFID reader interrogation zones (usually the dock doors, conveyor or sort stations, and the like). One drawback to this static testing methodology is that it is difficult to find the location of any interference.

The next step toward increasing the accuracy of your full Faraday cycle analysis is to take a roving data capture of AEN. To take a roving capture, you will need the following:

- A portable uninterruptible power supply (UPS) or similar battery backup device that should be able to power the spectrum analyzer for 20–30 minutes (available from American Power Conversion for under $200 at most computer stores)
- A golf cart, shopping cart, or similar means of wheeling your equipment around a warehouse safely
- A willing friend to act as a human tripod and carry the antenna around next to the golf cart

The spectrum analyzer is set up in the exact same manner as it is for the static capture, except the power source and the antenna are both mobile. For this test you need to pay close attention to the display as you are moving about the facility and watch for anything that shows up as noise in the ISM band. This test is particularly effective if you are sharing a facility with other tenants who may have systems running that are only separated by sheetrock walls.

If you do find a source of interference, make sure you note on your CAD drawing the exact location and the strength in decibels. The next step is to begin moving away from that original spot in 10- to 15-foot increments on four sides. In other words, move north 10 feet, go back to the original spot, move south 10 feet, go back, and so on. This will give you four read points equidistant around the original interference location to compare relative strength. If any one of the four points is stronger than the first in terms of signal strength, that is the direction the interference is coming from. The same process should be carried out to triangulate the source of the interference.

WARNING Many people incorporating RFID systems in a warehouse may find that there are wireless barcode systems that operate over the UHF unlicensed band as well. If this is the case, you can pretty much plan on calling your barcode vendor and asking them for an upgrade to 2.45 GHz.

The full Faraday cycle analysis is the foundation for building an RFID network; the goal is to make it a perfect foundation for the structures being put on top of it. You have tested the environment and now understand what you have to deal with. After the site assessment is done, it's like starting with a fresh canvas for your electromagnetic work of art:

- You have identified all of the AEN within the facility.
- You have logged data over the course of a full business cycle (all the shifts) and understand any changes that happen at different times of the day.
- You drilled down to specific interrogation zone sites, as well as roved around the facility to make sure you looked under every nook and cranny for rogue AEN.
- You have triangulated any sources of interference while roving about the facility.
- You took all the possible machinery and equipment that is likely to make its own electronic noise and ran it in the interrogation zone while recording the data to make sure that no potential source was overlooked.
- You addressed the potential interference found by either eliminating it or knowing that you will have to come up with some sort of creative work-around.
- You have mapped out the interrogation zones on CAD drawings or blueprints and have made sure that those areas are noise-free.

Now you have the basic starting point to begin designing the RFID network. The last step in the site assessment is figuring out how a perfect radio wave will behave in your real-world environment.

Micromanaging Your Waves

Now that you have a good understanding of the working environment, it's time to start designing the interrogation zones. The way to design an interrogation zone is to take a perfect

RF wave and propagate it around the area where you are proposing to set up your readers. This is done by using the following equipment:

Spectrum Analyzer A device to measure the relative strength and specific bandwidth of communication across a given range (in our case 902–928 MHz) and serve as the data-logging mechanism in the testing setup for your site assessment.

Signal Generator A specialized device to produce RF signals at preset frequencies, strengths, and durations. The signal generator is hooked up to a 1/4-wave dipole antenna via a coax cable and will be used to transmit the generated RF field.

Circularly Polarized UHF Antenna The antenna used by any UHF reader or ordered directly from a company such as Cushcraft or Sensormatic is exactly what you will need to attach to the spectrum analyzer to measure the RF field received from the signal generator.

1/4-Wave Dipole 915 MHz Antenna and Ground Plane Plate The antenna is attached to the center of a ground plane to properly load the antenna, and it also is attached to the signal generator by a coax cable. The antenna radiates an RF field in 360 degrees.

Two Tripod Stands The mechanisms that support the antenna in the center of the target location and the UHF antenna at the outside of the interrogation zone. A tripod should be sturdy enough to hold up the antenna and flexible enough to go from 1 or 2 feet off the ground up to 5 or 6 feet high. A high-quality camera tripod usually does the trick.

Laptop Computer The laptop is used to measure the relative strength of the signal produced by the signal generator. At the end of the testing, you will also take the data produced by the test and map them in a spreadsheet program such as Excel or Lotus.

Ever Think You Could Lose a Path?

After you are sure that there is no ambient noise polluting the interrogation zone, you can start to map out what each individual interrogation zone will look like. This process is called RF *path loss contour mapping (PLCM)*. It's pretty much self-explanatory—you are about to map out the RF path where it varies from a perfect RF field. The RF field propagating out of an antenna is shaped like a giant pear, with the stem part going out the back of the antenna and the fat part heading off into space in front of the antenna. The fat part is where the items with RFID tags on them should be moving through. This RF propagation bubble size and shape depends on the type of antenna, and changes dramatically when there is anything in or near the bubble to reflect or absorb the RF waves. The decibel (dB) scale is used to describe RF path loss. In relationship to power, the dB scale is logarithmic and graphically demonstrated in Figure 3.2. Notice the dramatic drop in power for the first few decibels; for every 3 dB reduction in RF power, the signal strength is reduced by half.

In some instances, large drops in power are discovered over the course of the PLCM processes. Seeing such a dramatic loss in power due to the immediately surrounding environment raises flags for ODIN Technologies' RFID design engineers and contributes to important design decisions including RFID rack placement, reader selection, and reader configuration.

PLCM deliverables include a diagnosis of how effective RFID can be expected to perform in the client's environment as well as guidance for how to configure the reader and antennas postinstallation.

Keep in mind that a 3 dB loss reduces the power level by one half, and it becomes easy to see how the environment can negatively impact the performance of an RFID deployment.

The RF PLCM will allow you to understand how that perfect shape is distorted by what is around the proposed interrogation zone. This information will tell you exactly where you have to place antennas and how much power should be used to create a signal.

The best way to investigate each interrogation zone is to take a look at what happens in the area one step at a time. Although the steps are similar to getting set up, which was discussed earlier in the chapter, the more data points you can find now before you start deploying readers, the better the final results will be. Follow these steps:

1. Place the 1/4-wave dipole antenna on the ground plane plate and attach both to the tripod stand so that the center of the antenna is in the center of the target area, as illustrated earlier in Figure 3.1.
2. Connect the 1/4-wave dipole antenna to the signal generator via the coax cable. Set the signal generator to a signal of at least –14 dBm so that the UHF antenna can pick up a reasonable signal.
3. Attach the laptop computer to the spectrum analyzer by using either an RS-232 connector or an Ethernet cable. Power up the laptop.
4. Power up the spectrum analyzer and tune it to a center frequency of 915 MHz and a span of 60 MHz. Attach the UHF antenna to the spectrum analyzer.
5. Finish setting up the spectrum analyzer by doing the following:
    - Set the span to 60 MHz.
    - Set the resolution bandwidth to 100 KHz.
    - Set the video bandwidth to 30 KHz.
    - Set the amplitude attenuation to 0 dB.
    - Turn off maximum hold.

The 1/4-wave antenna attached to the signal generator is going to pretend to be our tag with a mock signal bouncing back to be read by an antenna. This antenna is where we want to be reading our tags because the box with the tag on it crosses this zone. So think of the tag location as being at the center of a pie, and then dividing the pie into eight slices (the slices would be cut at 0, 45, 90, 135, 180, 225, 270, and 315 degrees). Figure 3.2 shows where the 1/4-wave antenna should be positioned in the center of the interrogation zone, and the eight spots around it show the location of the UHF antenna attached to the signal generator. Those eight corners are where we want to test the reaction of a 915 MHz propagation, or how well the RF wave travels back to be heard by the reader's antennas.

For the purposes of this first test, let's assume that you are trying to find out how a dock door and all the equipment around it will affect where you need to put antennas, which direction they will have to face, and how much power each antenna will need. The location could be any potential interrogation zone, from a conveyor belt to a stretch wrap station.

FIGURE 3.2 An antenna in the middle of a test zone for PLCM

	902	915	928
0	–38.4	–42.9	–42.2
45	–38.8	–43.5	–43.3
90	–41.4	–43.5	–44.3
135	–40.4	–43.2	–45.5
180	–38.7	–42.4	–40.9
225	–41.5	–43.1	–41.6
270	–41.9	–43.0	–44.8
315	–42.2	–42.9	–44.1
dB differential	-3.5	-1.1	-4.6

	902	915	928
0	–40.6	–47.1	–47.9
45	–45.1	–46.6	–46.3
90	–43.1	–47.2	–46.1
135	–54.3	–53.8	–52.2
180	–45.5	–55.2	–54.2
225	–44.0	–46.3	–50.8
270	–41.6	–44.6	–52.7
315	–39.7	–41.0	–43.5
dB differential	–14.6	–14.2	-9.2

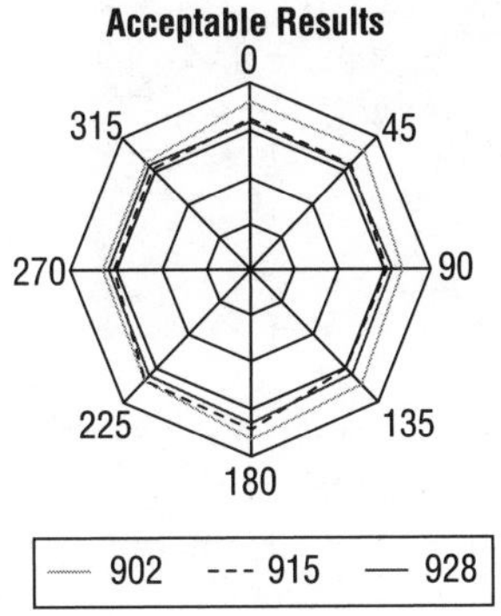

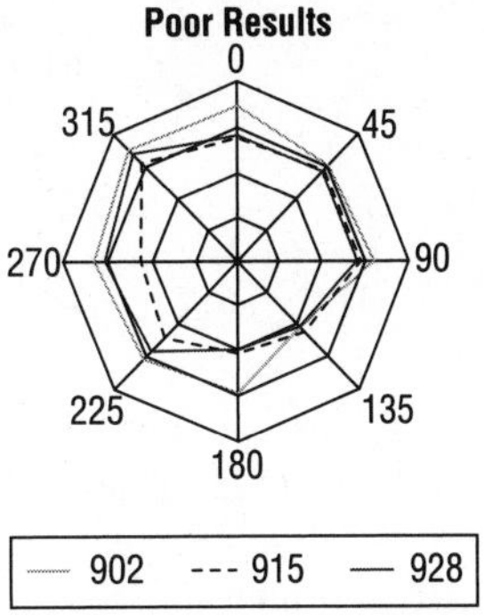

The steps to conduct the test are as follows:

1. Place the 1/4-wavelength dipole antenna, which is connected to the signal generator, in the center of the proposed interrogation zone.
2. Connect the UHF flat panel directional antenna to the spectrum analyzer and mount it at the same height as the 1/4-wave dipole antenna. Place it parallel to the dock door in the center (0 degrees in our pie). See Figure 3.3.
3. Turn the signal generator on, first to 902 MHz, and record the results on the spectrum analyzer. Keep the UHF antenna in the same location, set the signal generator to 915 MHz, and record the results. Repeat the same process with the signal generator set to 928 MHz. It is important to record the strength of the signal three times at each of the respective frequencies.
4. Relocate the directional antenna to the eight positions around the 1/4-wave dipole antenna, keeping the distance from the 1/4-wave dipole the same (usually the maximum distance you want to read from, or half the total width of the dock door) and the directional antenna always facing directly toward the 1/4-wave dipole. This will result in an eight-position contour of the RF field strength.
5. Record the signal strength at all eight locations around the stationary antenna.
6. Put these eight values into a spreadsheet program in the format shown in Table 3.1.

FIGURE 3.3 Positioning the antenna and spectrum analyzer

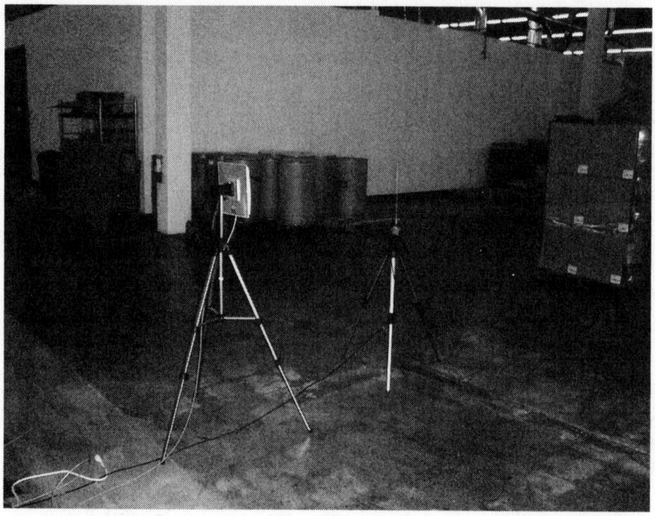

Input the results from your eight-position test into a radar graph in the spreadsheet program. The result should look something like the one on the left shown earlier in Figure 3.2. The result on the left is a perfect RF field in a vacuum. The information you are interested in is how the left and right figures are different.

TABLE 3.1 Typical Data from Testing around an Interrogation Zone

Position		Signal Strength	
	902 MHz	915 MHz	928 MHz
0	35	43	43
45	35	37	24
90	37	31	37
135	31	40	31
180	40	35	40
225	35	42	35
270	42	32	42
315	32	34	42

With the RF PLCM, what you now have is an important tool to design your reader interrogation zone. The ideal zone should be an equal bubble around the center pole (the left graph in Figure 3.2). What you need to compensate for are any areas that may not be equally powerful from that center. In other words, if you look back at the graph on the right in Figure 3.2, you will see that the graph is not an equal symmetrical distance around the center. It is up to the reader configuration to compensate for this loss, but doing a reader setup by using only trial and error would result in a dead spot as tags went through that area of the interrogation zone. The reason there is not as strong a signal is that something is either absorbing or deflecting the signal away from this area. To counteract that loss, the antenna located on that side of the dock door needs to receive additional power compared to power used on the other dock doors, or interfering items such as racks or desks may need to be moved.

Don't Forget the Details

The full Faraday cycle analysis and the RF PLCM are the perfect steps for setting up the optimal RFID network architecture. With those two tests completed, you can move on to the next key steps in deploying your RFID network. However, before you rush headlong into bolting down a reader and booting it up, you should plan for the installation, including adding your RFID racks and location onto your site plan. This can be done on the engineering drawings and also in a summary site survey report given to the client.

There are many mounting options from which you can choose for the interrogation zones, but keep in mind that you want a rack or cabinet that allows you to point the antennas without having to move the rack around and also protects your equipment from environmental issues such as dust or impact. Figure 3.4 shows the ODIN Technologies double RFID rack that can have antennas mounted on both sides and angling toward different dock doors.

FIGURE 3.4 An ODIN Technologies RFID double rack with covers removed to see the inside

Summary

This chapter gives you the groundwork for installing your RFID network. The site assessment, understanding how various RFID components are going to be installed, and determining what is likely to happen after they are installed are critical scientific data that can save you hours of trial and error and headaches when your system doesn't perform up to snuff.

The first topic you learned about was the "how"—how the business process is going to be documented and where RFID will fit into the process. Understanding and documenting will help you determine where all the touch points are and who needs to be involved. Remember, most likely you will be looking at three key areas: information technology, facilities, and business processes.

After you know how the business processes are executed, you need an understanding of the "where." The blueprints or engineering data will give you an accurate view of the facility and provide a clean slate for laying out the RFID network topology.

Last, you need the "why." Why is the system behaving the way it does? The reason, as you learned, is that there are a lot of invisible RF waves flowing through the air at any point, and you have to determine whether those are going to interfere with your RFID network, or vice versa. The path loss contour mapping will give you an opportunity to see exactly what would happen if you turned a reader on and fired it up at each interrogation zone.

Having the how, where, and why under control will allow you to lay out a plan for moving forward with your RFID deployment. This data also will help you provide a document to your client that shows what is happening in their RFID world and will give you a future reference in case you need to come back in and change or adapt the system later.

Exam Essentials

Know the business processes that surround the use of RFID. Map out the various functional roles within the organization at each location. Determine what happens when an item, case, or pallet comes into a facility, goes out of a facility, or both. Document the process by using swim lanes, which allow a visual representation of the facility's work flow.

Explain the various touch points of RFID. RFID impacts the information technology (IT) staff. Network connections as well as data storage and backup are required, and another device has to be managed on the network. Large objects are being permanently installed within a manufacturing facility, store, warehouse, or distribution center, and there need to be electrical outlets to support them, protective items such as bollards and racks bolted down, and specifications included in any system changes. Finally, the RFID network will impact the workforce and how they do their tasks—the business processes. Mapping out what happens when a tag is not read (an exception process), developing strategies to provide a visual alert by using a light stack, and determining where to put the readers all should be decided based on the business processes.

Understand how to read blueprints. Blueprints are a graphical representation of an actual building. Engineering drawings are blueprints with material handling systems shown as installed—conveyors, storage racks, and so on. Understanding that every set of plans has a scale that is consistent will help you measure interrogation zone locations, plan for cable lengths and distances, and graphically represent where each interrogation zone will be installed.

Explain how to perform a full Faraday cycle analysis site survey. A spectrum analyzer is set up to look within the specific frequency range that is being deployed, before any equipment arrives at the facility. The analyzer should run continuously in the facility for 24–48 hours at different locations to determine whether there is any ambient environmental noise (AEN) that might interfere with the RFID system.

Demonstrate how to find the source of AEN. Using the spectrum analyzer on a mobile cart, move around the facility in concentric circles and note when the signal gets stronger and weaker. Triangulate the strongest signal and pinpoint the source of the AEN.

Tell why a site analysis is important when using UHF. Most RFID, including UHF, operates within the Instrument, Scientific and Medical (ISM) band. This frequency band is unlicensed and can be used by any device meeting FCC part 15 rules. Therefore, there could already be devices in place that are using the same frequency band. Before an RFID system is installed and drowns out the signal of another system, or gets installed and doesn't work, the installation team needs to understand what is happening in the facility.

Explain why you need to look at the macro and micro environments. Understanding what is happening with other RF energy is critical to the overall system, but only by performing a detailed analysis at each location can you understand how each individual reader is going to function. Using science and not trial and error is the key to installing a successful RFID system.

Know how to read a PLCM map. The path loss contour map (PLCM) shows what happens to RF in a field when using the actual antennas a reader will use. Knowing that a perfect graph will show you where RF energy is being absorbed means you can tell where null spots are and can make plans to work around them.

Explain the basics of the ISM band and UHF relating to RFID. The ISM frequency band is an unlicensed band, so any device meeting FCC specifications can be used on this band. The ISM band for UHF is between 902 and 928 MHz in the United States. FCC rule part 15 requires any devices that communicate over that frequency to hop pseudo-randomly about that range.

Key Terms

Before you take the exam, be certain you are familiar with the following terms:

ambient environmental noise (AEN)

business process

data collision

Full Faraday cycle analysis

Industrial, Scientific, and Medical (ISM) band

intermodulation, or signals getting "crossed"

path loss contour mapping (PLCM)

Swim lane diagrams

Review Questions

1. What is a swim diagram?
   A. Map of the business process
   B. Map of the RF interference
   C. Map of the chain of management
   D. Map of the interrogation zone
2. What type of information can you get from a typical blueprint?
   A. Process flow information
   B. Information about materials the building is made of
   C. Sources of RF interference
   D. Floor plan of the building including dock doors, windows, rooms, and exits
3. What will you use the blueprint for? (Select two options.)
   A. As a basis for layout of the future interrogation zones
   B. As a map for the installers to know where to find restrooms
   C. To mark specific areas that need a closer look
   D. To make sure of having enough coax cables
4. Why do you need to measure the RF signal frequency and strength in the facility? (Select two options.)
   A. To find out what type of tags to use
   B. Because the management of the facility usually wants to see it
   C. To find and account for any possible interference
   D. Because RFID as well as other devices operate in unlicensed ISM bands
5. What device do you use to measure RF signals in the facility?
   A. Power analyzer
   B. Spectrum analyzer
   C. Faraday cage
   D. RFID tunnel
6. What is the best practice when connecting or disconnecting antennas from a device?
   A. Turn off the device before connecting or disconnecting the antenna.
   B. Turn off the device only before disconnecting the antenna.
   C. Do not turn off the device before connecting or disconnecting the antenna.
   D. Do not turn off the device before disconnecting the power cable.

7. What are the essential parts of the full Faraday cycle analysis? (Select two options.)
   A. Identification of ambient electronic noise
   B. Identification of sources of interference
   C. Identification of the frequency you will use for your RFID system
   D. Identification of dock door locations

8. What devices will you use for RF path loss contour mapping? (Select three options.)
   A. Spectrum analyzer
   B. Network analyzer
   C. 1/4-wave dipole antenna
   D. 1/2-wave monopole antenna
   E. RF signal generator

9. What can cause asymmetrical signal coverage in the interrogation zone? (Select two options.)
   A. Signal weakening
   B. Signal deflection
   C. Signal modulation
   D. Signal absorption

10. What should you do to counteract the loss of signal strength on one side of the dock door?
    A. Increase the power going to the whole interrogation zone.
    B. Increase the power going to the antenna on the opposite side of the dock door.
    C. Increase the power going to the antenna on that side of the dock door.
    D. Decrease the power going to the whole interrogation zone.

Answers to Review Questions

1. A. A swim diagram, or a swim lane diagram, shows how steps within a process are organized by systems, roles, locations, and business units. This diagram is used for business process mapping in the first part of the site analysis.

2. D. A blueprint is a bird's-eye view of a floor of the building where you will be installing an RFID network. The building is drawn to scale, and the blueprint shows where every door, loading dock, room, window, and other permanent components are located.

3. A, C. Blueprints should be used to lay out where the RFID network will be built. You need to determine where each RFID interrogation zone is going to be located, and after you mark out each interrogation zone you will understand the specific areas that need a closer look because of possible interference or changes in signal path contour.

4. C, D. You need to measure RF signal frequency and strength because other devices can use the same unlicensed ISM band such as cordless phones, long-range radios, barcode devices, alarm systems, real-time location systems, and the like. If these devices were operating on the same frequency and with certain signal strength, they would cause interference and data collisions and make your RFID network dysfunctional.

5. B. To measure the relative strength and specific bandwidth of communication across a given range, you need to use a spectrum analyzer. This device also can serve as the data-logging mechanism in the testing setup for your site assessment.

6. A. As a best practice, you should never connect an antenna to or disconnect it from a powered-up device, even if the device has fault protection. Although most of today's electronics have solid protection, connecting an antenna to a device with the power off is a good habit to get into that may protect your costly equipment.

7. A, B. Essential parts of the full Faraday cycle analysis are identification of the ambient electronic noise within the facility, logging all data over the course of a full business cycle, and understanding any changes that happen at different times of the day, as well as finding current or potential sources of interference.

8. A, C, E. For RF path loss contour mapping, you will need a spectrum analyzer to measure the relative strength and specific bandwidth of communication, and an RF signal generator to produce RF signals at preset frequencies, strengths, and durations. The signal generator is connected to a 1/4-wave dipole antenna via a coax cable and will be used to transmit the generated RF field. You will also need a circularly polarized UHF antenna, two tripod stands, and a laptop computer.

9. B, D. Signal coverage in the interrogation zone could be asymmetrical because the signal was deflected or absorbed by an object near or in the interrogation zone.

10. C. To counteract the loss of signal strength on one side of the dock door, the antenna located on that side of the dock door needs to receive additional power compared to power used on the other dock doors, or interfering items may need to be moved.

Chapter 4

Tags

RFID+ EXAM OBJECTIVES COVERED IN THIS CHAPTER:

✓ **4.1 Classify tag types**

- 4.1.1 Select the RFID tag best suited for a specific use case
  - 4.1.1.1 Pros and cons of tag types
  - 4.1.1.2 Tag performance
    - 4.1.1.2.1 Tag antenna to region/frequency
- 4.1.2 Identify inductively coupled tags vs. back-scatter
- 4.1.3 Identify the differences between active and passive

✓ **4.2 Given a scenario, select the optimal locations for an RFID tag to be placed on an item**

- 4.2.1 Evaluate media and adhesive selection for tags
- 4.2.2 Tag orientation and location
  - 4.2.2.1 Tag sticking (shadowing)
- 4.2.3 Package contents
- 4.2.4 Packaging
  - 4.2.4.1 Items
  - 4.2.4.2 Tags
  - 4.2.4.3 Labels
  - 4.2.4.4 Inserts
- 4.2.5 Liquids
- 4.2.6 Metal
- 4.2.7 Polarization

When I wrote *RFID For Dummies* a couple of years ago, there were only a handful of ultra-high-frequency (UHF) tags and about the same number of high-frequency (HF) tags. Now it seems like someone added water and plenty of fertilizer to the tag farm because there are dozens of tag types for all sorts of applications. As the industry grows, more and more choices will become available, so knowing the basics will be critical to selecting the right tag.

This chapter will teach you everything you need to know about tags and their characteristics, capabilities, and applications. This knowledge will be tremendously helpful in the designing stage of your radio frequency identification (RFID) system, when you will have to make the right tag selections based on the customer's needs and the desired performance of your system.

I'll also introduce you to various tag types—active, passive, and semi-passive tags—and discuss their functions, capabilities, and applications. Then I'll dive into communication methods that various types of tags use to receive interrogation signals from the reader and to respond.

In the middle of the chapter, you will learn about four primary frequency bands that are used for RFID systems and the function and application of tags operating within the specific bands. You will also discover that different frequencies within one band are used around the world, which can create challenges in an international supply chain. However, I'll show you how the differences can be overcome with clever tag design.

Finally, you will learn about tag construction, including techniques used to attach the chip to the antenna and methods of antenna manufacturing. You will also discover and evaluate tags intended for specific applications, explore the various types of tag packaging, and learn how to solve problems with materials and products that are not RF friendly. The latter can be done by using material-specific tags or by finding the correct placement on a product or its packaging and carefully testing this placement. You will learn that you can do this yourself or use various RFID testing facilities.

Tag Types

RFID tags can be categorized in many ways. They can be divided by communication methods, frequencies, classes, polarization, construction, or packaging. In this chapter, we will discuss all of these specifications and start with tag types according to the way they communicate.

If tags are able to transmit radio frequency (RF) signals to the environment without being near an interrogation zone or without needing power of some sort from an outside source, they are called *active tags*. If they are not able to transmit the signal by themselves, but need energy from the reader to do this, then they are called *passive tags* or *semi-passive tags*. I know you're thinking it can't be that simple or CompTIA wouldn't have created a whole section of the test just for tags—and you're right, so let's take a deeper look at tags and how they work.

Active Tags

As mentioned earlier, active tags can *actively* transmit an RF signal carrying data to the environment. They can broadcast this radio signal to the outside world because of how they are made. Active tags carry a transmitter and a battery, in addition to a chip and an antenna that are common to almost all tags. The battery is used to power the chip's circuitry as well as the transmitter. This enables the active tag to transmit its signal far into the environment (I have seen tags that could reach distances close to 1,000 meters) and to respond to a much lower-level interrogation signal than passive tags can handle. Because of the presence of a battery, active tags can also carry large amounts of memory and various sensors, and perform processing functions. An active tag has all the functionality of a minicomputer, without the keyboard, video, and mouse components.

Active tags can be programmed to *beacon*, which means that they broadcast their information to the environment, saying, "I am here, I am here" at regular intervals. Tags can beacon continuously or in preset time intervals. Setting the broadcast is determined by the application or "use case." Active tags can wait for an interrogation signal from the reader (*reader-talks-first,* or *RTF*) or send out the signal first (*tag-talks-first,* or *TTF*). They respond only after the reader contacts them.

TIP When deciding how often you will want your tags to beacon, keep in mind that beaconing discharges the tag's battery. Continuous beaconing not only uses more energy, but also may create unwanted RF noise in the environment.

Many techniques are used to program active tags. You can set them up to beacon until they are in the interrogation zone of a reader. After the communication link is established, the reader can issue commands to the tag and the tag will respond accordingly. Or, the reader can use the beacon signal only as a sign of the tag's presence and then will continue polling for other tags.

Active tags can operate on several frequencies; most often you will see them working at 433 MHz or 2.45 GHz. The most common active tags are the ones used by the U.S. Department of Defense (DoD) and made by Lockheed Martin's Savi Technology group. They operate at 433 MHz, and are on every container that the DoD sends outside the continental United States (OCONUS).

Active tags are significantly more expensive than passive and semi-passive tags because of how sophisticated their processing and capabilities are. The DoD has been using active RFID tags for almost two decades for container management, supply-chain management, equipment and asset tracking within a business process, and unit deployment efforts. Other commercial uses of active RFID technology include transportation companies and railroads using the tags in much the same way the DoD does for identifying goods within the transportation pipeline, asset tracking, and business process tracking, which is most commonly found within manufacturing processes of expensive industrial equipment. A newcomer to active RFID is real-time location system (RTLS), an exceptionally powerful tool that provides the ability to physically locate an item within 1 or 2 meters of its position. (RTLS providers usually guarantee accuracy for 7 to 15 feet.)

NOTE You can find more details about RTLS in Chapter 6, "Peripherals."

The following are examples of active tag applications:

- Hospitals track the inventory and location of medical equipment (medical carts, heart-monitoring machines, and so forth) by using RTLS.
- The military and industries such as transportation and retail use active tags for container tracking and location. This could be combined with monitoring of environmental conditions as well as route and container access and yard management.
- The automotive industry uses key fobs for remote car locking and unlocking, alarm activation, starting up the car, and so on.

The users benefit not only from the long read ranges, but also from the tag's memory, which can carry information such as tag ID, container number, content of the container, dates of departure and arrival, route, and so on, up to several megabytes. Active tags can also be used with a global positioning system (GPS) as well as other satellite systems or cellular communication networks. The tag is able to collect, for instance, data about its route or data from environmental sensors that track temperature, humidity, and other information. These data then can be communicated in real time to the back-end system, sent in batches, or downloaded at the end of the tag's assignment. Another critical component that makes active tags attractive is that they don't need to be hooked up to the Internet to get useful information. Even in the middle of a desert with a handheld reader, a soldier can determine the contents of a shipping container without opening it, because the data are entirely on the tag.

Passive Tags

Passive tags differ greatly from active tags. They do not carry a battery or a transmitter and are not able to transmit an RF signal by themselves to the environment. Passive tags use the signal received from the reader to power their chip circuitry and send a response back to the reader. To communicate with a reader, passive tags use either inductive coupling or passive backscatter techniques (both of which will be discussed further later in this chapter) depending on whether they are getting energy from a magnetic field or an electric field.

The construction of a passive tag is quite simple. A passive tag consists of a chip (integrated circuit, or IC) and an antenna, which are connected and placed on a substrate. These three components together are often called an RFID inlay. Usually, the RFID inlay is not used by itself but is integrated into some kind of packaging or media, most often labels but sometimes buttons, cards, or wristbands. Because a passive tag has a very thin profile, often as thin as a sheet of paper with a small bump for the chip, it also can be integrated into product packaging or in some cases inside the product itself.

Passive tags can operate on various frequencies, from 135 kHz to 2.4 GHz, and their characteristics differ by the frequency used. Generally, passive tags have a considerably shorter read range than active tags. Passive tags can communicate in distances up to 10 meters (30 feet) under ideal conditions, but usually their read ranges are shorter, and they vary by frequency and communication method used and the type of material the tags are attached to.

Because of their relatively simple construction and fast manufacturing, passive tags are the least expensive types of tags. (I have been referred to as the Great Tagnac recently because of my ability to predict price. For those of you who read *RFID For Dummies,* you'll see that I accurately predicted the price of tags dropping below 10 cents by 2006 and being close to 5 cents by the end of 2006. Chalk that up to even a blind squirrel finding a nut occasionally.) Passive tags are easily produced in large quantities and are suitable for use on high-volume, low-cost products. Passive tags are used for tracking pallets, cases, or items throughout military, retail, automotive, pharmaceutical, and other industry supply chains; for inventory management; and for access control, personnel identification, parking, subway toll collection, theft prevention, and many other applications. Just to give you an idea about the flexible uses of passive RFID tags, here are a few examples:

Retail Passive tags are used for tracking pallets and cases, and sometimes items. Tags are used for theft prevention, inventory management, promotion management, product display, and availability, as well as a multitude of other applications.

Pharmaceutical Industry Tags are used for item tracking to provide the drug pedigree (history of the drug and its progress throughout the whole supply chain from the manufacturer to the retailer or hospital) and prevent counterfeiting. For this application, tags are placed on vials with pills, as well as on cases.

Garbage Collection Tags are placed on garbage bins. The tag ID is cross-referenced with a database carrying data about paid and unpaid accounts.

Automotive Industry Passive tags are used in keys to provide key/vehicle/owner identification. When the key is positively identified, it can turn on the ignition. Tags are also used for inventory control and tracking of various parts to provide a history.

Hospitals Babies are tagged to provide identification as well as theft prevention. Patients are tagged to provide identification, medical records, and a list of medicines provided.

Access Control Badges and access cards are equipped with tags that can be read without being swiped through a reading device. This is used for access control to buildings, parking garages, secure areas, and the like.

Libraries Tags are placed in books, CDs, and DVDs to prevent theft, track inventory, provide location, prevent mis-shelving, and speed up checkout.

Animal Tracking Tags are usually placed on the animal's ear when tracking cattle. For household pets, tags are implanted under the skin.

Amusement Parks Tags can track children as well as match them with their parents. Their wristbands with embedded tags are scanned at each attraction; therefore, you can identify where they were at what time.

Ski Resorts Tags are embedded in ski passes.

Airport Tags are used for baggage tracking and identification.

Semi-passive Tags

Semi-passive tags are also called *battery-assisted passive tags*; they are a hybrid of passive and active tags. (Occasionally they are referred to as "semi-active tags," which is not correct terminology; usually it's coming from what I call RFID pirates. The way to distinguish them is that they refer to R-F-I-D as Arrrr-fid!) Although semi-passive tags have a battery, they do not transmit an RF signal by themselves and they use passive communication methods (mostly passive backscatter and in a few cases inductive coupling) to talk to the reader. In semi-passive tags, the battery is used to power the chip's circuitry, as well as possible sensors and memory, but it does not assist with signal transmission. Semi-passive tags usually have longer read ranges than passive tags (up to 100 meters), but only because the chip needs a lot less power from the reader in order to wake up (it responds to a much weaker signal) since the additional power is supplied by the on-board battery.

Semi-passive tags vary a lot by size, capabilities, read range, casing, and of course price. (Their price is usually close to the price of an active tag.) Although they carry an on-board power source (which is usually very small, in the form of a battery used in watches or a printed battery), semi-passive tags can come in very small sizes that could compete with passive tags.

Semi-passive tags can operate on various frequencies, from 135 kHz to 2.4 GHz. Because the tag can detect different conditions and save the record even if it is not in the reader's field, it can be used for monitoring, activation, and deactivation of alarms, seals, thermostats, valves, and other devices and systems. Semi-passive tags are also used for temperature tracking in shipping trailers with environmental control (for instance, to avoid produce spoilage or thawing of frozen products) as well as for pressure, chemical, and tamper detection.

Table 4.1 provides an in-depth look at the pros and cons of the three types of tags I've discussed in this chapter.

TABLE 4.1 The Pros and Cons of Different Types of Tags

Tag Types	Pros	Cons
Active tags	Long read ranges (up to a kilometer) Can beacon, and carry sensors and large memory Possible processing capabilities Work well in difficult environments Sturdy construction RTLS	Expensive (prices vary from $5 to $150) Relatively large size due to battery Lifetime limited by battery life

TABLE 4.1 The Pros and Cons of Different Types of Tags *(continued)*

Tag Types	Pros	Cons
Passive tags	Cheap (prices start at 7 cents) Virtually unlimited lifetime (manufacturers claim unlimited reads and about 100,000 rewrites) Fast production in large quantities Fast and easy application with automatic label applicators	Short read ranges (up to 10 meters) Small memory Orientation sensitivity More susceptible to damage than active and semi-passive tags
Semi-passive tags	Relatively long read ranges (up to 100 meters) Can carry sensors and large memory Possible processing capabilities Sturdy construction	Relatively expensive (prices start at $5)

Communication

As mentioned before, RFID tags differ by their communication methods. Active tags communicate with a reader directly because they have their own transmitter that sends a signal to the environment in order to contact the reader or respond to its inquiries.

Passive and semi-passive tags, on the other hand, do not have this option. They can communicate with a reader only by using the same energy sent by the reader. These tags respond by "reflecting" some of the reader's original signal back, modified to carry the tag's data.

The tag uses the reader's signal for data as well as energy. The tag receives the energy from the reader and uses it to power its chip as well as to send a response signal back to the reader. When the tag's chip receives a signal from a reader, it demodulates it to recognize the data from the reader (usually commands or queries). The tag then modulates this signal to include its own data as a response to the reader's inquiry and sends this data to a reader by using the energy provided by the carrier wave received from the reader.

There are two main methods of passive communication, which differ by whether they use a magnetic field or an electric field. These methods are inductive coupling and passive backscatter (or capacitive coupling).

Inductive Coupling

With *inductive coupling*, the tag knows it is going to be in the magnetic field of the reader and is ready to respond appropriately. Inductive coupling utilizes the magnetic field that is created by changing current in the reader's antenna. When a tag enters this magnetic field, the field induces an electric current in the tag's antenna, which then powers the tag's chip. Data between the reader and a tag are transferred by fluctuations in the magnetic field. This method is used by low- and high-frequency systems (and in some ultra-high-frequency systems) and requires an induction coil within tags (see Figure 4.1).

Because of the nature of the magnetic field, this communication method allows for only near-field communication and therefore short read ranges, usually less than 1 meter.

FIGURE 4.1 Examples of various types of tag antennas

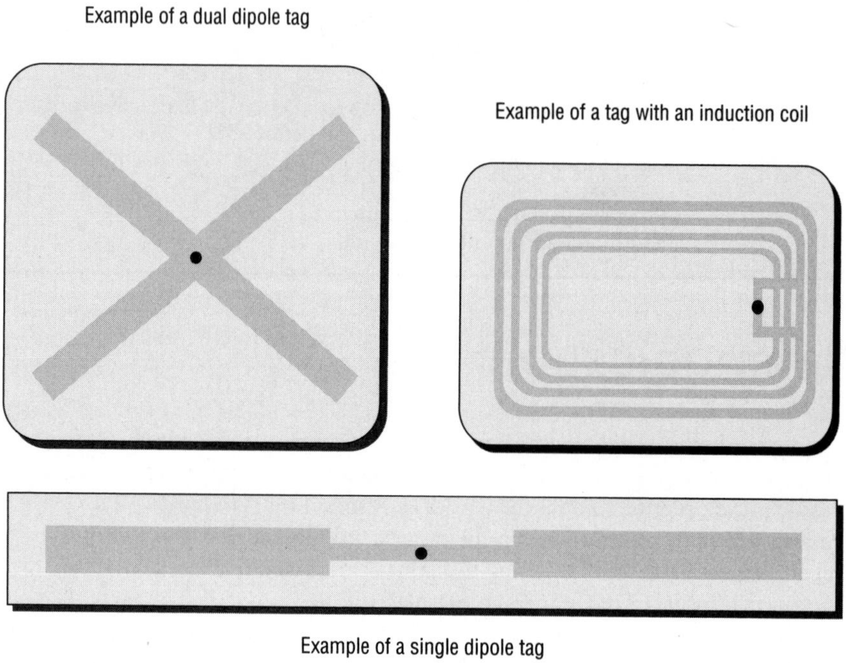

Passive Backscatter

Passive backscatter communication is based on an electric field, which is out past the magnetic field. When a tag enters the electric field produced by the reader's antenna, the field creates an electric current in the tag's antenna, which powers the tag's chip. The electric field is used not only for energy transfer, but also for data transfer. The tag's antenna does not have to be a closed loop (such as an induction coil), but can be made into various shapes to achieve the best read rates possible; usually it is a dipole antenna or dual dipole. Passive backscatter is used mainly by ultra-high-frequency and microwave tags. Because of the nature of the electric field, these tags can achieve longer read ranges than tags of the same size utilizing a magnetic field.

Table 4.2 compares the attributes of inductive coupling and passive backscatter.

TABLE 4.2 Differences between Inductive Coupling and Passive Backscatter

	Inductive Coupling	Passive Backscatter
Field Used	Magnetic	Electric
Tag Antenna	Induction coil (conductive loop)	Antenna of any shape (single dipole, dual dipole)
Read Range	Short	Long
Performance around Liquids and Metals	Good	Bad
Frequencies	LF, HF (UHF possible)	UHF, microwave

Frequencies

When R.E.M. (and less famously *RFID For Dummies*) asked, "What's the Frequency, Kenneth?" the answer was pretty cut and dried because Wal-Mart demanded UHF. The world of RFID has changed a lot since the Wal-Mart mandate in 2003. RFID systems operate at various frequencies, which have been allocated by the International Telecommunication Union (ITU) and regional regulatory organizations such as the U.S. Federal Communications Commission (FCC). Although specific frequency bands differ by country or world region, four general frequency bands are used by RFID systems: low frequency, high frequency, ultra-high frequency, and microwave frequency. RFID tags working in each of the bands have different constructions, capabilities, and performance. Each frequency has its own advantages and disadvantages, and no frequency is perfect for all applications, despite what the greeter in the blue smock might tell you.

Low-Frequency Tags

Low-frequency (LF) tags operate at a frequency from 125 kHz to 134 kHz. Passive LF tags are constructed with an induction coil and use near-field inductive coupling for power and communication. An advantage of a low frequency is that the RF waves have great penetration ability, and metals, liquids, or any other "difficult" materials do not pose a problem. This fact also could be a disadvantage because LF waves are hard to shield. However, LF tags are less susceptible to interference than are the tags of other frequencies.

Read ranges of LF passive tags are typically less than half a meter. The read range is highly dependent on the area of the tag's antenna: the larger the area, the longer the read range. LF tags have slower data-transfer rates and are usually *read-only*. That means that they carry a pre-encoded tag ID, which is then matched to a database in order to retrieve information related to the tag. This feature provides higher data security. Recent developments within the LF tag technology have provided write/rewrite and anticollision capabilities.

The main applications of LF tags are as follows:

- Animal and livestock identification and tracking
- Access control
- Vehicle immobilizers (tags in key fobs)
- Point-of-sale (for instance Mobil/Exxon Speedpass)
- Various applications in closed-loop systems, for example tracking of electronic equipment such as laptops, PCs, or terminals

High-Frequency Tags

High-frequency (HF) tags operate at 13.56 MHz, which is globally accepted and implemented. Passive HF tags include an induction coil and use near-field inductive coupling for power and communication. Passive HF tags provide relatively good performance around liquids and metals, but have short read ranges, usually fewer than 1 meter, most of the time under half a meter. They have higher data-transfer rates than LF tags but are more susceptible to interference. Passive HF tags can be read-only as well as read/write and have anticollision capabilities, which are based around International Organization for Standardization (ISO) standards.

To date, HF tags are the most used tags globally because of their application in smart cards. Other applications include the following:

- Item-level tracking in supply-chain applications
- Access control
- Libraries
- Healthcare and pharmaceutical industry
- Smart shelves

Ultra-High-Frequency Tags

Thanks to the biggest retailers in the world and the largest supply chain in history (the U.S. DoD), there is a new star in the world of RFID—UHF. Passive *ultra-high-frequency (UHF)* tags operate anywhere from 860 MHz to 960 MHz, while active tags usually operate around 433 MHz. UHF tags have higher data-transfer rates than LF and HF tags and provide many additional capabilities, such as better anticollision and the possibility of locking and killing the tag, which were mostly implemented with *electronic product code (EPC)* Generation 2 technology.

There are two main types of passive UHF tags. The first type utilizes far-field communication (above one wavelength). The second type, which will be in production in 2007, uses near-field communication (within one wavelength).

Far-field passive UHF tags are made with an antenna that can be etched, stamped, or printed into various shapes. These tags use passive backscatter technology to communicate. A main advantage of these UHF tags over HF and LF tags is their read range, which reaches up to 10 meters, although it typically is around 3–5 meters. Far-field UHF tags do not penetrate water or metals and their performance around these materials is largely diminished, which makes them less suitable for item-level tagging.

Applications of far-field passive UHF tags include the following:

- Case-level and pallet-level tracking (retail, military, and so forth), sometimes item-level
- Baggage tracking
- Toll collection
- Asset tracking
- Antitheft protection

Near-field passive UHF tags were patented back in the mid-1990s but are just now coming into production. The tags have an antenna that is slightly similar to that used in an HF tag, except UHF requires only one loop, so it's not nearly as loopy as an HF tag, and it uses near-field inductive coupling for power and communication. The advantage of using near-field technology is the possibility of water penetration and a better performance around metals; however, it comes with a disadvantage of shorter read ranges. The range should be dictated by the laws of physics, which say that the magnetic field boundary layer is equal to the wavelength divided by 2 times pi. This would mean that the read range of UHF in the near field should be about 33 cm divided by 6, or around 5 cm. However, manufacturers are claiming the ability to read up to 3 feet using UHF near field, although this might be achieved with the help of a small far-field antenna or, more accurately, by using a PE mode wave guide, which may not even be legal according to the FCC—but that's way more detail than you need to know for the CompTIA exam.

This type of tag is being investigated to improve the capabilities of UHF tags that are largely used and mandated in the retail supply chain but historically provided bad performance in conjunction with liquids and metals. Near-field passive tags can be made to support the EPC Generation 2 protocol, and because of their purported performance and read range could be ideal for item-level tagging for such products as apparel and liquor.

Applications of near-field UHF tags include the following:

- Item-level tracking
- Possibly other applications that currently use HF

NOTE You are probably thinking, what is so great about this tag, if the HF tag can do the same thing? Well, near-field UHF tags have much faster data-transfer rates than HF tags (one of the manufacturers claims they're up to 64 times faster) and they can be used for tagging products that are under the UHF mandates. It also provides all the features of the Generation 2 protocol, another innovation that could be a breakthrough in the industry over the next few years.

Microwave Tags

Microwave tags operate at frequencies around 2.45 GHz and sometimes 5.8 GHz. Because of the frequency properties, microwave tags have the highest data-transfer rates of all tags, but the worst performance around liquids and metals. Passive microwave tags use passive backscatter to communicate and have limited read ranges, usually up to 1 meter. This is usually overcome by using active tags, which can achieve longer read distances. Because of fast data transfer, active microwave tags are suitable for use with toll-collection systems.

Table 4.3 provides a comparison of the pros and cons of all four types of frequencies.

TABLE 4.3 Comparison of Frequencies and Related Tag Capabilities

Frequency	Band	Typical Read Range*	Pros	Cons	Applications
Low	125–134 kHz	Under 0.5 m	Best performance around water and metal	Slow data transfer Short read range*	Animal tracking Immobilizers Access control Speedpass
High	13.56 MHz	Under 1 m	Global standard Higher data-transfer rate than LF	Short read range*	Smart cards Smart shelves Access control Libraries Pharma
Ultra-high	860–960 MHz* 433 MHz	Around 3 m (up to 10 m)	Higher data-transfer rate than LF and HF Longest read range out of all passive tags*	Susceptible to interference Far-field tags have bad performance around water and metals*	Retail and DoD mandates* Case-level and pallet-level tracking (near-field tags for item-level)* Electronic toll collection
Microwave	2.45 GHz, 5.8 GHz	Under 1 m	Highest data-transfer rates	Short read range*	Electronic toll collection

* Applies to passive tags

Frequencies Used around the World

Because of international, regional, and local regulatory and standardization organizations and the frequencies allocated for a wide variety of purposes, radio frequency bands for RFID differ in various regions of the world. Frequencies were allocated by the ITU to three regions: Region 1, which contains Europe (including the former Soviet Union), the Middle East, and Africa; Region 2, which contains North and South America; and Region 3, which includes Asia, Australia, and Oceania. Within the first two regions the frequencies do not significantly vary by country, but this is not true about Region 3. Table 4.4 summarizes the frequencies per continent or country (as applicable).

TABLE 4.4 RFID Frequencies by Region

ITU Region	Continent or Country	LF	HF	UHF	Microwave
2	North America	125–134 kHz	13.56 MHz	902–928 MHz	2400–2483.5 MHz and 5725–5850 MHz
2	South America	125–134 kHz	13.56 MHz	915 MHz (typically accepted)	2.45 GHz
1	Europe	125–134 kHz	13.56 MHz	865–868 (up to 870) MHz	2.45 GHz
1	Africa	125–134 kHz	13.56 MHz	865–868 (up to 870) MHz (north) 915 MHz (south)	2.45 GHz
3	China	125–134 kHz	13.56 MHz	917–922 MHz (temporary)	2446–2454 MHz
3	China (Hong Kong)	125–134 kHz	13.56 MHz	865–868 and/or 920–925 MHz	2.45 GHz
3	India	125–134 kHz	13.56 MHz	865–867 MHz	2.45 GHz
3	Japan	125–134 kHz	13.56 MHz	952–954 (955) MHz	2.45 GHz
3	Korea	125–134 kHz	13.56 MHz	908.5–914 MHz	2.45 GHz
3	Australia	125–134 kHz	13.56 MHz	918–926 MHz	2.45 GHz

TABLE 4.4 RFID Frequencies by Region *(continued)*

ITU Region	Continent or Country	LF	HF	UHF	Microwave
3	New Zealand	125–134 kHz	13.56 MHz	864–868 MHz and 921–929 MHz	2.45 GHz
3	Singapore	125–134 kHz	13.56 MHz	866–869 MHz and 923–925 MHz	2.45 GHz
3	Thailand	125–134 kHz	13.56 MHz	920–925 MHz	2.45 GHz
3	Taiwan	125–134 kHz	13.56 MHz	922–928 MHz	2.45 GHz
3	Malaysia	125–134 kHz	13.56 MHz	868.1 MHz and 919–923 MHz	2.45 GHz

The idea of global supply-chain visibility is more difficult to realize at the UHF level when you look at the variance in UHF spectrum around the world. Generally, a UHF tag that operates on the U.S. frequency will not function adequately in Europe; a tag used in Europe will not work in Korea or Thailand. Fortunately, there is a solution for this problem. Some tag manufacturers (such as OMRON or UPM Raflatac) have or are developing a global tag that works on several different frequencies (within the UHF band), and therefore product manufacturers and distributors will be able to use only one tag for their goods anywhere in the world. The difficulty from a physics perspective is that as the bandwidth gets wider, the ability to tune a tag to respond gets more difficult.

Tag Classes (EPC)

Just like kids at school, RFID tags are divided into classes. These classes were developed primarily by two industry standards organizations—EPCglobal (a division of GS1) and the ISO—in order to classify and unify function and capabilities of RFID tags. EPCglobal has done its best to promote the use of EPC.

NOTE EPCglobal and other standardization organizations will be discussed in more detail in Chapter 9, "Standards and Regulations," but EPC classes and related tag capabilities belong in this chapter because they are so specific to tags.

Time to blow the dust off the RFID history book. In early 2000, two RFID companies started to produce RFID tags. One of them was Matrics (later bought by Symbol Technologies) and the other was Alien Technology. Matrics came up with a tag that was read-only; therefore, the data had to be encoded at the point of manufacturing and could not be rewritten by the user. The design came from some very smart engineers from the National Security Agency (NSA). These tags belonged to EPC Class 0. Matrics tags came with a dual dipole antenna starting at a size of 4″ × 4″ and performed very well.

Alien offered a tag that was *write-once read-many (WORM)*, which means that the tag's data or number could be written by the user. This tag became the basis for EPC Class 1. Alien tags came with a single dipole antenna in a squiggly format and the name "squiggle" tag. Although the standard for EPC Class 1 specifies that this tag is WORM, in reality it could be rewritten several times. Matrics saw the shortcomings of their read-only tag and introduced a WORM tag, which was unofficially called Class 0+. This tag was also fully rewritable, but was not compatible with other vendor equipment; therefore, it could not be rewritten by any reader other than Matrics. Class 0+ never became an EPC standard.

In the meantime, EPCglobal developed a new standard based on the capabilities of both EPC Class 0 and 1 tags, enhanced with many new features and functions. These tags became EPC Class 1 Generation 2 (a.k.a. Gen 2). This standard was submitted to the ISO for ratification under ISO standard 18000. After the ISO approval, Generation 2 will become one unified international air-interface protocol as well as the data standard for UHF RFID tags, and eventually for HF tags as well.

EPC Class 1 Generation 2 tags offer many new and enhanced features, such as the following:

Faster Data Transfer The Gen 2 protocol supports a data-transfer rate from tag to reader of up to 640 kilobits per second (Kbps). In contrast, Generation 1 Class 0 could transfer up to 80 Kbps and Class 1 up to 140 Kbps. Gen 2 also supports much faster writing, approximately 800 bits per second.

Higher Read Rates In the United States, read rates could reach (under ideal conditions) up to 1,500 tags per second; in Europe, because of regulatory restrictions, the rate could be up to 600 tags per second. For comparison, Generation 1 tags were capable of reads about 10 times lower.

Better Access Control and Security Gen 2 tags provide better access control and security because of 32-bit Access and Kill passwords. Gen 1 used 8- and 24-bit passwords.

Capability to Generate and Respond with Random Numbers Based on a Value Q Given by the Interrogator (Q Algorithm) This not only makes the Gen 2 tags more secure, but also gives the reader the ability to inventory tags even if they have the same EPC.

Proven Air Interface Gen 2 tags use *FM0* or *Miller subcarrier* encoding for backscatter. FM0 is fast but more sensitive to interference, whereas Miller subcarrier encoding fits the tag responses in between the channels used by the reader. This latter method is slightly slower but is more resistant to interference.

Memory Divided into Four Memory Banks Bank 0: *Reserved memory*—carries 32-bit Access and 32-bit Kill passwords

Bank 1: *EPC memory*—includes EPC number of a flexible size (16 to 469 bits) and various protocol controls

Bank 2: *Tag identification (TID) memory*—consists of information about the tag itself, such as tag ID

Bank 3: *User memory*—provides a space for user-defined data

Reduced Ghost Reads Gen 2 tags and readers use several methods to avoid ghost reads. Tags are programmed to respond with a certain delay in a small uncertainty window. If the tag responds outside this window, the reader ignores it. Or, the tag can send a preamble (unique wave). After this preamble is validated by the reader, the communication can begin. The third method involves the reader checking a data stream coming from the tag for a valid EPC format.

Sessions Each tag can operate in four *sessions*. This is useful when the tags are inventoried by more readers. Each reader or group of readers is assigned a different session and they do not interfere with other readers when interrogating tags.

AB Symmetry *AB Symmetry* provides the tags with a capability to be in a state A or state B. A reader changes the state after it reads the tag. This method replaces the Gen 1 method, which put tags to sleep after they were read to avoid interference with interrogation of other tags. (Sometimes they never woke up, and sometimes the waking up took valuable time.)

Smaller Chips Most of the Gen 2 chips are smaller in size compared to Gen 1 chips, which allows for smaller power consumption and faster data processing due to smaller gates on the chips. Smaller size also means that more chips can be produced from a single wafer, with the idea of reducing costs.

Improved Dense Reader Mode The frequency band is divided into several smaller bands, which allows for the readers and tags to have their own section. Tags and readers are not permitted to share a band, which prevents them from interfering with each other. Readers are required to stay strictly within their band to avoid leaking their energy into the tag section.

The Gen 2 protocol was built to leave open options for additional EPC classes. The tags with these functions already exist; however, they are not standardized by EPCglobal yet:

- Class 2 would include tags that would be fully rewritable, carry a large memory, and support encryption.
- Class 3 would include semi-passive tags with possible sensors.
- Class 4 would standardize active tags with the ability to communicate with other tags.
- Finally, Class 5 would provide guidelines for tags based on Class 4 but with added reader capability. These tags would function as readers as well as tags.

Tag Construction

As we discussed earlier, RFID tags can have a different construction depending on their functions and application. Two components are common to all tags: a chip—also called a microchip, an integrated circuit (IC), or an *application-specific integrated circuit (ASIC)*—and an antenna. These tag parts can be manufactured and attached in many ways; each method has its advantages and disadvantages that affect tag performance.

The Chip, or IC

The widespread acceptance of the EPC architecture is based on the ability to mass-produce a 5-cent RFID tag. This concept was originally driven by the fact that supply-chain applications require you to tag so many items that tag cost would be paramount in determining the business case outcome. Although the emergence of many new asset-tracking solutions and the use of RFID on higher-value goods can challenge this assumption, there is no doubt that lower cost is a benefit to business cases of all kinds. To achieve low-cost RFID tags, it is critical that material and manufacturing costs are minimized. This translates directly into small chip sizes and memory. With this as the primary design criterion, the IC offers bare-bones logical functionality:

On-Chip Memory Is Limited Gen 2 tags are required to store at least a 96-bit EPC number accompanied by a 16-bit cyclic redundancy check (CRC) for error checking. This number is then used to *point* to additional data about the product stored in a networked database. This is not enough memory to provide details other than the most basic product identification and serial number. For companies looking to track lot codes and expiration dates, this information must be stored externally.

Tags Must Respond in Collision-Free Channels When multiple tags are in the field simultaneously, they must talk in turn to prevent data collision at the receiver. Generation 2 EPC tags utilize a slotted ALOHA algorithm to prevent collisions. The characteristics of these protocols have a significant impact on the rate at which tag data can be collected.

The IC also holds responsibility for converting RF energy into usable electric power and for modulating the backscatter signal. Design parameters related to power requirements include the following:

Small Onboard Chip Memory Reduces Power Needs Because storage requirements have been minimized, the power required to read EPC tags is very low, on the order of microwatts ($1\times 10E^{-6}$ W).

The Efficiency of the Power Circuitry The IC receives energy for the tag antenna in the form of oscillating current at the frequency of the reader transmission. This current must be down-converted and rectified by using circuitry tuned to a specific frequency. The precision of these components and how well they are matched determines power conversion efficiency.

The Impedance Match of the Chip and the Antenna Impedance can best be described as opposition to the flow of current in an electrical system. To illustrate, think of water flowing through an open pipe vs. through a pipe that is clogged and leaky. If an impedance mismatch exists between the chip and the tag antenna, power will be reflected away from the chip and unavailable for use on the tag.

The Ability of the Chip to Alter the Impedance of the Antenna Backscatter modulation (or simply reflecting usable signals back to the receiver from the tag) occurs as the IC alters the impedance of the tag antenna at specific time intervals. The chip's ability to change the impedance abruptly and in sync with the reader determines signal clarity and strength.

Tag Antenna Production

There are three main methods of manufacturing a passive tag antenna: etching, stamping, and printing.

The etching process starts with a sheet made of three layers: a substrate, metal film (usually copper), and a photopolymer layer. A special mask "burns" an image of a future antenna into the photopolymer layer. The sheet is then washed by a chemical solution that dissolves all metal around the burned image. The burned photopolymer is removed from the image by another chemical solution to expose the etched metal antenna. The antenna then goes through a special process to prevent oxidation of the metal.

This method produces high-quality metal antennas with great conductivity. However, it has a main disadvantage: producing chemical waste. Etching uses chemical solutions for dissolving the remaining metal as well as the photopolymer layer, and these require special handling.

The stamping method uses a metal foil (usually aluminum) and a "cookie cutter" in the shape of an antenna, which is attached to a roller. When the roller stamps out the antenna in the foil, the unused foil is removed and potentially reused. This method produces high-quality antennas that are also relatively cheap (because of the reused aluminum), and also eliminates the need for any chemicals and reduces waste.

Antennas also can be printed using conductive inks. This is a very fast method and does not require sheet metal. Conductive inks are made of liquid containing solvents, binders, and very fine metal particles. Ink is applied through a mesh screen with a cut-out opening in the shape of an antenna. The rest of the mesh is sealed off. This method produces an antenna of comparable conductivity to pure metal antennas via a high-speed manufacturing process. There are concerns regarding printed antennas' durability as compared to pure metal antennas, but there is absolutely no waste.

Chip Attachment

When handling RFID tags, you probably noticed that not only do they have various shapes of antennas, but also some of them have a different chip attachment. There are two primary methods of affixing the chip to the antenna. A chip can be connected to an antenna by using a strap or it can be directly attached.

When using a strap technique, the chip is first attached to a strap. The strap is made of conductive material and is then connected to an antenna. An advantage of this method is the ability to handle very small chips and enables a high-volume production compared to direct attachment. However, a possible disadvantage can occur if the strap is not made of highly flexible material. (This is the reason to avoid using tags manufactured a couple of years ago.) If the tag is bent, the strap could interrupt the connections to the antenna or totally fall off, which would render the tag useless. This used to happen in early stages of the strap attachment technique, but today this problem has been eliminated. Another potential disadvantage is that the strap creates a slight "bump" on a tag, which makes it prone to damage during handling of a tagged product.

NOTE

There are many methods for placing the chips onto the straps; some innovative designs not yet put into practice are trying to increase throughput and reduce cost. One of them, developed and patented by Alien Technology, is called Fluidic Self Assembly (FSA). This approach uses chips floating in a liquid over a base that has cut-out gaps in the shape of the chips. After all gaps receive a chip, the base is then sealed and cut into straps. A similar technology called PICA uses vibration and was patented by Symbol Technologies.

The direct attachment approach uses a robotic hand with a high-precision vacuum nozzle that places the chip onto an antenna. The chip has to be flipped over to allow for attachment to the antenna, and for this reason this method is sometimes called "flip-chip." When the chip is placed onto the antenna, it is then bonded with it by using pressure and heat to cure the electrically conductive epoxy on the chip's surface.

Modulation: Why It Matters

This would be a good time to take a deep breath, stretch your medulla oblongata, and get ready for some heavy but important technical talk. The EPC Generation 2 specification provides unprecedented levels of flexibility for tuning readers in accordance with customized business processes designed to fit with existing operations. But beware: selecting the wrong *modulation scheme* is analogous to driving an Indy 500 race car, when you should be nestled securely in an Abrams battle tank. Do you need a fast exchange between readers and tags to enable the use case that integrates seamlessly with your existing business processes, or a robust interface impenetrable to sources of RF interference that would otherwise rain destruction on your RFID system?

The modulation flexibility found in the Gen 2 protocol makes RFID more customizable to your application, translating into superior performance potential. This improvement will enable applications that improve operational efficiencies, saving end users time and money.

Selecting a modulation scheme determines how information is communicated on an RF wave. The Gen 2 protocol allows readers to use multiple modulation schemes in both the reader-to-tag link and vice versa. What you need to understand is how a Gen 2 UHF tag responds to a query command issued by a reader.

Gen 2–compliant tags have two built-in modulation operations, FM0 baseband and Miller subcarrier, as mentioned earlier. The reader tells the tag which scheme should be employed.

When FM0 is activated, the tag is instructed to use the same frequency as the reader to communicate its EPC information. This exchange is very quick, but problematic because the reader's signal is a million times stronger than the tag's and can drown it out. Alternatively, Miller subcarrier modulation moves the tag's response away from the reader's strong carrier signal, making the reader less susceptible to interference due to its own signaling.

The option of multiple modulations is available to enable superior reader optimization. In cases where many readers (a dense-reader environment) or other strong sources of interference are present, the Miller subcarrier modulation scheme should be employed. The trade-off is that Miller subcarrier data rates are significantly slower than FM0 by a factor of two, four, or eight. At the very least, understanding the key differences between the two will help you design a better system, or at least provide some fodder for cocktail parties when you want to bring a conversation to a screeching halt—just start talking about the various Gen 2 RFID modulation schemes.

Q Factor

Without getting into my penchant for James Bond movies, suffice it to say that Q is one of my favorite names. Q in this case is for Quality. The *Q factor* is often used as a classification of the quality or efficiency of a resonant circuit, which also applies to RFID tags.

Tags are tuned to operate at a certain frequency and respond to frequencies that are the closest to their own frequency. The higher the Q factor, the higher the amount of energy that could be transferred between the reader and a tag. The most efficient energy transfers (with the highest Q value) take place when the frequency is very close to the tag's resonant frequency. This means that a high Q factor comes with the slight disadvantage of a smaller bandwidth. In other words, an HF tag will have a higher Q factor than a UHF tag (13.56 MHz bandwidth vs. the 902–928 MHz wider spectrum). I know this may be a bit confusing, but if you remember that you can have either high Q or high bandwidth, but not both, you will have the basic concept.

Tags for Specific Applications

Tags can come in various forms, and each form is particular to a specific application. Of course, generic types of tags can be used for many applications; however, there may be situations in which you are not getting satisfactory results with all-purpose tags and you need a custom solution. Many manufacturers offer tags intended for specific applications, or they can customize the tag according to your needs and requirements.

Tags for specific applications differ by tuning (they are tuned to work better with certain materials such as metal, glass, liquids, and so forth) or they can have varied packaging designed to support their performance or withstand various environmental and handling conditions. Understanding the physics and material composition of an item to be tagged helps people leverage science to create a tag specific to that application. For instance, good RF engineers can measure the frequency response off of a sheet of metal and determine how that will affect the resonant frequency of a tag; then they can change the resonant frequency to account for that change, essentially using the metal object as a backplane of the tag component. Once again, physics makes it all happen.

Tag Packaging

You've learned about all the components that are necessary for the tag to function, except for one critical part: the tag packaging. Although the types of tag packaging conceivably can be limitless, I've put together a list that shows you the types of tag packaging, the applications they are used for, and their advantages and disadvantages:

Label (Also Called a Smart Label) An RFID inlay is integrated into a thin flexible paper or plastic sheet with an adhesive side. Labels usually come in the form of rolls or fan-folds, and are used in RFID printers and label applicators. Labels are manufactured in various sizes, most commonly 2″x 4″, 4″x 4″, and 4″x 6″, but you can also encounter labels of other dimensions. Labels are used mostly for tagging cases and pallets in the retail supply chain, but also are used for product (item) tagging, library books, and movie rentals. Labels are easily accessible, are relatively low cost, and offer fast and precise application methods, but they are not very sturdy.

Card (Also Called a Smart Card) An RFID inlay is integrated into a plastic card, and usually looks like a standard credit card. These types of tags are often used for access control to buildings, secure areas, and parking garages. Cards are more durable than labels but are a bit more expensive to produce.

Button An RFID inlay can be encased in sturdy plastic packaging in the form of a button, usually around 1 inch in diameter. The button can have an adhesive side or one or more holes for attachment. Buttons are usually attached to garments or sewn into them and are used for applications in laundry, dry cleaning, or clothing rental. There are machines available on the market that can automatically apply tags in the form of buttons.

Wristband A thin plastic strip carrying an RFID tag is usually placed on a wrist or other body part. The strip often uses adhesive or notches to connect the ends. Wristbands are used, for instance, in hospitals for patient identification or theft prevention (see the following "Proud Daddy" sidebar).

Real World Scenario

Proud Daddy

When my daughter was born, my thoughts turned away from RFID for a change, and I was focused on being the proud daddy. I was thinking only about cuddling her and giving her mom a much-deserved rest as I walked (on air) around the hospital corridors. Out of nowhere, alarms started ringing and the pudgy security staff with Taser guns were lumbering toward us, clearly upset by an interruption of their Dunkin' Donuts moment. (Well, they didn't really have the Tasers, but I was still feeling woefully outgunned holding a one-day-old.) After a couple of disoriented moments, I realized we had wandered near the exit door with RFID readers and antennas, and that "innocent" band my daughter had on her ankle was there to make sure that she did not leave the infant ward! So, although I couldn't steal my baby without facing down a chocolate-frosting-lipped constable, I did feel better knowing that no one else could either.

Glass Bead An RFID tag can be placed into a small cylindrical vial. The glass bead is used for animal tracking (mainly for pets) because it can be easily injected under the skin. Glass beads are also used for human tracking, such as for members of military special forces.

Key Fob A tag is integrated into a key fob used for vehicle access and immobilizer activation and deactivation.

Casing An RFID tag is inserted into a rugged plastic (or other RF-neutral material) container. This container can be of various sizes, depending on the tag and other components such as sensors, battery, and so on. Usually you will see active and semi-passive tags in casing. Tags in casing usually have to be attached manually. Encased tags are used in high-stress environments, where the tag has to be protected, as well as in applications common to semi-passive and active tags (container tracking, RTLS, etc.).

TIP There are many ways to attach an encased tag. Sometimes the casing has openings; therefore, you will be able to use screws or zip-ties. If the casing has no holes, you can utilize adhesive Velcro, double-sided tape, or brackets to hold the tag in place.

Embedded Passive tags can be embedded into certain RF-neutral materials that provide protection for the tag's parts and/or spacing from a product surface, enabling them to function when they are placed on various materials. These tags include tags for use on metal that can have a ferrite layer or tags embedded in epoxy to protect them from damage. We've had calls to embed tags in everything from ceramic for a metal smelting business to salmon for tracking their spawning habits—but there was something fishy about that last company (sorry, I couldn't resist).

Integrated into Product Packaging RFID inlays can be integrated into a product or its packaging. For example, the inlay can be embedded into a carton, box, plastic container, bottle cap, or product label. The advantage of this method is fast tagging and usually better protection of tags against damage. However, if the tag fails, it may be difficult to repackage the product.

As you design the incorporation of the tag into the overall system and business process, you will have to choose how the tag is packaged. As you evaluate types of tag packaging, base your choice not only on size, application, and attachment method, but also on the tag's sturdiness. You may be interested in the cheapest tag possible that is easily applicable but does not last forever (in this case you are most probably going to choose smart labels) or you may be looking for a tag that will survive extreme conditions. When examining the tag for its rigidity, you must find out what environmental and handling conditions it will withstand, such as pressure, humidity, temperature, multiple attachments, and other factors. Sometimes this information is available from the manufacturer, but sometimes you will have to test it. There are some interesting attachment methods, such as OMRON's global tag that does not use adhesive (which is more susceptible to expansion and contraction in temperature changes), but rather an electronic weld to make the attachment very rugged.

Just as with humans, the environment can dictate how well tags work. Some items may require deep freezing or heat sterilization, so you will need tags that will not only survive these processes, but also function during and after. Not all tags will. Typically, the tags that are present in standard smart labels are intended for use in temperatures from –25°C (–13°F) to 70°C (158°F) and can be stored in temperatures from –40°C (–40°F) to 85°C (185°F). Some manufacturers produce tags that can withstand temperatures up to 250°C (482°F), which can be used, for instance, on medical items that are subjected to heat sterilization or in industries where extreme temperatures are common, such as the metallurgical industry. The operating and storage temperatures can differ by manufacturer, tag type, or tag packaging.

Real World Scenario

Labels and Extreme Temperatures

You might be thinking that if the tag was built to tolerate extreme temperatures, the packaging should be too. Several years ago I took this for granted as well, until I witnessed the manual application of labels in a near-desert warehouse without temperature control. You can imagine the dramatic change in temperatures not only season to season, but also day to day. During the hottest days, the labels would come off their backing almost without the adhesive, which "melted" and remained on the backing. In the coldest days, the labels would not stick properly on certain products because the adhesive was less tacky in low temperatures. The label converter had to be informed about this issue and had to change the properties of the label adhesive to avoid these problems in the future, and the client was left with a stock of tags that could be used only in good weather.

Material-Specific Tags

You're already at Chapter 4, so you know that some materials (such as liquids or metals) pose a problem for UHF RFID tags. Not only are some of these materials hard or impossible to penetrate by RF waves (liquids absorb the RF waves, metals reflect them), but they can also impair a tag that is placed on a surface of such material. The presence of this material could detune the tag, which would result in a drastically shorter read range. Detuning shifts the tag's operating or resonant frequency. If the tag's frequency were moved entirely out of the band of the reader's operation, the reader would not be able to read this tag at all.

To put it another way, a typical UHF tag has a resonant frequency of 915 MHz in the United States. The tags are designed with antennas that can pick up a signal starting at 900 MHz (15 MHz below the resonant frequency) and expanding up to 930 MHz (15 MHz above the resonant frequency), covering all the area in between where a tag may be frequency hopping (see Chapter 2, "Interrogation Zone Basics"). If a tag is put on a metal surface, the resonant frequency may change to 800 MHz and the range it can receive a signal on would then be 785 MHz (–15MHz) to 815 MHz (+15 MHz).

To increase performance in tough situations, manufacturers have developed tags that are intended for use with specific materials. These tags are specially tuned to be used with these materials and are enclosed in special packaging to support their function. For instance, there are special tags for use on metal, glass, containers with liquids, and minerals.

In very simple terms, if an engineer knows that a tag is being affixed to metal that will drop the tag's resonant frequency from 915 MHz to 800 MHz, a change of –115 MHz, she can design a tag that in free air would have a resonant frequency of 1030 MHz (+115 MHz). Then, when the tag is affixed to the metal object, the tag would return to the EPC standard resonant frequency of 915 MHz and be read from 902–928 MHz. If all of this makes sense to you, have no fear, you'll pass this exam with flying colors!

TIP

As a general rule of thumb, you should not use tags intended for one material on a product made of another material unless it has the same or similar chemical properties. Otherwise, the tag will not work well or may not work at all.

NOTE

Although liquids generally absorb RF waves, you should know that the surfaces of liquids can be great reflectors (you can see yourself in the surface of water, after all). Metals are generally reflectors; however, they can also absorb some of the RF energy and dissipate it across the metal surface.

Tag Placement

To receive the best possible performance from your tag, you must not only choose the right tag for your product, but also determine its best placement on a particular item or its packaging. Sometimes the tags are already preselected, and then it is up to you to make them work. There are several general rules that you should follow to do this successfully:

Use Physics and Scientific Tools to Test Your Products There are several tools, from signal generators and spectrum analyzers to specialized tag-testing software and RFID-designed probes, that can be used to leverage science rather than trial and error to find the optimal tag and location. One such tool is EasyTag (available at `www.odintechnologies.com/store`), which allows someone with very little training to accurately test for the RF response of a particular product and tag combination. Figure 4.2 shows the starting screen for EasyTag.

Utilize Air Gaps as Much as Possible This is especially important when you are tagging products or packaging containing RF-difficult materials, such as cans of soup (metal) or bottles of soft drinks (liquid).

When you are tagging cases of products, look at how the items are positioned in a case. For instance, the lean bottlenecks create large air gaps at the top of the case. This will be the best space in which to place a tag. These air gaps are called static air gaps because their location in the case does not change with movement.

FIGURE 4.2 EasyTag tag-testing software

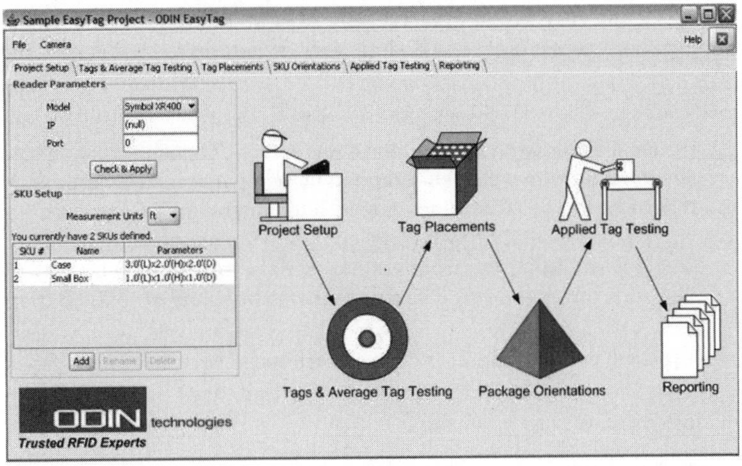

When tagging some items, you will often encounter dynamic air gaps, which are air gaps that change with product movement and orientation. For instance, an air gap created at the top of a box of Milk-Bone dog biscuits will disappear when my Newfoundland helps herself by flipping the box off the counter and dropping it onto the floor. The air gap could be on any one of the sides depending on how it lands and where the bones settle. Dynamic air gaps are impossible to utilize, but you can make them somewhat static by stabilizing the product orientation (for instance, ensure that the bottles are standing upright when passing through an interrogation zone).

When tagging a single bottle, one of the best practices is to embed the tag into the bottle cap; however, you have to make sure that the cap or bottle spout does not contain a metal lining. Placing the tag into a bottle cap has several advantages. The tag is protected from external damage, it has a slight distance from the contents of the bottle (even if it is just a couple of millimeters of plastic), and it can be integrated into the cap during its manufacturing.

If you do not have air gaps large enough to accommodate a tag or if you cannot integrate it into packaging that would not restrict the tag's performance but rather support it, you will have to use a tag intended for the tagged material. Be aware that specialized tags are usually a lot more expensive than generic tags, so you have to evaluate carefully all the possibilities of how to make a generic tag work before resorting to these.

Build a Pallet Correctly This rule ties in closely with the air gap rule. When you are building your pallet, you should try to position the items so that the tags are facing outside the pallet. If this is not possible, try to stack the products to create air gaps in between them. Do not forget that the products may have air gaps inside their packaging. When building a pallet or stacking items or cases on shelves, you should not only utilize air gaps, but also try to avoid shadowing.

Shadowing occurs when one tag is positioned in front of another tag. When the tags are interrogated, the first tag collects the signal from the reader and uses it to respond, while the second tag receives only very little or no signal and therefore does not have enough energy to respond to interrogation. The second tag is in the shadow of the first tag. To avoid shadowing, you should position tags so that they are not placed right behind one another, although this may be quite difficult, especially when there is a high density of tags on the pallet or a shelf is high.

TIP

Possible shadowing can be overcome by motion, especially by rotation. Pallets are commonly stretch-wrapped by using a stretch-wrapping machine that turns the pallet around its axis. If the interrogation zone is placed at this station, pallet rotation will often eliminate the shadowing problem and you will receive high reads from your tags. Plus, the tags will be in the interrogation zone longer so you'll have a higher probability of reading them.

Stacking tags close to each other could also cause interference between them. This could be avoided by the already discussed techniques, but also by using tags that have been tested to perform well in close proximity to other tags.

Ensure Proper Tag Orientation You must make sure that you know what types of antennas are used as well as their polarization in the interrogation zones the product will travel through, because this will affect your tag choice.

Single dipole tags will be easily accommodated by a circularly polarized antenna, regardless of the tag's orientation, as long as the tag is facing the antenna (see Figure 4.3). However, if the antenna is linearly polarized, you will have to make sure that the tag's antenna is parallel to the reader's antenna and is in the same plane as the reader's antenna wave propagation (see Figures 4.4 and 4.5). You will also have to ensure that the tag's orientation is the same on every product that crosses the discussed interrogation zone. The constant product orientation and position can be achieved mainly on manufacturing lines.

A dual dipole tag will be easier to implement, because it is less orientation sensitive. This tag will perform well at any orientation with a circular antenna as well as a linear antenna. Of course, the tag should face the antenna. Dual dipole tags are well suited for use on items that will be traveling on conveyor belts and whose position cannot be unified.

Tags using near-field coupling (LF, HF, and some UHF tags) are also orientation insensitive, unless you approach perpendicular to the reader's antenna, in which case the tags "disappear" altogether.

WARNING

The first thing you should do before you jump into tag testing is to check out the environment and make sure it is "clean." I suggest setting up a spectrum analyzer and looking at the area being tested, making sure you are reading in the entire frequency range. If no interference is recorded when using the spectrum analyzer, the second thing you should do is make sure that you have ample room (20 feet) behind the product, on all sides, and above. This will limit the possibility of standing waves and nulls.

FIGURE 4.3 Orientation with circular antenna

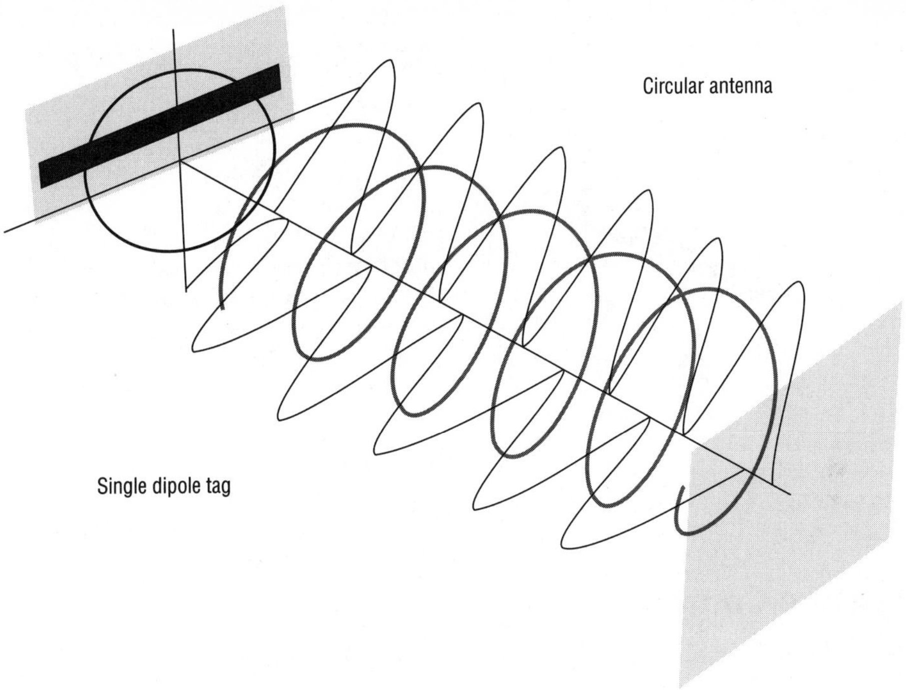

FIGURE 4.4 Correctly oriented tag

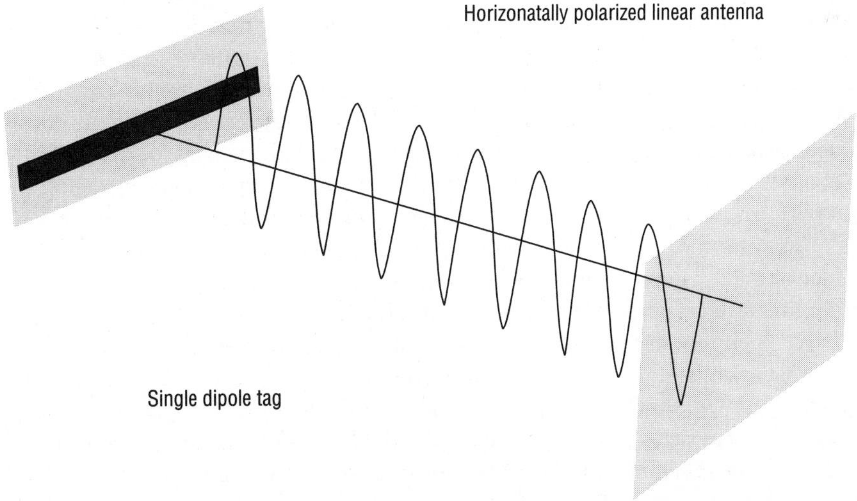

FIGURE 4.5 Incorrectly oriented tag

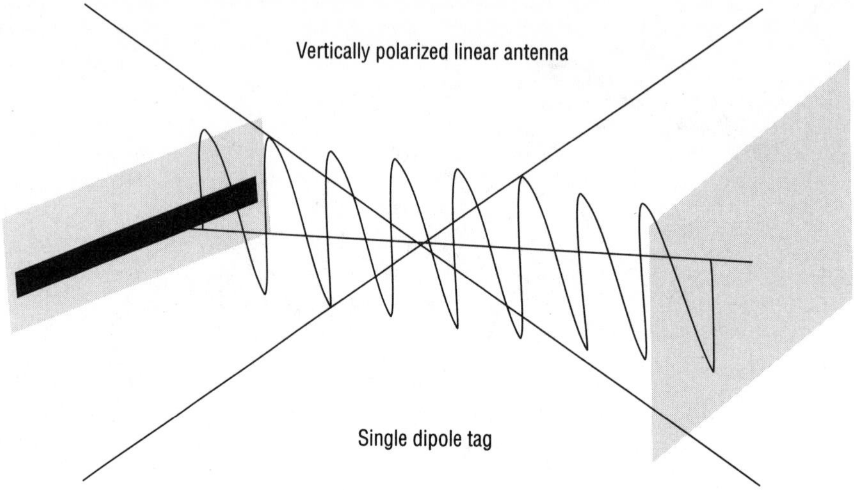

Package Contents

This RFID stuff is awfully confusing I know: not only does it matter what type of material the tag is actually affixed to, but it also matters what's inside the box. So cardboard is easy and a great product to tag, but liquid or metal inside that cardboard can really throw a wrench in the works. Although the packaging may be an easily penetrated corrugated cardboard, the product within can contain metals, water-based liquids, or other RF-difficult materials, which could either detune the tag or prevent the interrogation signal from reaching it. There are three main groups of products and packaging: product or packaging that does not include any RF-difficult materials, product or packaging that does not include liquids or metals but includes other RF-difficult materials, and product or packaging that includes liquids and metals.

Product or packaging that does not include any RF-difficult materials usually consists of corrugated cardboard, paper, foam, or dry food such as cereal, tea bags, or flour. You will be able to choose from a broad range of tags to tag this group of products and packaging. Generic tags will perform relatively well and their placement on the product can be chosen for convenience of application or space, but it will not be critical for tag's performance.

Product or packaging that does not include liquids and metals but includes other RF-challenging materials could contain glass, wood, thick layers of plastic or paper (which are normally RF-friendly), dry dog food in high volumes, and various chemicals (including washing powder). All of these materials and products will affect the RF field distribution, and therefore you will have to perform tag placement testing, utilize possible air gaps, or choose tags that are either specially tuned or work in a wider frequency band.

Product or packaging that contains liquid or metal is the most difficult to tag because not only do these substances detune the tags, but they also are opaque to RF waves. Such products include bottled drinks, cans, food in metal-lined packaging, liquid hair products, electrical equipment, and laptops and PCs. When tagging such items, you will have to heavily utilize the air gaps in the packaging, test the tag placement, and ensure that the product will go through the interrogation in a correct position. This principle has to be applied to pallets as well; because of the product's impenetrable nature, the items in the middle of the conventionally built pallet will not be read.

TIP Make sure that you place the whole tag, including the antenna, into the air gap.

NOTE Although the Generation 2 tags have enhanced capabilities and perform much better with RF-difficult materials than the previous generation, you should still follow these best practices and perform all necessary testing to ensure the best possible performance of your tags and the whole system.

Tag Placement Testing

To locate and verify the best possible spot to place your tag, you will have to perform scientific-based testing. You can do this by yourself if you have the location and testing equipment, or you can send the products to a specialized testing facility. Testing labs differ by the range of available testing equipment, testing methods, and services they provide. ODIN Technologies has been testing products for years and has completed literally hundreds of thousands of tests, so what you are about to learn is without a doubt industry best practices.

Some labs perform testing in a "clean" environment without RF noise and interference and under ideal environmental conditions; this is done in an anechoic chamber. The performance results coming from these facilities will be the best possible results you can achieve with that type of tag and your product, and are the best way to ensure 100 percent read rates. If you don't get 100 percent read rates, the data you will get from you, and your partner's, RFID networks will be incomplete, and therefore less valuable. However, with testing in an anechoic chamber you are not getting the "real world" impact on the tag and product. That's why this type of testing is not really applicable to the real world; however, it can be a helpful first step, especially for tough to tag products. A tag's ability to handle outside interference and noise is a critical performance factor. If you have a product of paper, Styrofoam, rubber, or similar RF-friendly characteristics, however, this test is entirely unnecessary.

If you know that your RFID system and tagged items will reside in an environment with high levels of RF noise, interference, high humidity, extreme temperatures, or other conditions that are far from ideal, your best bet is to choose a lab that performs the testing in a "dirty" or "noisy" environment. This means that the lab simulates the conditions that will be encountered in the customer's facility, and the testing results will be very similar to results achieved in reality.

The steps to identify the perfect tag and location are as follows:

1. Use a spectrum analyzer with a tracking generator and a probe to determine the RF signature of the product under test.
2. Select 4–5 different tags to test and obtain quantities of at least 100 tags of each.
3. Test each tag and note the minimum effective power to receive a signal back from the tag.
4. Plot the distribution of tags to determine the standard deviation and the power of an "average" tag.
5. Select six average tags of each model and test those on the sweet spots using a reader with a scientific testing tool such as EasyReader.
6. Verify results by incorporating dynamic testing in real-world use cases.

The first step in static testing is using a spectrum analyzer with a built-in tracking generator and a special probe or probe table that has a very small antenna (to simulate the tag) connected to the test gear. From this test equipment you can get an RF profile of the sides of the case to be tested. This will help you determine where to put the tags.

After you identify these sweet spots by using the scientific testing equipment, you can test the tag types to find an "average" performing tag. Make sure you test at least 100 tags of each type so that you will have statistical significance. This is important for two reasons: first, you need to find out which tag types have the lowest performance variability (or the highest manufacturing quality) and second, you need to make sure that you are not testing with a particularly good or bad tag, which will throw off your results. Using a reader and a set of different tags with tag-testing software will make this go very quickly. A tested product (or case) is placed a certain distance from a reader's antenna (usually around 2 meters). The tag-testing software will then use an algorithm to lower the power on the read to determine the lowest possible power that gets a tag response. This is superior to a methodology of moving the case, because you will always be in the same location relative to the RF wavelength and outside influences. All results are recorded for later comparison. This process is repeated for every evaluated tag on every type of product, and results in a narrow selection of best performing tags.

TIP Each of the testing facilities has developed various automated processes to achieve the same goal of finding the best tag for a particular product. If you have an RF-friendly product such as paper towels and would like to do this yourself, you can achieve reasonable results with minimal equipment: a reader, an antenna, tag-testing software, and time. (I can already see some folks from the test labs grinding their teeth when they are reading this, but the truth is some materials do not need the expertise of an RFID lab.)

After the most suitable tags are selected, their best possible placement has to be identified and verified. This is referred to as *dynamic testing*. Dynamic testing is usually performed on a conveyor and through a dock door. Maybe you are surprised about the conveyor use. The reason for this is not only a discovery of a good way of evaluating the performance of tags in motion, but also a necessity to verify compliance to various mandates. (Some retailers, such as Wal-Mart, require 100 percent tag reads on a 600-feet-per-minute conveyor.)

When testing a tag placement on a case, the case is divided into numbered sections forming a grid. Several sections will be left out of testing because they carry a bar code, product name, warnings, or other information that cannot be covered for merchandizing, marketing, or safety reasons. The tags are then placed one by one into every remaining section on the case (or into the sections that are presumed the most suitable), which is then circulated on a conveyor. The number of reads per each pass through the interrogation zone is captured in a testing log. After all tags are tried out with selected grids, the log should verify which location is optimal.

Summary

In this chapter, you learned everything you need to know about tags to be able to select the most suitable tag for a specific application and find a correct placement on the product or packaging.

First, you discovered different types of tags based on their function. Active tags have a battery and broadcast a signal into the environment, whereas passive and semi-passive tags need to be in the presence of a reader's signal in order to communicate. You also learned that active tags, although they are the most expensive type, have long read ranges and can be used with sensors, GPS, and cellular networks. Passive tags have a simpler construction and lower price, but have shorter read ranges.

In the next section, you learned about various communication techniques of passive tags. Passive tags can use either inductive coupling, which utilizes a magnetic field, or passive backscatter, which utilizes an electric field. Tags using passive backscatter can have a lot longer read ranges than the inductively coupled tags.

Hopefully you enjoyed the summary of different frequency bands and the tag performance characteristics based on their frequency. Low-frequency tags have short read ranges and slow data-transfer rates but good penetration of water and metals, and are used mainly for animal tracking or access control. High-frequency tags also have short read ranges and relatively good performance around water and metals, and are used in smart cards, smart shelves, pharma, and item-level tracking. Ultra-high-frequency tags have long read ranges and relatively high data-transfer rates but bad performance around water and liquid. They are used for product tracking throughout the supply chains, in libraries, in stores, and for inventory control. The last type of tags based on frequency are microwave tags. These are used mainly as active tags for toll collection because of their fast data-transfer rates.

After discussing the characteristics of different frequencies, I specified how the frequencies within a band differ around the world. U.S., European, and Asian frequencies are not the same; therefore, some manufacturers came up with a tag that works globally.

In the next section, you learned about EPC tag classes and their capabilities. EPC Class 0 is a read-only tag, and EPC Class 1 is a WORM tag. These classes are now called Generation 1. Generation 2 came with many improved and new features such as higher data-transfer rates for reading and writing, longer passwords, better anticollision, and dense reader mode.

After this, you discovered the components hidden behind the tag, such as the microchip and antenna. You found out how the chip can be attached to an antenna and the antenna manufacturing techniques. I also described Q factor as a measurement of a tag's efficiency.

In the section discussing tags designed for specific applications, you learned that tags can come in different types of packaging or be embedded into the product itself. There are specific tags for various types of materials, especially the materials that RF waves find difficult to penetrate or materials that detune the tag and decrease its performance.

In the following section, I discussed how to place a tag onto a product or its packaging related to the physical and chemical properties of the item, how to evaluate a correct tag placement, and which facilities can do the testing for you.

This chapter has given you a good level of knowledge about various types of tags and their applications and has equipped you with comprehensive knowledge to help you select the right tag during the design stage of your RFID system.

Exam Essentials

Know the differences between and characteristics of active, passive, and semi-passive tags, their specific use, performance, and pros and cons. Active tags have a battery and a transmitter, which support long read ranges (up to a kilometer). They can carry sensors, support large memory and processing capabilities, and work with GPS, cellular, and other networks. They are expensive but are less susceptible to interference and are suitable for tracking high-value goods. They are heavily used by the U.S. DoD as well as various transportation companies and railroads for container tracking, trailer tracking, and the like. Active tags are also used for RTLS.

Passive tags do not carry a battery or a transmitter and communicate by "reflecting" the energy received from the reader. They are inexpensive and have read ranges from 0.5 to 10 meters, depending on the type. Passive tags are used in item-level, case-level, and pallet-level tracking in retail supply chains, as well as for many other applications.

Semi-passive tags carry a battery but communicate in the same way as passive tags. The battery powers the chip and sensors but does not enable broadcasting the signal to the reader. Semi-passive tags are often used for their sensors, which can monitor temperature and other conditions. Their read ranges can be up to 100 meters.

Know the difference between inductive coupling and passive backscatter. Passive and semi-passive tags receive power and communicate using inductive coupling and passive backscatter. Inductive coupling uses a magnetic field, whereas passive backscatter uses an electric field. Inductive coupled tags (LF, HF, and certain kinds of UHF) have an antenna, usually in the form of an induction coil, whereas tags using passive backscatter (UHF and microwave) have dipole antennas (single or dual dipoles). Inductively coupled tags have short read ranges (a maximum of half a meter); passive backscatter tags can reach distances up to 10 meters.

Distinguish between frequencies and know tag performances within each frequency, including pros and cons. Low-frequency tags have read ranges up to half a meter (passive) and slow data-transfer rates. They penetrate liquids and metals well. They are commonly used for animal tracking, access control, and tracking of RF-difficult items such as laptops in closed-loop systems. They are mostly read-only and without anticollision capabilities; however, there are LF tags that offer these features.

High-frequency tags have read ranges up to a meter (passive) and a data-transfer rate faster than HF but slower than UHF. They work relatively well around liquids and metals. They are commonly used for smart shelves, smart cards, item tracking in pharma and movie rentals, and access control.

Ultra-high-frequency tags have read ranges up to 10 meters (passive) and a data-transfer rate faster than LF and HF. They do not work well around liquids and metals unless they use near-field communication. Passive UHF tags are mandated by the DoD and major retailers and are used for case-level and pallet-level tracking in retail supply chains, as well as for other applications.

Microwave tags have read ranges up to a meter but are usually active (read ranges in hundreds of meters). They have the highest data-transfer rate of all tag types but do not work well around metals and liquids. They are used mostly for toll collection.

Know the regional differences between frequencies used in RFID. Low frequency (125–134 kHz), high frequency (13.56 MHz), and microwave frequency (2.45 GHz) are used globally. Ultra-high frequency differs by region. The United States uses 902–928 MHz (South America, South Africa, China, and Australia use a similar band), whereas Europe uses 865–868 MHz up to 870 MHz (as do North Africa, India, Hong Kong, New Zealand, and Singapore). Japan operates at 952–954 MHz, which is outside of the U.S. and European bands. Active tags usually operate on the UHF frequency around 433 MHz internationally.

Know the contents of EPC Generation 2 memory. Gen 2 tags have four memory banks. Bank 0 is a reserved memory and holds the Access and Kill passwords (each 32 bits). Bank 1 is an EPC memory that holds the EPC number (96 bits or more) and protocol controls. Bank 2 is a TID memory that holds tag ID and other tag information. Bank 3 is a user memory, which can be defined by the user.

Ensure a correct tag orientation for a reader's antenna. Tags should face the antenna (parallel to the antenna's radiator) for maximum performance. When using a single dipole tag and a linear antenna, the tag antenna should be in the same plane as the plane of wave propagation. When using a circular antenna, or when using a dual dipole tag, the orientation does not matter.

Distinguish between various methods of chip attachment. Chips can be attached to an antenna directly (flip-chip technique) using a robotic hand with a vacuum nozzle that picks up the chip, flips it over, and using pressure and heat affixes the chip to the inlay. Chips also can be attached first to a strap, which is then attached to an antenna. This technique is suitable for very small chips.

Evaluate the package contents and select the right tags and their locations. Although packaging generally is made of cardboard, the contents can be either RF friendly or RF unfriendly. If you are dealing with RF-unfriendly contents such as liquids, metals, chemicals, moist food, or glass, you should utilize the air gaps in the packaging as much as possible and place your tag in the gap, avoiding contact with the product. If you are tagging items or you must place the tag on an RF-unfriendly surface (metal cans, glass bottles), try to use a tag specially designed (tuned) to perform well on these materials. When selecting the tags and their locations, you must test and record everything. You can do this testing yourself or use testing facilities.

Know different types of tag packaging and their possible uses. Tags can come integrated into labels (for use with RFID printers and label applicators), buttons (for clothing maintenance and rentals), cards (used for access control, payment, or memberships), glass beads (animal tracking), wristbands (hospital patient tracking, amusement parks), key fobs (for vehicle access and immobilizers), case (mainly for active and semi-passive tags), or integrated into packaging or the product itself.

Key Terms

Before you take the exam, be certain you are familiar with the following terms:

AB Symmetry

active tags

application-specific integrated circuit (ASIC)

battery-assisted passive tags

beacon

dynamic testing.

electronic product code (EPC)

EPC memory

FM0

High-frequency (HF)

inductive coupling

Low-frequency (LF)

Microwave

Miller subcarrier

passive backscatter

passive tags

Q factor

reader-talks-first,

read-only

reserved memory

RTF

semi-passive tags

sessions

shadowing

tag identification (TID) memory

tag-talks-first

TTF

ultra-high-frequency (UHF)

user memory

write-once read-many (WORM)

Review Questions

1. Which types of tags carry a battery? (Select two options.)
   - **A.** Active tags
   - **B.** Passive tags
   - **C.** Semi-passive tags
   - **D.** All of the above
2. Which memory bank includes the EPC number in Generation 2 tags?
   - **A.** Bank 1
   - **B.** Bank 2
   - **C.** Bank 3
   - **D.** Bank 0
3. Which tags are the most suitable for use with smart shelves?
   - **A.** Active UHF
   - **B.** Passive HF
   - **C.** Passive microwave
   - **D.** Passive LF
4. Where would you place a passive UHF tag on a carton box of corn flakes?
   - **A.** Only on the top of the box
   - **B.** Only on the bottom of the box
   - **C.** Only where the air gap is located
   - **D.** Anywhere on the box, avoiding bar codes and logos
5. Where would you place a tag when tagging a six-pack of lemonade in glass bottles? You are using a passive UHF tag. The six-pack case is made of cardboard.
   - **A.** On the front of the case
   - **B.** On the bottom of the case
   - **C.** On the handle of the case
   - **D.** Anywhere on the case, avoiding bar codes and logos
6. What type of tag is the most suitable to use in a toll-collection system on a highway so that the cars do not have to slow down or stop?
   - **A.** Active LF
   - **B.** Active microwave
   - **C.** Passive UHF
   - **D.** Passive microwave

7. What type of field does the inductive coupled system use?
   - A. Magnetic
   - B. Electric
   - C. Electric and magnetic
   - D. Circularly polarized

8. Which type of a passive tag would you use on thin and tall cases of a clear plastic wrap used in the kitchen? Orientation of the cases cannot be ensured. Circular antennas are installed throughout the entire RFID system.
   - A. Single dipole UHF tag
   - B. Dual dipole UHF tag
   - C. Single dipole HF tag
   - D. Dual dipole microwave tag

9. Which tags use passive backscatter to communicate information? (Select two options.)
   - A. Active UHF
   - B. Passive UHF
   - C. Semi-passive UHF
   - D. Passive HF

10. What is Miller subcarrier?
    - A. A type of carrier frequency
    - B. A type of backscatter encoding used by Generation 2
    - C. A type of tag antenna used for global tags
    - D. A type of microchip used in Gen 2 tags invented by J. Miller

11. A generic passive UHF tag was placed on an empty glass bottle. During testing this tag could not be read farther than 30 centimeters (1 foot) away, even if it was directly facing the reader's antenna. What do you think is the problem?
    - A. The tag is "bad" and should be replaced.
    - B. UHF tags are not suitable for tagging glass; it has to be replaced by an HF tag.
    - C. Glass detuned the tag. It should be replaced by a tag specially tuned for use on glass.
    - D. Glass contains large quantities of metal. The tag should be replaced by a tag especially tuned for use on metal.

12. What is the advantage of Gen 2 tags over Gen 1? (Select two options.)
    - A. Gen 2 tags have bigger and more-efficient microchips than Gen 1 tags.
    - B. Gen 2 tags have higher data-transfer rates than Gen 1 tags.
    - C. Gen 2 tags can read through metal, whereas Gen 1 tags cannot.
    - D. Gen 2 tags are more secure than Gen 1 tags.

13. What is the most common use of low-frequency (LF) tags?

A. Animal tracking

B. Military supply-chain tracking

C. Container tracking

D. Smart shelves

14. What type of tag would you use to track temperature inside a freezer truck and report this information to the shipping company headquarters?

A. Active tags with sensors connected to GPS

B. Semi-passive tags with sensors connected to GPS

C. Passive tags with sensors and wireless network capability

D. Active tags with sensors connected to a cellular network

15. What types of passwords are available for EPC Class 1 Generation 2 tags? (Select two options.)

A. Lock password

B. Access password

C. Kill password

D. Un-kill password

16. What could be a reason to use a read-only tag?

A. There is no reason to use them; they are not even manufactured anymore.

B. They have better performance than read-write tags.

C. They are more secure.

D. They are smaller.

17. You are a U.S. manufacturer and have a contract to ship goods to Europe. Will you be able to use the same tags you are using to comply with the Wal-Mart mandate?

A. Yes.

B. No. The U.S. uses the 902–928 MHz frequency, whereas Europe uses 865–868 (870) MHz. Two tags would have to be used.

C. Yes, if the tags are made to operate on both frequencies.

D. Yes, if the European customer used the U.S. readers.

18. How would you tag large plastic bags containing washing powder that will be palletized? How would you organize the pallet?

A. Place the tag on the front or the back of the bag. Organize the pallet in a common way.

B. Place the tag on the sides of the bag. Organize the pallet so that the tags are facing outward.

C. Place the tag on the handle part of the bag. Organize the pallet in a common way.

D. Place the tag anywhere on the bag. Organize the pallet so that the tags are facing outward.

19. Which types of tags can use near-field as well as far-field communication?
    - A. Passive UHF
    - B. Passive LF
    - C. Passive microwave
    - D. All passive tags
20. What is the Q factor?
    - A. Measurement of the quality of a tuned circuit
    - B. Measurement of the size of a tag's antenna
    - C. Measurement of the time it takes the tag to respond
    - D. Feature of EPC Class 1 Generation 2 tags

Answers to Review Questions

1. A, C. Active tags carry a battery to power their microchip and broadcast the signal to the environment. Semi-passive tags have a power source in the form of a battery as well, but only to power its chip circuitry and possible sensors; they cannot actively transmit signals.

2. A. The EPC number is located in memory bank 1, which is called EPC memory.

3. B. For smart shelf applications, the most used and most suitable tags are the passive high-frequency (HF) tags, because of their short read range, small size, and relatively good performance around RF-difficult materials.

4. D. Corn flakes in a thin carton are dry and easy to penetrate for RF waves. Therefore, you can choose to locate your tag anywhere on the box, avoiding the bar codes, logos, and other information specified by the product manufacturer or distributor.

5. C. When tagging a six-pack of beverages, you have to realize that the water and glass are RF-unfriendly materials; therefore, you need to avoid placing the tag on them or near them. Although you could place the tag on the case, the tag would be hard to read if its position caused the reader to have to penetrate the liquid in order to get to the tag. The best spot to place the tag on a six-pack is on its handle or inside it to avoid damage.

6. B. The most suitable type of tag for use in toll-collection systems is an active microwave tag, which has a long read range (as all active tags do) and high data-transfer rates. Therefore, a car could drive through an RFID-enabled toll booth at a relatively high speed.

7. A. Inductive coupling utilizes the magnetic field created by changing current in the reader's antenna. When a tag with an induction coil gets into this magnetic field, the field induces current in the tag's antenna, which powers the tag's chip.

8. A. For any thin and tall cases without enough surface area to accommodate dual dipole tags, you should use a single dipole tag, especially when the RFID system uses circular antennas throughout. When using circular antennas, you do not have to worry about the tag's orientation as much as if you had linear antennas installed.

9. B, C. Passive and semi-passive UHF tags use passive backscatter to respond to the interrogator's signal. Active tags broadcast the response directly to the reader by using their own transmitter. Passive HF tags use inductive coupling to communicate.

10. B. The Miller subcarrier technique is used for backscatter encoding by EPC Class 1 Generation 2 tags. This technique fits the tag responses between the channels used by interrogators for transmission, which makes it less susceptible to interference.

11. C. When the tag was placed onto a glass bottle, the glass detuned the tag; therefore, it could not respond as efficiently. If the short read ranges are a problem, you should consider placing the tag on the bottle cap, embedding it into the cap (only if the cap does not contain metal or a metal lining), or integrating it into the bottle's label. The label should have an insulation layer so that the tag does not touch the glass.

12. B, D. Generation 2 tags have higher data-transfer rates that reach up to 640 kilobits per second. Due to this feature, Gen 2 readers can read up to 1,500 tags per second, whereas Gen 1 readers read about 10 times fewer tags per second. Gen 2 tags are also more secure, because they use 32-bit Access and 32-bit Kill passwords and are able to generate and respond with random numbers based on a value Q using a Q algorithm.

13. A. Low-frequency tags are used frequently for animal and livestock tracking because of their great body penetration ability.

14. D. Active tags with sensors and connection to the cellular phone network will be the most suitable for tracking the temperature and reporting the values to the shipping headquarters. If these tags used only GPS, the headquarters would receive only the tag's location; the temperature would have to be recorded and reported when the truck gets into the reach of an appropriate RFID reader.

15. B, C. Gen 2 tags carry two passwords: Access and Kill. After the Access password is input, the tag can be locked or unlocked and other operations can performed.

16. C. Read-only tags are still being manufactured (for example, some LF tags or microwave tags), and they are used because of their security and their need for only a simple infrastructure. The tag carries its serial number. When this number is read, it has to be matched to a database to relate it to the object. Therefore, if an unauthorized person interrogated the tag, he or she would receive only the serial number; without access to the database, this number would be useless.

17. C. Some manufacturers have developed tags that can work on various frequencies within the UHF band. These tags are the best to use on goods for international trade because they can be read by equipment in the United States as well as Europe and Asia.

18. B. The best way to tag the bags with washing powder (or dog food, garden soil, and so forth) is to attach the tags to the sides of the bag and when building a pallet, trying to make sure that the tagged side faces the outside of the pallet. If you put the tag on the front or back of the bag, you could not position these sides to face out of the pallet. These tags would then have to be read through several layers of powder, which includes chemicals and moisture and poses a challenge for RF waves. Although Gen 2 tags achieve better performance even with challenging products, you should still follow the general rules to achieve consistent results.

19. A. Passive UHF tags can use far-field communication as well as near-field. Near-field UHF tags utilize the UHF frequency for faster data transfer and can be used for item-level tagging and fulfillment of mandates with one type of frequency. However, as opposed to far-field UHF tags, the near-field tags have better performance around liquids and metals.

20. A. The Q factor is a measurement of the quality or efficiency of a tuned circuit. The higher the Q factor, the more efficient the energy transfers between the reader and the tag.

Chapter

5

Designing the RFID Network

RFID+ EXAM OBJECTIVES COVERED IN THIS CHAPTER:

✓ **5.1 Given a scenario, predict the performance of a given frequency and power (active/passive) as it relates to read distance, write distance, tag response time, storage capacity**

✓ **5.2 Summarize how hardware selection affects performance (may use scenarios)**

- 5.2.1 Antenna type
- 5.2.2 Equipment mounting and protection
- 5.2.3 Cable length/loss
- 5.2.4 Interference considerations
- 5.2.5 Tag type selection (e.g., active, passive, frequency)

Imagine yourself as Leonardo da Vinci staring at a complex problem such as why the moon glows at night. You have some scientific equations, a few specialized tools, and then some creativity and good problem-solving skills. After meditating on it for a while and maybe sketching a painting just to stir up a conspiracy theory or two, you come up with a solution that combines scientific knowledge and a bit of artful intuition. Designing a successful RFID system is a bit like that. Da Vinci used that combination to discover that what we can see of the moon is really the sun reflecting off of it. Old Leonardo would have been great as an RFID technician.

The beginning of this chapter will answer the first basic question you need to sort out when designing an RFID system: what's the best frequency for your specific business application? You'll learn the basics of frequency and some of the behaviors of the various ranges. This is where understanding Chapter 1, "The Physics of RFID," will tie together nicely to give you full understanding of how RFID can really be leveraged.

This section also focuses on something that most of those who are preparing to take the CompTIA exam will be asked to determine at some point in their career: what's the best UHF reader? Understanding what happens when you test readers not only will help you pick the correct reader, but also will give you insight when you begin to set them up. You'll see some of the science behind the individual metric testing and you'll get a flavor for the art with the use-case testing as well.

After the reader, the next thing that falls naturally in the analysis is the cable. This chapter will show you some of the basics, and again give you the equations to determine the right choice for a 100 percent accurate RFID system.

You'll then follow the path from the reader to the cable out to the antenna. Although we covered antennas in Chapter 3, "Site Analysis," this overview will serve as a good refresher on what you've already learned.

Last, I'll give you a little bit of insight on middleware. This chapter's final section will cover just the basics because the middleware component is evolving so rapidly and is not a big part of the CompTIA test.

Determining the Proper Frequency for Your RFID System

Most of the hype in the popular press concerning RFID centers around the U.S. Department of Defense (DoD), Wal-Mart, Target, Albertsons, METRO Group, Tesco, and other companies mandating the use of UHF RFID systems. These systems incorporate the electronic product code (EPC) numbering scheme and data construct. The EPC UHF systems have grown exponentially in popularity since 2000, which tends to make people forget that there is a whole other world of RFID out there beyond UHF and EPC. Work-in-process (WIP) systems and manufacturing automation have used high-frequency (HF) systems for decades. Toll-collection lanes, shipping containers, and similar structures have used active or semi-passive tags for nearly as long.

The contactless transfer of data and the ability to read without line of sight gives RFID numerous applications in commerce and industry. Most RFID systems operate in RF bands requiring no license. In the United Sates, the Federal Communications Commission (FCC) refers to these as nonlicensed for Instrument, Scientific, and Medical (ISM bands) uses. When designing an RFID system, the requirements of the application, trading partners who may be participating in the extended RFID network, standards and regulations governing a given geographical region, and cost can be all dictate which RF band and RFID system needs to be used.

RFID systems are commonly classified according to the properties of the data carrier, or tag. Each RFID system can be broadly classified by those tags, therefore you would refer to a system as using an active, passive, or semi-passive tag, as shown in Table 5.1.

NOTE

CompTIA classifies tags that are passive but assisted by a battery as being semi-active. This is an incorrect classification, as the tags are semi-passive, in that they require a reader's interrogation zone to make them work—like every other kind of passive tag.

Here's a brief explanation of the active and passive systems:

Active RFID *Active RFID* tags operate at 433 MHz or 2.45 GHz. Powered by a battery or an external power source, they have a higher energy signal and can communicate at greater distances. Because the active tag has its own transmitter and power source, the tag can be instructed to send its data at periodic intervals, often referred to as broadcasting intervals, without being interrogated by the reader. Because of an external power source, active tags can support sensors, large memory sizes, data loggers, and more. These tags have a finite working life (typically 3–5 years) because of the need for a battery. Metal can possess some nominal interference. Because of the complex tag design, the implementation costs of such systems are relatively high, with tag prices ranging from $10 to $100. Because of the battery and additional data-carrying capability, active tags also can be fitted with sensor and measurement devices for vibration, temperature, and other effects.

Passive RFID *Passive RFID* tags are powered when they enter the radiated field of a reader. The reader powers the tag by providing a continuous wave after the query signal. A *continuous wave* is an electromagnetic wave of constant amplitude and frequency. Because the passive tag activates and communicates only when the reader interrogates and powers the tag, the read range and the signal strength of tag response is relatively smaller than for active tags. Passive tags also have limited memory size, because the memory read and write is a highly power-hungry process. Compared to active tags, passive tags are much smaller and can be manufactured in very large quantities at a very low cost. For this reason, passive technology has been largely adopted and deployed in several applications such as supply chains and manufacturing.

Passive RFID uses the following two power-transfer techniques:

Inductive coupling Transfer of energy from one circuit component to another through a shared magnetic field. Inductive coupling favors transfer of lower frequencies. LF and HF technologies use inductive coupling to transfer energy between the tag and reader.

Capacitive coupling, or E field coupling Transfer of energy from one circuit to another by means of the mutual capacitance between the circuits. UHF and microwave technologies use capacitive coupling to transfer energy between the tag and reader.

The semi-passive tags use the same type of communication methodologies as a regular passive tag, but have a battery on board to help create a stronger signal and get a greater read distance. Having a battery on board a passive tag also allows for taking measurements from built in sensors as well.

Table 5.1 summarizes the various types of RFID technologies.

TABLE 5.1 Types of RFID Systems

Passive Technology	***LF or Low Frequency***	***HF or High Frequency***	***UHF or Ultra-High Frequency***	***Microwave***
Frequency Range	125 or 134 KHz	13.56 MHz	860–960 MHz	2.45 and 5.8 GHz
Approx. wavelength	87988.07″	870.79″	12.9″	4.81″
Max. Read Range (Passive)	Less than 1 foot	Less than 3 feet	Less than 30 feet	Less than 10 feet
Approx. Maximum Tag Populations	16 (w/ anticollision tags)	50	200 +	
General Characteristics	Relatively expensive, even at high volumes, because it requires a longer, more-expensive copper antenna. Additionally, inductive tags are more expensive than capacitive tags.	Less expensive than inductive LF tags. Best suited for applications that do not require long-range reading of multiple tags.	Because of its adoption in supply-chain and new silicon and inlay manufacturing techniques, costs have come down. Offers a good balance between range and performance—especially for reading multiple tags.	Similar characteristics to the UHF tag but with faster read rates. Offers the most directional signal, which is ideal for certain applications.

NOTE Although not exhaustive, the RFID technologies in Table 5.1 are the most popular and also the ones CompTIA is most concerned with for the test.

Choosing the Right Reader for Your RFID Network

Hopefully you have the feeling by now that I preach about three primary components to an RFID system:

- The tag
- The reader
- The software

So why the definitive heading for this section that implies the other two primary components are chopped liver? The reason is simple: the reader (and antennas) and the tags have the biggest impact on the upper performance threshold. The software can only mess things up; it can't make them better. So why then does the reader matter more than the tags? Another good question, grasshopper.

There are four primary reasons that RFID readers are the workhorse of an RFID network:

- Readers are the lynchpins of data collection.
- Readers are the most complex system component.
- Readers are an expensive device to maintain.
- Deployment decisions are expensive to reverse.

At this point in the process, you have enough information to determine the proper reader. Your business process analysis will provide details on where the RFID system will collect data. The site survey has armed you with details about the electromagnetic environment and what challenges you need to overcome. Choosing the frequency has given you the information you need to now look at various types of RFID readers. But before you go on to testing and choosing a reader, it might help if you knew a little something about the basics.

Basics of an RFID Reader

You may know a person in their late 70s or early 80s who was in World War II. If you can think about how long that person has been around and what they have seen in their lifetime, you might be surprised to discover that they may have been using RFID during their time in the service. This is especially true for aviators. In WWII the British first innovated the use of RF signals to detect friendly aircraft from "unfriendlies." Because of all the hype and coverage

RFID has received, it might seem like a new innovation at the turn of this century, not a 60-year-old technology.

Even though the technology is more than half a century old, it is still very complex and includes a high degree of complex physics. Fortunately, today's reader manufacturers and software vendors have simplified much of that complexity for you, the RF technician. For the CompTIA test you don't need to know all the details of the reader and the intricacies of what happens under the hood. However, having an understanding of what makes up a software-defined radio (SDR) and an application processor back end will help you understand what is happening when you plug an Ethernet cable into the back of a black box. Figure 5.1 shows the basic layout of an RFID reader.

FIGURE 5.1 Basics of an RFID reader

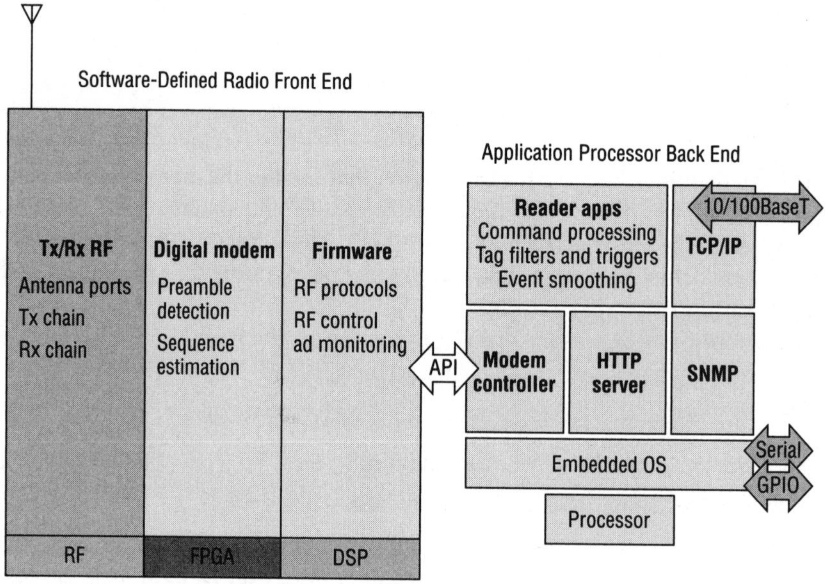

As you can see from Figure 5.1, an RFID reader is nothing more than a sophisticated radio driven by some software. Keep in mind that even though there are global standards such as those from the ISO for determining what a reader should do, that doesn't necessarily mean they all do it the same. Think of the radio in your car. If you're driving a 1976 Pinto, you might have a $25 AM radio that gets little more than static and the occasional runway clearance when you're near an airport. However, if you're styling in a 2005 Ferrari 360, you're likely to have a several-thousand-dollar system that's thumping not only you, but the whole neighborhood. The difference is the sophistication of the components and the quality of the firmware. RFID readers are the same basic thing under the hood—just as an internal combustion engine is basically the same thing in various cars, yet that Pinto and Ferrari will get much different results from their engines.

There are two key terms that you will hear a lot about in RFID: the field-programmable gate array (FPGA) and the *digital signal processor chip*, or *DSP*, which is a specialized chip that performs very fast mathematical calculations). As you can see in Figure 5.1, they are the two other critical components to creating that high-performing reader. The FPGA is a modem that translates the RF into a lot of digital signals. The DSP is a fancy name for a processor that is really good at math.

Choosing the Proper Components in a UHF System

CompTIA began the RFID+ certification program because many of the DoD, Wal-Mart, and Target suppliers were looking for someone who knew about RFID to help meet a mandate. Most of those suppliers are looking for information about UHF. So I'll devote the next section to what both CompTIA and many of the large users of RFID are focusing on: the UHF Generation 2 (Gen 2) reader.

RFID was branded as overhyped in 2003 when Wal-Mart first made its announcement requiring suppliers to use RFID tags. Unfortunately, much of that ballyhoo still continues, and that is part of the reason CompTIA is trying to create a base-level standard of understanding. It is clear that Gen 2 far outperforms Gen 1 and creates a unified global specification. This is particularly true now that ISO standard 18000-6 interoperates with Gen 2. However, some RFID manufactures are overstating the true performance of Gen 2 quite unnecessarily. End users are generally forced to rely heavily on media sources and marketing from hardware vendors when shaping their opinions about RFID. Unfortunately, this approach seldom produces winning results.

There is a particular mode of Gen 2 that allows many readers operating in close proximity to not interfere with each other as much as they were before this new dense reader mode was written into the protocol. Gen 2 dense reader mode does a nice job of addressing the problem of reader-to-reader interference within a dense reader environment. To illustrate, reader A cannot use the same channel that reader B is using to receive a tag response if both readers are set up for dense reader mode.

1,600 Tags per Second? Only in Theory

Gen 2 is leading the industry toward improved security, friendlier dense reader environments, and rapid tag interrogation. Unfortunately, the number of possible tag reads has been embellished by at least two fold. Today's readers far outpace their Gen 1 counterparts, interrogating as many as 50 tags per second. But don't make the mistake of relying on media sources and vendors claiming Gen 2 read rates of 1,600 tags per second, which is possible in theory only. Simply Google "1,600 tags per second" to see some of the vendors' claims.

Tag vendors would have you believe that the reader is only half the equation. Dense reader mode does not address the question, however, of interference at the tag. How does Gen 2 tag silicon (which employs relatively unsophisticated filtration) handle several readers hopping on the same channel? Some vendors have claimed that Gen 2 silicon can discriminate between competing readers and respond to only the strongest signal.

NOTE At ODIN Technologies, we decided to put this claim to the test by placing two readers at 4.5 feet and 9 feet away from the same tag at the same power level. Leveraging our licenses granted by the FCC, we programmed each reader to transmit at a single fixed frequency to see whether the tag would respond to only the strongest reader signal. Not only was the tag unable to identify the stronger reader, but it failed to respond altogether. The reader interference caused a disabling conflict at the tag, making it clear that silicon and Gen 2 design are not as advanced as some manufacturers claim.

Scientific Testing

There are five critical tests that can determine the performance of a reader:

- Distance testing
- Power output analysis
- Receive sensitivity testing
- Interference rejection testing
- Tag acquisition speed

After years of testing readers at ODIN Technologies, we learned that these five critical parameters need to be isolated in a scientific methodology and compared before doing actual use-case analysis. All of these tests should be performed in an experienced laboratory, so that the isolation of each variable being tested can be assured. An anechoic chamber is often where much of the testing takes place. However, you need to make sure that some tests are purposely performed in a real-world environment to find out how the reader responds outside of a lab.

TIP ODIN Technologies has performed hundreds of thousands of tests and published the results in our RFID Benchmark Series. This series goes into much greater detail than this book about the tests performed and how they were done.

Performing Distance Testing

Distance testing is a simple metric that end users have used for years to compare reader performance. By setting up two readers in the same location and slowly backing a tag away from the readers, an end-user can determine which reader has the best read distance.

This sort of testing, however, offers limited value, because it is impossible to decouple the core drivers of performance over distance (transmit power accuracy and receive sensitivity, for example), which are covered in the other tests. Additionally, in tons of deployments, I have yet to deploy a dock door of greater span than 10 feet, making read performance at 15 feet of limited value. Still, distance testing is helpful for comparing the performance of today's readers with those of several years ago and provides an easy-to-understand method of discussing reader performance.

To perform this test, place 20 tags in a test grid format on a corrugate substrate. The grid should be placed at four distances: 3, 5, 10, and 15 feet from the interrogation antenna of the reader under test (RUT). The total number of tags read at each distance should be recorded as well as the number of reads for each tag over a 30-second time interval. Make sure no other readers are active during the test and make sure that you don't compare results based on read rate, rather on relative performance, because each reader vendor uses its own software to record read rates.

Performing Power Output Analysis

This simple yet important test is often overlooked by integrators deploying RFID, since they tend to trust the reader manufacturers. However testing the level of power that each reader port emits is critical prior to any RFID deployment.

Power output analysis is at the root of potentially putting an RFID reader company out of business if they violate the FCC rules by broadcasting more energy than legally allowed. The issue of power management is often overlooked by end users who are unfamiliar with regulations and do not have the scientific equipment required to take power measurements at the port or in the far-field.

Effective power management is critical to RFID reader performance because it determines the range and consistency of tag capture. Overdriving or going above legal limits of reader transmit power is tempting for reader vendors because extra power often achieves better results in a single portal situation. For those readers providing Gen 2 compliance, power management is particularly important because dense reader mode (DRM) has specific power management requirements that contribute to better performance.

To create this experiment, you need to have a real-time spectrum analyzer (RTSA). The RTSA provides highly precise measurements and spectral triggering not common to other less-sophisticated instruments. Standard cabling fabricated for this testing should be used. Power measurements at the reader port are taken by using a fixed 10 dB attenuator to avoid overloading the RTSA. Radiated power measurements are then captured at 5 feet from the interrogation antenna by using a low-gain antenna.

The first power measurement you investigate should focus on peak RF power output at the reader port. These measurements should be taken with the reader in a factory default setting; no special configuration commands should be used. The FCC requires that power emitted by an "intentional radiator" not exceed 30 dBm. Some vendors have interpreted this to mean that the power output at the reader port shall not exceed 30 dBm. Others have assumed this to include losses due to cabling, so they drive the port above the 30 dBm mark based on the assumption that several decibels will be lost in the cabling. In practice, it seems that the FCC is ultimately concerned that the radiated power not exceed 36 dBm, which includes a 6 dBi gain antenna.

In addition to peak power, end users should understand *frequency hopping* and the channels of reader transmit power. The FCC regulation (part 15.247) states that the reader needs to hop from channel to channel pseudo-randomly over at least 50 channels within a 10-second time period. Transmit power is one of the most important factors in defining success between a reader and tag(s) in almost any use case. Readers that enable higher power output to compensate for losses due to cabling will be more successful in the field if they are to be operated at full power. Although this capability does require that power measurements be taken at the end of each cable to ensure FCC compliance, it guarantees that the best performance possible will be realized.

Performing Receive Sensitivity Testing

The receive sensitivity takes into account one of the other big factors in RFID system performance: the tag. Tag consistency has a profound impact on performance of an RFID network. Unreadable tags often lead to expensive exception-handling processes and slow supply-chain throughput, so getting the best read rate of weak tags can be a big time and money saver. Until production quality improves, it's up to the readers to make up for the shortcomings inherent in the poorer-quality tags. Tag quality is a common and known problem, but it is only part of the equation; the reader's receive sensitivity or how well it can "listen" for tag responses is another key factor.

Every reader design team faces the formidable challenge of designing a system that transmits 1 watt (continuous wave) to power a tag, while simultaneously listening for a faint tag response that is 1 millionth of that power as strong. Success is driven by the ability to carefully filter the tag response from the transmission signal so that these two signals do not interact destructively within the reader. It's kind of like trying to hear a pin drop at a KISS concert.

As you might have guessed, because this is one of the more formidable challenges that a reader overcomes, the testing of receive sensitivity measurements is nontrivial. Many readers today transmit and receive on the same RF port making the process even more difficult and less accurate than having a dedicated send and receive port. This characteristic is known as "mono-static" antenna sequencing and requires specialized RF engineering equipment to separate received tag responses from the transmission signal to determine the receive sensitivity. This is one of the tests that is easiest and best to outsource to an RFID laboratory.

If you do have a lab perform the test, knowing the interpretation of the results is germane to designing a great-performing RFID system. A 30 dB difference in receive sensitivity is identical to saying that one reader is 1,000 times more sensitive than another. The stark contrast displayed in testing the cross section of today's readers demonstrates how different one reader is from the next, and those types of variations routinely have been recorded in the ODIN labs.

Keep in mind that a high receive sensitivity can be both a blessing and a curse. The reader may be optimized for interrogating a single tag, but how effective is the reader at filtering out additional readers and tags, which is common in a field deployment? Given the option, however, the more sensitive the reader, the better the performance.

Performing Interference Rejection Testing

The next area to test is the level of interference that a system with many interrogation zones is capable of withstanding. This type of system is usually called a dense reader mode (DRM) environment. DRM was created to deal with implementations that will continue to scale as the industry unfolds over the coming years. End users are beginning to understand the value associated with deploying RFID throughout an enterprise, migrating RFID implementations beyond the warehouse into manufacturing, and raw-materials tracking. Other companies are simply adding readers to their existing RFID network as their volume of tagged products and assets grows.

When additional interrogation zones are brought online, existing RFID reader infrastructure faces growing interference pressure. Many end users are overlooking an important question as they select RFID technology components: "Are the readers I'm deploying today sufficiently robust to reject the interference generated by my planned and unplanned RFID infrastructure 2–5 years from now?" I always advise end users to consider this impact when designing and deploying RFID solutions at the beginning—design with the end in mind. You do not want to be forced to replace your whole RFID network because it cannot scale to meet your or your clients' needs over time.

As I mentioned, DRM has been designed as part of the Gen 2 specification to help readers and tags address the problem of growing numbers of readers in the same environment. Although many readers are dense reader mode compliant, some implement the protocol far more effectively than others. Interference rejection testing is designed to study the effects that interfering reader signals have on the performance of a RUT. This test should be performed with a single tag attempting to be read, and an increasing number of interfering readers added to the environment. By pointing the interferers directly into the RUT, the full interference rejection capability of that reader can be determined.

Dense reader mode is often thought of as the most important feature of a Gen 2 reader, especially by retailers who are actively deploying 40–60 units per store and 100+ units at distribution centers. Product manufacturers will quickly face these same issues as they continue to scale their RFID footprints to meet increased shipping volumes and the need to track tagged goods at more read points. There are also many examples of RFID installations in manufacturing environments that include dozens or even hundreds of RFID readers in a single facility. As many of these implementations migrate to UHF RFID technology, dense reader mode will be a critical component of project success.

Performing Tag Acquisition Speed Testing

The final test of the five scientific evaluations is for acquisition speed. This refers to how fast tags can be read by a reader.

The ability to interrogate large tag populations is critical to many applications, but not all. As I've been alluding to (unfortunately, for unsuspecting end users), not all readers are created equal. Some of the people who designed the EPC protocol—including Dr. Daniel Engels of the University of Texas, who contributed to this book—have said there is a theoretical maximum of 1,600 tags per second. In reality, this number is just not achievable with today's technology. However, reading large-enough populations of tags for most business uses is possible today.

Real World Scenario

Nothing Runs Like a Well-Tuned RFID Network

A few of our engineers at ODIN were hired to deploy a work-in-process tracking system for a well-known U.S.-based industrial machine manufacturer. A primary concern when we designed the system was using a reader that could scale as the manufacturer moved from a handful of readers up to hundreds of readers. The testing we did around interference rejection will allow them to add readers without degrading performance as they expand to meet the needs of their business.

If you think of an application for which tag acquisition is critical to success, it is reading cases on a pallet coming through a dock door such as a common dock door portal, or aggregating cases to a pallet and associating them to a specific pallet tag (for example, at the end of a manufacturing process), or reading runners at the start or finish of a race. If you're concerned about runners, you don't need 15 feet of read range, but you do need acquisition speed.

At ODIN technologies we've deployed systems which are designed to read 320 cases on a pallet. To get those kinds of results, careful component selection, design, and implementation are critical.

TIP All readers implement an "anticollision" algorithm to define how a reader will interrogate more than one tag in the field. Although the Gen 2 air interface protocol defines an anticollision sequence known as "slotted random anticollision," many design variables are left to firmware engineers regarding its implementation. The speed of tag interrogation is driven primarily by the unique anticollision algorithm developed by each vendor.

To establish the limitations of each reader's anticollision algorithm, it is best to place a tag grid composed of 400–500 tags in the interrogation zone of the RUT. The RUT should then be placed in continuous read mode for five seconds and the total number of unique identifiers captured. This simple but effective test should be repeated five to ten times for statistical significance. It is important to the results that you normalize the data so that you will not be thrown off by the reader manufacturer's software. I've mentioned this in other sections of the book, but one manufacturer's "read" can often be very different from that of another manufacturer.

Now that you have the basics of scientific testing and you may know the top two or three readers that will meet your needs, the best thing you can do is set up a mock-up of the specific environment you'll be testing, or actually test those readers in that environment. If you are planning on reading all the cases you put on a pallet, think of the best place you can capture all those reads. The amount of time each case sits on the pallet while being stretch-wrapped and the change in tag orientation relative to the antenna all make the stretch wrapper one of the best locations. This should be one of your use cases.

Each time I design an RFID solution, I leverage scientific data similar to the results outlined in this section. This provides an easy-to-defend scientific rationale for supporting technology-selection decisions. The scientific tests are specifically designed to isolate a single variable (power output, receive sensitivity, and so forth) so that readers can be compared. This points to a short list of viable reader options. The next step is to test the top readers in the use case that will be deployed as a final proof of concept.

Use-Case Testing

Scientific testing does the heavy lifting when it comes to testing anything RFID. However, a little peace of mind verifies your testing methodology and can confirm a thesis based on the scientific testing. It can also help put one reader ahead of another if the scientific testing results are similar.

The most common uses for UHF RFID today fall under three simple applications, or use cases:

- Conveyor
- Stretch wrapper
- Dock door

Certainly no one industry, such as fast-moving consumer goods, is going to have a use-case scenario that fits everyone's needs. But given the focus of many of today's RFID adopters, it at least makes sense to start your design process thinking about these parameters. The three have very different requirements largely based on the dwell time (amount of time the tag is in the interrogation zone) and the number of tags being read at any one time.

The conveyor use case is one of the most widely deployed to automate internal sorting processes as well as to conduct inline verification of applied RFID tag performance. Even more commonly, it is used in the process of capturing material receipt information, particularly among major retailers. Although not the most challenging use case, it is among the most important. This testing should be conducted by using either a fast-moving conveyor (up to 600 feet per minute, or fpm) or, for superior control over object orientation relative to the interrogation antenna and to ensure scientific accuracy, a device that can accelerate the product above 600 feet per minute in the interrogation zone while ensuring dwell time is around one second. What you will find is that even the middle of the speed range (400 fpm) is fast by most standards, and there are only a couple of readers that can actually perform at 600 fpm. The readers that do not perform well at this speed are likely to be those that conduct heavy filtering on board. This is telling, because if a tag is read even once, it appears in the results. The reader's activity and reporting to the applications can sometimes not be in real time, this is said to be a synchronization issue. It is a discrepancy between the time at which the reader is searching for a tag and the time that the tag is actually present.

Next is one of my favorites for deployment, the stretch-wrapper use case. It has become an important point in manufacturing and warehouse operations to verify tagged cases and associate them to a specific pallet. An interrogation zone at the stretch wrapper is often employed to save processing time and maintain throughput levels after RFID is introduced into operations. Figure 5.2 is a sample ODIN Technologies' stretch-wrapper deployment with the rack cover removed to show the three-antenna configuration.

FIGURE 5.2 Stretch-wrap test setup

This testing is quite simple to conduct. A standard pallet is placed on a stretch wrapper and rotated three times. The number of reads captured for each unique tag is recorded. The trial should be conducted five times for accuracy, and the data should be normalized to make up for reader vendors' software differences in interpreting a tag read. This analysis makes it easy to identify how each reader compares in this use case and whether each reader has an affinity for a particular tag type (which they usually do, so having your tag testing done first is essential). If tags are being shipped to a third party such as a distributor or retailer who will also be attempting a tag read, then it will be important to select tags that are likely to perform well with that reader. This is in your best interest because you directly benefit from higher read rates and better data quality at your downstream supply-chain partner. Finally, if you are a distributor or retailer or do not have control over which tags are used, you will want to look at readers that perform consistently across tag types. This will allow you to maximize your read rate performance regardless of what type of tags you start receiving into your facility.

The adjacent dock door use case is where end users from many industry verticals are harvesting business value from fixed RFID portals. The value proposition ranges from automated receiving to ship verification to more-efficient put-away processes. Yet with this value comes complexity. Distribution centers outfitting every dock door with RFID leads to a serious level of RF noise that leads to a high likelihood of two readers activating the same channel simultaneously and missing read opportunities. One size does not fit all when it comes to designing and deploying a dense reader environment.

In addition, adjacent dock doors lead to confusion of a different type called cross talk. Cross talk occurs when a reader in portal A reads case tags moving through portal B. Resolving this issue, while ensuring a robust use case, requires special tuning tools to optimize reader configuration, leading to the best performance possible. The other way to approach this testing is manually, by employing a signal generator and spectrum analyzer.

Testing for adjacent dock doors requires at least five of the same type of reader. The RUT should be placed in the center portal and four interfering readers placed on the outside of the two adjacent dock doors. This setup will simulate the effects of three adjacent dock doors. This testing is similar to what has been conducted by major retailers as they have assessed RFID reader performance.

What you will find is that even if a reader is Gen 2 compatible, only a handful actually perform adequately in this test, for a large-scale RFID deployment. Bear in mind that as additional interfering readers are brought online in your environment, reader performance will continue to degrade. Scaling an RFID implementation is by definition expensive and difficult to reverse. If ever there was a time to leverage physics in your decision-making process, this is it. I always recommend that testing be conducted in accordance with the scale of your implementation prior to making a final reader selection decision. I have conducted testing similar to the preceding for clients who wanted the piece of mind that comes with measuring twice and cutting once.

Choosing the Correct Cable Type

I've already mentioned the big three components in an RFID network: the reader (and antenna), tag, and software. However one of the most overlooked components of the entire system is the cabling. Cabling is a vital aspect of designing a quality RFID network and yet is the least understood topic in the system design. Even after having the highest-quality RFID components, if the RF signal is not transmitted by using a proper medium, the entire system will suffer. By using a proper cable and installation technique, you can improve the performance of the entire RFID system.

Figure 5.3 shows the cutaway view of a coaxial (or coax) cable. A *coaxial cable* is one that consists of two conductors that share a common axis. The inner conductor is typically a straight wire, either solid or stranded, and the outer conductor is typically a shield that might be braided or foil.

FIGURE 5.3 Cutaway view of coax cable

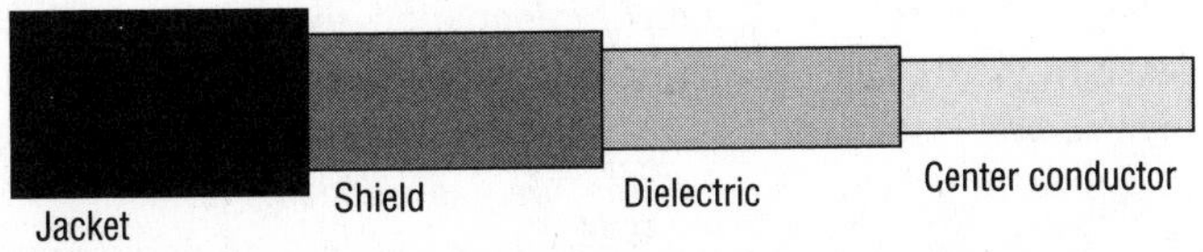

In a *coaxial cable*, the RF signal is carried between the cable shield and the center conductor. Coaxial cables are typically characterized by the impedance and cable loss. The length has nothing to do with coaxial cable impedance. Characteristic impedance is determined by the size and spacing of the conductors and the type of dielectric used between them. For ordinary coaxial cable used at reasonable frequency, the characteristic impedance depends on the dimensions of the inner and outer conductors. Most common coaxial cable impedances in use in various applications are 50 ohms and 75 ohms, but 50 ohms is predominantly used in RFID systems.

If you select an incorrect coaxial cable, that mistake can degrade the overall signal transmission and/or allow outside electromagnetic or radio frequency interference to be introduced into the main signal. This causes high noise levels, which in turn can result in poor read rates. Using the wrong coaxial cable is common with poorly trained RFID technicians. In an RFID system, the most important factor to be considered is that there is proper impedance match between the reader, coaxial cable, and the antenna for maximum power delivery. If this is not done, there will be signal loss and reflection resulting in short distance transmission and poor RF signal quality. Figure 5.4 shows a well-matched RFID system.

FIGURE 5.4 A well-matched RFID system

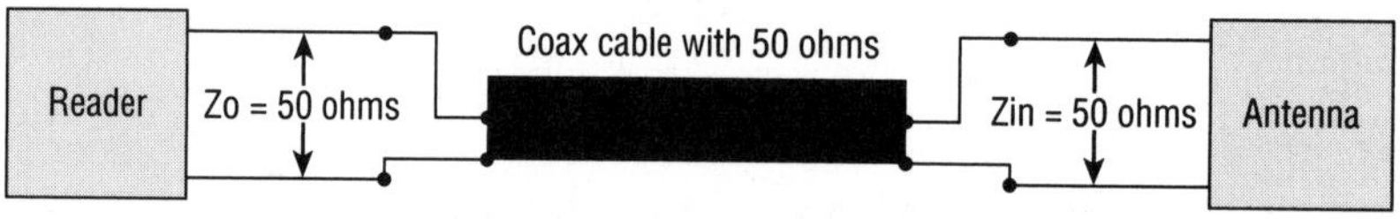

If the cable is such an important part of an overall RFID system, how do you go about making sure you have the right one for the job? Like everything else in RFID, you can use science and a strong foundation in physics to plan for the optimal RFID network. The parameters to consider while selecting a cable are as follows:

Mechanical Characteristics These can include center conductor material, dielectric material, shield type, and jacket material.

Electrical Characteristics These include resistance, capacitance, impedance, and attenuation.

The center conductor, dielectric, type of shielding, and jacket all play important roles in deciding the preceding parameters.

Is What You Have What You Want?

Often when you order an RFID reader and antenna combination from a hardware manufacturer, you will be given the option, and often the recommendation, to purchase their cables. This is not always the best option. At ODIN Technologies, after setting up and deploying thousands of antennas and cables, we've taken a different approach to cabling. We have in-house teams that make up our cables, or for very large orders we use a specific outsourcer who builds just the cables for us. Often we'll use three or four types of cables on a deployment, and sometimes two types of cable on the same reader.

The higher the frequency of the RF signal, the more the signal travels on the outer surface of the conductor. This phenomenon is known as the *skin effect*. Hence, depending on the frequency of use, a certain type of center conductor needs to be selected. Dielectric material and its physical dimensions and composition decide the electrical characteristics such as capacitance, impedance, attenuation, and velocity of propagation of the cable. It is essential to also consider the type of shielding the cable has, because it determines how well the center conductor carrying the RF signal is isolated from the ambient environmental noise (AEN). The shielding also needs to act as a low-resistance ground path. Depending on the environment where the cable needs to be installed, the cable with appropriate jacket needs to be selected.

LMR are the letters that proceed a number (like LMR-400) when ordering a thickness of cable. The higher the LMR number the thicker the cable and the lower the loss. LMR doesn't seem to be an acronym for anything, rather it seems to have cropped up as an industry way of describing cable types.

The first step in selecting a superior-performing RFID system is getting the tags, readers, and antennas correct based on what you learned from your site survey and tag testing. Depending on your frequency selection and system requirements, you should choose the right type of cable. Choosing the right cable is only as good as choosing the right reader—if not deployed properly, then it can ruin what might be a perfectly designed RFID network.

NOTE Cable manufacturers have a very specific measurement when it comes to laying out cable. This is true not just for RFID, but also Internet networks, fiber-optic, and other similar transmission mediums. The manufacturer will give you the radius measurement, which cannot be exceeded. A team of ODIN engineers went on-site to a third-party logistics provider (3PL) to perform an RFID Rescue. The 3PL was hamstrung with low read rates and wanted to improve them. One of the first things our team noticed was cable stuffed into racks at very tight radii to accommodate all the equipment. This tight bend was interrupting the flow of RF energy and a partial cause for the poor read rates.

Our team at ODIN has a checklist a mile long of things we are careful to avoid when it comes to deployments, but here are the highlights for installing the cable for the system:

1. Evenly distribute the pulling tension over the cable and never exceed the minimum *bend radius* or the radius that you can bend the cable around and still get maximum performance. Exceeding these factors can result in permanent mechanical and electrical damage to the cable.
2. When laying out cable, try to protect it from harsh environments by installing the cable in conduits. When pulling the cable from the conduits, try to lubricate the cable before pulling and also deburr the ends of the conduit. Failing to do so can damage the external jacket and shielding.
3. Always lay the cable without any tension and leave some extra cable to incorporate any changes or correction.

Appropriate end connectors are required to connect the reader and antennas to the cables. The required connector types will depend on the reader and antenna being used. The cable selection (thickness) can be limited by the connector. Sometimes longer cable lengths cannot be implemented since the thicker low-loss cables are unusable. The thicker cable may be unusable because of the connector types being used by the reader or the thickness of the cable housing not working with a bigger cable. There are several methods to make the cable and connector connection, but the most common are as follows:

Solder Method This method provides the most robust mechanical and electrical connection. The technician needs to have extensive *soldering* experience to make a good connection. The main disadvantage of this method is that there can be a dry or cold solder joint which requires more time to make a solder joint.

Crimp Method This *crimping* method provides an average mechanical and electrical connection by squeezing the connectors onto the end of the cable. The main advantage is that it requires less time to make a termination compared to the solder method. A tight fit on the cable is important; hence proper crimping tools are a must. Doing it incorrectly can damage the connector or the cable, resulting in degraded electrical properties.

Standard coax cable connectors used in RFID systems are as follows:

Series	Frequency GHz	Power Watts*	Typ. Diameter Inches	Relative Cost
BNC	0–4	80	0.6	Low
N	0–11	300	0.8	Moderate
SMA	0–18	100	0.4	Moderate
TNC	0–11	100	0.6	Low

* At 1 GHz

Some commonly used 50-ohm cables are as follows:

Type	Frequency MHz	Diameter inches	Relative cost
RG-58	0–3000	0.2″	Low
LMR-240	0–2000	0.4″	Moderate
LMR-400	0–2000	0.4″	Moderate

Cable attenuation at various frequencies are as follows:

Attenuation (dB per 100 feet)

MHz	30	50	100	146	150	440	450	1000	2400
LMR-100A	3.9	5.1		8.8	8.9	15.6	15.8		
RG-58A/U	2.5	4.1	5.3	6.1	6.1	10.4	10.6	24.0	38.9

Attenuation (dB per 100 feet)

MHz	30	50	100	146	150	440	450	1000	2400
LMR-200	1.8	2.3		3.9	4.0	6.9	7.0		16.5
LMR-240	1.3	1.7		3.0	3.0	5.2	5.3		12.7
LMR-400	0.7	0.9		1.5	1.5	2.7	2.7		6.6

Approximate values shown for comparison purposes only.

The following are some important definitions and formulas you need to be familiar with:

Attenuation *Attenuation* is the decrease of a signal over distance in the direction of propagation. Attenuation may be expressed as the scalar ratio of the input magnitude to the output magnitude:

$$\text{Attenuation} \frac{dB}{m} = 10 \log \frac{Pout}{Pin}$$

Capacitance *Capacitance* is the ability of a dielectric material between two conductors to store electric energy. For coaxial cables, capacitance per meter is as follows:

$$C = 3.336 \_ 103 \sqrt{\frac{e_r}{Zo}}$$

where, e_r = dielectric constant, and Zo = impedance

Impedance (Zo in ohms) *Impedance* is the characteristic property of a transmission line describing the ration between electric and magnetic fields. For coaxial cable, the characteristic impedance is basically given by the permittivity of the dielectric and the dimension of the conductors:

$$Zo \frac{60}{\sqrt{e_r}} \_ \ln \frac{D}{d}$$

where, e_r = dielectric constant

Choosing the Correct Antenna and Design

The antenna is the broadcaster to the outside world. If it has the correct design and implementation, you will get out exactly the signal you want at exactly the right size. There are thick books dedicated to the design and creation of RF antennas. Suffice it to say that a base-level knowledge should be good for what you are likely to deploy. There is a critical trap to look out for however: most readers ship with one or maybe two types of antennas. The antennas shipped with a reader are not always the best ones for your particular application.

As you become more familiar with readers, antennas, and RFID deployments, you will start to form a picture in your mind of what an antenna "lobe" looks like, even though you cannot see the radiation pattern coming from the antenna. A UHF antenna has two types: linearly polarized and circularly polarized. The linearly polarized is highly concentrated and highly orientation sensitive. You can think of it as a slice of RF that is very vertically focused, like the type of light that might seep in through two slats of a window blind. Because of this narrow RF lobe, the tags have to be in just the right orientation to be read. Linearly polarized antennas are highly sensitive to the direction and orientation of the tags they are reading, but they provide a more-concentrated RF signal and therefore can read tags at a greater distance than circularly polarized. Circularly polarized antennas send a vortex of RF in either the clockwise or counterclockwise direction, and the lobe usually looks like an inverted pear or apple propagating from the antenna. Circularly polarized are a lot less susceptible to orientation and cover a wider area.

HF antennas are the other type of antenna you are likely to work with. They require that the tag be coupled with the antenna and therefore read at a much closer range. They are also much easier to make and tune, because the typical HF antenna is just a whole bunch of wire looped around again and again and tuned to the proper frequency (13.56 MHz). The loop antenna can be designed, therefore, in many shapes and sizes depending on the application.

The last part that you need to know about antennas is the installation. Many companies make specialized RFID racks. Symbol Technologies and Alien Technology have racks that fit their readers and antennas, although they do not have much control and flexibility in moving antennas and adding peripheral devices such as UPS systems.

NOTE

At ODIN Technologies we make a rack that works with any reader or antenna combination and allows antenna shaping and tuning. There are also many custom shops that, although more expensive, can create a rack specifically to your needs.

Understanding Middleware Considerations

Middleware is one of those things that requires understanding and integration beyond the RFID network. No matter how good you are as a physicist or RF engineer, without a proper software background you are unlikely to be able to comprehend the subtleties of middleware beyond the basics. CompTIA understands this and consequently does not have extensive coverage of the middleware component of RFID. What they want you to know are just the basics. So in this last section I will take you through the components of middleware, what it does, and what is important to the end user.

Middleware bridges the gap between raw data from a tag to the business applications that create actionable data. An RFID reader at its basic level has no intelligence imbedded on it. As far as a reader is concerned, there is no difference between six million reads and one read. However, to a business application there is a huge difference. This is why data filtering is the key aspect of RFID middleware.

To give you an example of how middleware can help out, imagine it's 9:15 AM and time for a coffee break. The forklift driver who is unloading a truck stops within the interrogation zone for his break. The reader on the portal is going to read continuously, perhaps every 300th of a second. That's 3.3 reads per second, and if the forklift sits there for 15 minutes, the same tags are going to be read almost 3,000 times. The business application needs to know only whether the tag came in the dock door. In other words, did the facility receive the case? So that requires only one read. Reading the tag data is not an extensive burden. However, if someplace is receiving hundreds of thousands of tagged items each day, then the difference between reading something once and sending that data to a central data base, and reading it 3,000 times and sending all that data to the same place, would be material. The middleware filters all those unnecessary reads and smooths out the data that is sent up to the higher level applications.

Middleware can also control a reader and devices attached to the readers such as light stacks and motion detectors. This capability is not inherent on all middleware packages. However, the more-mature programs, which can also control barcode readers and other handheld devices, usually have advanced functionality built in.

RFID middleware selection requires several steps. The critical first step is to finalize the detailed design and business process steps. The detailed design will include what happens at what particular steps in the process when RFID is introduced into a system. That is why the swim lane diagrams in Chapter 3, "Site Analysis," are so important. The design process finalizes screen flows for the middleware design—in other words, what happens at a particular step in the process if something is read by an RFID reader, and what happens if it is not read and is supposed to be. This set of activities then proceeds to configuring the work flows, rules, screens, data model, and integration. After the system is fully configured, it is unit tested in a controlled environment prior to full system testing on-site. It is important to conduct the controlled testing off-site first because basic functionality can be evaluated and bugs fixed prior to on-site installation. This saves time in troubleshooting and reduces the installation time on-site. If the system is being deployed across multiple facilities and supports multiple work flows, each facility will be system tested in turn and then the entire network will be tested as an enterprise.

There are more than a dozen middleware applications that are commercially available in 2006, and none of them are ready for deployment "out of the box." Even the more-mature middleware components require custom integration with a client's systems to make it truly effective. I also think the middleware market for RFID is going to disappear over the coming years—the functionality is not that complex from a software perspective. This is why reader manufacturers are putting more intelligence on their readers, and software vendors such as Oracle and Microsoft are putting RFID functionality in their applications. This pressure from the top (application) and pressure from the bottom (readers) will squeeze specialized middleware applications out of the market.

Summary

In this chapter, you learned everything you need to know about design and selection of the RFID network. With the understanding of physics and the specifics of the readers and tags that you have already gained, you should now be able to work with your team to understand the client needs and create an RFID network that is both the proper scientific and business combination to meet those needs.

The first step in that design is figuring out the best frequency for their needs. Sometimes this is plainly obvious, such as if you are designing a system for a DoD or Wal-Mart supplier—you know it is going to be UHF, and you know they are going to incorporate the electronic product code (EPC). There are, however, many other applications that would use the other available frequencies for RFID. This chapter showed you some of the strengths and weaknesses of those systems.

Next I gave you the basics of an RFID read, showing what was key about functionality and how a reader works. There is no mystery around the fact that an RFID read and an RFID tag are both essentially radios communicating with each other.

You also learned some of the trade secrets around selecting the proper RFID reader. This should be particularly valuable as you move out into the real world of RFID reader selection and begin choosing hardware for yourself or your clients. I covered the basics of scientific tests that attempt to isolate a single variable and then went into specific use-case testing for your particular needs.

After working with the different readers, you need to move to getting that connection out into the atmosphere—so you learned all the details around cable selection and deployment. This is one of the most overlooked facets of an RFID deployment and can make or break a well-designed and planned-out RFID network.

After the cable section, I reviewed the details of the antennas and talked about when you might use the various types of antennas in different applications. This section brought the conclusion of the portal design with mention of RFID racks—the devices used to hold RFID readers, antennas, and cabling at a portal installation.

Finally the last section gave a quick overview of RFID middleware. The important thing to glean from this section is that RFID middleware is a very specialized functionality for filtering and smoothing data, but is not difficult to build. Because of this, many application vendors will begin incorporating middleware into their existing programs.

This chapter should have helped bring together the various pieces of design and deployment.

Exam Essentials

Know the differences between and characteristics of the various frequencies (LF, HF, UHF, and microwave), their specific use, performance, and pros and cons. LF systems are used for applications requiring very short read distances. LF has the advantage of working through water, metal, and other challenging applications. It is often used for access control and automobile security (embedding tags in a car key with a reader in the steering column).

HF is the system that has the most maturity. It has been used for decades in industrial applications, from tracking totes carrying work in process to tracking cows and pigs. It uses inductive coupling and can transfer relatively high data rates over distances up to three feet. The readers are not very expensive. However, the tags are more expensive because they require several loops for the antenna to function.

UHF has been brought to prominence by the U.S. Department of Defense requiring its 50,000 plus suppliers and Wal-Mart requiring its 7,000 plus suppliers to use the technology developed out of the Massachusetts Institute of Technology called the electronic product code (EPC). UHF has very fast data-transfer rates and long read ranges. The tags also have the potential to be the cheapest of all systems, with the holy grail being the 5¢ tag. UHF is affected by water and metals in a way that HF is not.

Microwave functions like a UHF tag, although microwave systems are not nearly as prevalent and are therefore more expensive. As the frequency increases, the read rate and data-transfer rate increases. However, the challenges around metal and liquids also increase. Microwave systems work well for closed-loop applications in which speed is critical—for example, automobile toll tags.

Know the key criteria for antenna selection. The two basic types of UHF antennas are linearly polarized and circularly polarized. A linearly polarized antenna has a more-focused and concentrated beam of energy. A circularly polarized antennas is like a tornado of RF. Linearly polarized are best to use if the tag's orientation is going to be constant vis-à-vis the antenna. The linearly polarized antenna will allow you to keep a tight beam and not read adjacent tags if you do not want to read them. The circularly polarized antenna will allow many different tags and orientations to be read—for example, when a case of items comes in through a dock door and the tags are all over the place.

HF antennas are coiled loops of wire (usually copper) that can be made in many shapes and sizes and then tuned based on where they are set up and installed—for instance, in a smart-shelf type of application.

Know the proper way to select an RFID reader. All RFID readers are not created equal. Understanding the key functionality for your business requirements will help you select between the trade-offs of various readers. After you know the key differences among readers (cost, read distance, interference rejection, and so forth), you can determine the one or two parameters that are most important to you and your business requirements. Knowing how to test for those parameters will make you a better RF technician and more capable of setting up an accurate RFID network.

Be aware of the important considerations when choosing and installing a cable from reader to antenna.

The cable composition and thickness both determine how well a signal is carried across the cable to the antenna. The longer the cable run, the more insulation the cable requires to prevent signal loss. When using LMR cable, the thickness is designated by the number after LM. It ranges from LMR-100 to LMR-1700, with the number designating measurement in 1/100th of an inch. The other thing to keep in mind is not to exceed the manufacturer's recommended radius for bending the cable during install. You should also make sure to use cable lengths that are in increments of 1/4 wavelength.

Know the regional differences between frequencies used in RFID. *Low frequency* (125–134 kHz), *high frequency* (13.56 MHz), and *microwave frequency* (2.45 GHz) are used globally. *Ultra-high frequency* differs by region. The United States uses 902–928 MHz (South America, South Africa, China, and Australia use a similar band), while Europe uses 865–868 MHz up to 870 MHz (as do North Africa, India, Hong Kong, New Zealand, and Singapore). Japan operates at 952–954 MHz, which is out of the U.S. and European bands. Active tags usually operate on the UHF frequency around 433 MHz internationally.

Understand the basics of RFID middleware. RFID middleware simply filters the thousands of reads that would happen each second down to a handful of important reads. The filtering and smoothing of data is the primary function of RFID middleware. Some of the more-sophisticated programs can control RFID peripherals such as light stacks and motion sensors, or can set up reading based on time sequences (a work shift) or with a manual switch.

Ensure a correct tag orientation for a reader's antenna. Tags should face the antenna (parallel to the antenna's radiator) for maximum performance. When using a single dipole tag and a linear antenna, the tag antenna should be in the same plane as the plane of wave propagation. When using a circular antenna, or when using a dual dipole tag, the orientation does not matter.

Key Terms

Before you take the exam, be certain you are familiar with the following terms:

active RFID
attenuation
bend radius
capacitance
coaxial cable
continuous wave
crimping
digital signal processor (DSP) chip
frequency hopping
high frequency (HF)
impedance
LMR cable
low frequency (LF)
microwave frequency
passive RFID
semi-passive tags
skin effect
soldering
ultra-high frequency (UHF)

Review Questions

1. What determines the electrical characteristics of coaxial cable?(Select two options.)
   - **A.** Capacitance
   - **B.** Dielectric material composition
   - **C.** Dielectric material physical dimensions
   - **D.** Velocity of propagation
2. What is a broadcast interval in reference to an active tag?
   - **A.** The time between signals that are sent out from the tag
   - **B.** The amount of time between reads from an active reader
   - **C.** The time between each wavelength
   - **D.** None of the above
3. A pharmaceutical company that manufactures cough syrups would like to track every bottle manufactured in the supply chain. It needs to select a tag that can read through liquids at a low cost. What tag would you recommend?
   - **A.** Microwave
   - **B.** UHF
   - **C.** HF
   - **D.** LF
4. In a supply-chain application, you like to track cases and pallets made of corrugate. Each pallet has about 80 cases. What type of tags would you use?
   - **A.** Thermal label
   - **B.** LF
   - **C.** HF
   - **D.** UHF
5. You go to a hardware store and make a copy of your car keys. You then try to start your vehicle with the duplicate keys, but the car does not start. What kind of tag needs to be present in the duplicate key?
   - **A.** Key ring
   - **B.** LF
   - **C.** HF
   - **D.** Active tag

6. What does FCC regulation part 15 specify?
   A. Frequency hopping
   B. Antenna gain
   C. Cable loss standards
   D. Tag data requirements
7. What is cross talk?
   A. Waiting for one reader to read before another begins reading
   B. Reading outside of the intended interrogation zone
   C. Reading half of one tag and half of a different tag
   D. None of the above
8. Which use case has the longest dwell time?
   A. Pharmaceutical manufacturing line
   B. Highway tollbooth
   C. Forklift unloading a trailer
   D. Stretch-wrap machine
9. What is the best type of antenna to use for a UHF system that is reading laptops as personnel carry them through an entrance door in their briefcases?
   A. Linearly polarized
   B. Circularly polarized
   C. Inductively coupled
   D. Declonian design
10. What is the best choice for a 30-foot cable run from a UHF reader to a linearly polarized 6 dB gain antenna?
    A. LMR-100
    B. LMR-400
    C. CAT-6
    D. All of the above
11. What is the most complex component in an RFID network?
    A. The tag
    B. The antenna
    C. The reader
    D. The cable

12. Where would you use a UHF RFID network? (Select two options.)
    A. Pharmaceutical item-level tracking
    B. Luggage tracking
    C. Livestock tracking
    D. Retail store supply chain

13. What must you consider when selecting an antenna for a UHF system?
    A. Tag orientation
    B. Distance to be read
    C. Speed of tags through the interrogation zone
    D. All of the above

14. All middleware can control which of the following reader functionalities?
    A. Data filtering
    B. Light stack functionality
    C. Motion detectors
    D. Manual triggering of reads

15. When does a passive tag receive its power to communicate?
    A. When it is plugged into a battery
    B. When it is triggered by a motion detector
    C. When it enters the radiated field of a matched RFID reader
    D. All of the above

16. What is the most common operating frequency for an active RFID tag?
    A. 7 MHz
    B. 433 MHz
    C. 915 MHz
    D. 13.56 MHz

17. What does RFID middleware do?
    A. Filter and smooth data
    B. Provide a GUI to end users
    C. Print to RFID labels
    D. Monitor the health of the RFID network

18. What is a continuous wave?

A. A wave that has the same power throughout its lifespan

B. A wave that reflects off a surface and comes back out of phase

C. The turbulence created by multiple frequencies

D. None of the above

19. Which of the following best explains the skin effect relative to cable performance?

A. The thicker the skin, the more ribbing it can take.

B. The higher the frequency, the more signal travels along the outer surface of the conductor.

C. Mismatching of impedance will result in a melting of the cable's outer surface.

D. If the skin is rubbed too thin, the signal will short to ground.

20. Why do readers matter the most in an RFID network? (Select two options.)

A. They are the only system component you have control over.

B. They are the most complex system component.

C. They are expensive to both buy and maintain.

D. They last only a few months.

Answers to Review Questions

1. B, C. Capacitance and velocity of propagation are two of the characteristics that are important in choosing the right coaxial cable. However, the key performance drivers are capacitance and the impedance which are determined by B and C the correct answer.

2. A. An active tag, with its on-board battery, is set to broadcast its information at a certain interval so that an interrogator knows that a tag is in the field and can retrieve whatever data happens to be on that tag.

3. C. HF tags are less susceptible to liquids and can be manufactured in bulk at a lower cost. Hence HF tags would be the best choice for the pharmaceutical company.

4. D. Normally in a supply-chain use, case pallets are read at dock doors or stretch wrappers. The pallets and cases are about 3 to 6 feet away from the read point. Also the pallet has over 80 cases; hence UHF will be the best choice. The second reason for selecting UHF is because of the low tag costs.

5. B. Current car manufacturers use LF tags in the butt of the key. Car immobilizer circuits present in the car ignition circuits query the tag in the keys provided by the car manufacturer. Usually keys made at hardware stores won't work because they do not have LF tags embedded in the key. Such keys can be obtained only from the car dealer or manufacturer.

6. A. FCC regulation part 15 states that in the UHF ISM band a reader must hop pseudo-randomly across at least 50 channels in the frequency range 902–928MHz.

7. B. Cross talk occurs when multiple interrogation zones are set up in close proximity to each other, and the system is poorly designed. If the system is not properly designed, a reader in one portal could unintentionally read tags going through an adjacent portal.

8. D. The stretch-wrap machine usually turns a pallet for several revolutions, plus getting on and off. This keeps the tags in the interrogation zone for an extended period of time and also has the added benefit of moving the tag orientation to ensure a high probability of read success.

9. B. You are not sure what orientation the tag is likely to be presented to the antenna, because people will carry their laptops in different bags, and will hold them on their person in a different manner. Therefore, you want to limit the system's sensitivity to orientation and should install a circularly polarized antenna that is made for UHF.

10. B. The higher the LMR number, the more shielding or insulation to prevent loss on long cable runs. LMR-400 would provide adequate insulation for a long cable run.

11. C. The reader has many sophisticated components that turn a digital signal into an analog wave, listen for a much weaker signal in response, and turn that signal into useful information. It is by far the most complex part of an RFID network.

12. B, D. If there are large items to be tracked at fast speeds over relatively long distances, they are likely candidates for UHF tracking. Pharmaceutical item level is best suited for HF, where the metal and liquids would not cause an issue, and livestock is also suited for HF because there is a lot of liquid associated with living beings.

13. D. The three primary criteria of antenna selection will drive whether you choose a linearly polarized or circularly polarized application.

14. A. The only true commonality in middleware is the ability to filter out data and present it up to the application layer. Other capabilities such as device configuration, peripheral control, and monitoring are not common to the various programs.

15. C. A passive tag receives its power from the energy output broadcast by a matched RFID reader. A UHF reader will not power up an HF tag, and vice versa.

16. B. Most active RFID systems are based on a standard working at 433 MHz.

17. A. RFID middleware at its basic level filters and smooths the data coming off an RFID reader before it gets sent up to a business application such as a warehouse management system (WMS) or enterprise resource planning (ERP) software.

18. D. A continuous wave is an electromagnetic wave that has both the same amplitude and the same frequency. If you were to measure it as a visible graph, you would see the same height and width constantly repeating itself.

19. B. Lower frequencies are transmitted inside the center conductor, and therefore if it is a lower-frequency system, the choice of material for the core becomes more important than the outer conductive surface.

20. B, C. The largest capital outlay and the most variation in the system occur when selecting the RFID reader. At an average price ranging from \$700–\$4,000, they are also the single most expensive piece of equipment in the network.

Chapter 6

Peripherals

RFID+ EXAM OBJECTIVES COVERED IN THIS CHAPTER:

✓ **9.1 Describe the installation and configuration of an RFID printer (may use scenarios)**

✓ **9.2 Describe ancillary devices/concepts**

- 9.2.1 RFID printer encoder
- 9.2.2 Automated label applicator
- 9.2.3 Feedback systems (e.g., lights, horns)
- 9.2.4 RTLS

If you think of bubble gum, baseball caps, or batting gloves, you're thinking of peripherals for a baseball player. Radio frequency identification (RFID) systems are no different—the tags, readers, and antennas are the main aspects of RFID, just as the bats, mitts, and baseballs are the equipment of baseball. But just as the game isn't a game without its peripherals, an RFID network isn't an RFID network without peripherals, either.

RFID peripherals are devices that provide the RFID system with the capability to encode and verify tags, trigger interrogation, or react to various events created by data that are generated by the interrogation zones. Some readers/interrogators have evolved into "smart" machines like sophisticated computers; their capabilities have grown not only to filter, process, and store data coming from RFID reads, but also to directly manage most of the peripheral devices through input/output (I/O) ports.

RFID peripherals include RFID printers/encoders that encode the RFID tag with data and print visible information on the label; label applicators that apply labels to products; diverters, which are used mainly with conveyors for routing products to various destinations; triggering devices such as motion sensors or infrared sensors; and feedback devices such as light stacks, alarms, diverters, and other devices that might be part of an RFID network.

In this chapter, you'll learn about the following:

- The function, installation, and configuration of an RFID printer/encoder
- The function and working principles of different kinds of label applicators
- The working principles and reasons for using triggering devices
- The working principles and reasons for using feedback systems
- The concept of real-time locating systems (RTLS)

RFID Printers/Encoders

RFID printers/encoders became symbols of the quick integration of RFID technology into existing business processes, mainly as a response to mandates from major retailers or the U.S. Department of Defense (DoD). Buying just a printer allowed people to quickly create RFID labels with an electronic product code (EPC) number encoded on them. This process has been called *slap-and-ship*: an RFID printer prints and encodes shipping labels with RFID tags that are then placed on products before being shipped to a mandating customer such as Wal-Mart, Target, or the DoD. In this case, RFID is not fully integrated into the company's business process and it is not used for internal benefit. This is one of the reasons people complain of RFID having no value; in this slap-and-ship instance, it is purely a cost.

However, more and more companies are using RFID as a strategic competitive advantage, and have done a detailed analysis to find value drivers by using RFID. What that means is that they are investing in full RFID integration, with RFID printers being used at various points of the business process for printing, encoding, and validation of RFID labels. Printers are often either used in conjunction with automatic label applicators or applied manually during exception processing.

Most RFID printers/encoders evolved from a barcode printer. Companies such as Zebra Technologies, Printronix, Intermec, and Paxar evolved their barcode printers by integrating an RFID reader board onto them. RFID printers/encoders have gone through several iterations and improvements during their development life cycle, from the early days when I saw printers that literally had an RFID reader bolted to the back of them.

The current version of RFID printers not only prints information on the label, but also encodes and validates the RFID tag in the label via wireless data-transfer protocols. If the tag's function is not positively verified, the printer prints the word "void" or a large "X" on the label to inform the operator that this tag does not work, and automatically issues a new replacement label. The main reasons for a rejected label to be marked "void" are the following:

- The label medium does not carry an RFID tag, or the tag works on a different frequency than the printer. (For example, a high-frequency tag would not be recognized by an ultra-high-frequency printer.)
- The label medium contains tags that, although they operate within the correct frequency, size, and location, operate under different air interface protocols.
- The printer was not calibrated for the location of the tag's antenna on the label. The printer manufacturers publish label and tag specifications, and you should have your RFID labels made according to these guidelines. If your labels do not comply with the printer's default specifications, the printer has to be properly calibrated.
- The tag was damaged after the manufacturing and verification process or faulty from production. Damage could have been physical or by electrostatic discharge (ESD). ESD is discussed further later in this chapter.

Printer Installation

Although each printer is different and each manufacturer will supply a manual that will guide you through a printer installation, let's look at some common techniques and best practices that you may find useful in your future printer deployments. There are several things that need to be taken into consideration when installing and working with an RFID printer; one of them is the issue of ESD, which I will discuss once we go through the printer installation guidelines.

Guidelines

When you are installing an RFID printer/encoder, you should adhere to the following guidelines:

- Unlike putting together toys for your kids at Christmas, when working on RFID equipment you should always read the printer manual supplied by the manufacturer (this is important for any device you work with). This will allow you to avoid mistakes when installing this device and ensure its proper function, and you are less likely to have leftover screws and bolts.

- Place the printer on a solid, level surface and ensure proper ventilation. Heat and humidity can be one of the big killers of RFID equipment.
- Make sure that you will have enough space to open the printer and change the print supplies, as well as access to all buttons, ports, and cables. Sometimes it is a good idea to place the printer on a cart to improve its accessibility and mobility.
- Find out what ports you have and need to connect to other devices or networks. Printers usually come with standard communication interfaces such as RS-232 serial data port, bidirectional parallel port, USB 2.0, RS-422, and sometimes RS-485 port. For an Ethernet-based network connection, you may have to use a print server that has an Ethernet port. Several printer manufacturers also provide additional communication capabilities through Bluetooth or 802.11 wireless networks. (Bluetooth and 802.11 wireless capabilities usually require appropriate print servers, but these options can be integrated into some printers.)
- Make sure that you have an accessible, grounded power outlet for the printer to plug into.
- A power cord may or may not be included with the printer. If your printer does not come with a power cord, consult the manufacturer's manual for guidelines regarding selection of a proper type and length for the power cord. You will usually need a three-conductor HAR (harmonized) cable with an IEC 320 connector certified by an international safety organization. This is what most desktop computers use these days, so you are likely to have one somewhere.
- Select the correct media (printer ribbon and labels) for your printer. This depends on the printing method you will use as well as other label and tag requirements.

Electrostatic Discharge

When installing a printer, you should take *electrostatic discharge (ESD)* into consideration and protect your device as well as personnel against its effects. ESD refers to the rapid release of charge that has accumulated on a person or object. Most materials can be electrically charged by friction; the amount of charge is highly dependent on the material, speed of contact and separation, and environmental humidity. Electrostatic discharge can cause damage to any unprotected device, and this damage can induce either immediate or later failure of the device or its components. ESD can also harm your team, so be careful!

NOTE

According to the Electrostatic Discharge Organization, walking across vinyl tile can create a static charge of 250 volts at 65 percent to 90 percent humidity. The same action will generate 12,000 volts at 10 percent to 25 percent humidity! Electronic components can be damaged or destroyed by discharges lower than 100 volts, in some cases even by discharges lower than 10 volts!

ESD can cause problems in RFID printers, where the movement of unwinding media and the printing ribbon through the printer generates an electrostatic charge. The discharge could damage the printer as well as the tag's chip and cause malfunctions. This has been solved by implementing special ESD bristles inside the printer and by proper grounding. If you use a proper power cable for your printer (the cable should have a ground line and a total of three prongs), and the power outlet or power strip you connect to is properly grounded and complies with all electrical building grounding regulations, you do not usually need a second ground. As a matter of fact, in this situation, a second ground could lead to a ground loop that could damage the device.

ESD also can be generated by peeling the label off its backing. This charge can be temporarily stored on the label or it can be discharged onto the product that the label is applied to. The released charge can then cause damage to this product or to the RFID tag within the label. Some label manufacturers produce labels that dissipate static and reduce the possible product and component damages.

Generally, you must always use proper grounding, and possibly humidifiers in severely dry environments, as a means of ESD protection for your personnel. You may also need other devices such as static mats or special shoes or bracelets.

NOTE: Today, many types of tags have a near-field loop as a part of their antenna design. This helps create a balance in static electricity for both sides of the tag and reduces the possibility of ESD and its damaging effects on the tag.

Printing Methods

There are two major printing methods used with RFID printers. They are *direct thermal* and *thermal transfer*.

Direct Thermal

The direct thermal printing method requires heat-sensitive RFID media and no printing ribbon. Information is printed as the printhead applies heat directly onto a heat-sensitive label.

The advantages of the direct thermal printing method include the following:

- No need for a ribbon. Sometimes the manufacturer recommends using a ribbon with the direct thermal method to protect the printhead; however, this is not a rule and it may cause errors in some printers.

The disadvantages of the direct thermal printing method include the following:

- Heat-sensitive media are more expensive.
- Print is less durable, especially when the printed labels are subjected to heat. In high temperatures, the print on the label will fade away (similar to a receipt from a gas pump left in a car during the summer).

NOTE Direct thermal printing is often used by mobile printers because this method has proven superior and more cost-effective for immediate "in the field" application of RFID/barcode labeling.

Thermal Transfer

The thermal transfer printing method requires RFID media (labels) and a printing ribbon. The ribbon is a wax- and/or resin-coated plastic strip that is available in rolls. The coating is transferred by a printhead onto a label, creating the printed information.

The advantages of the thermal transfer printing method are as follows:

- Print is more durable (especially when using a ribbon with a resin coating).
- Labels are not as heat sensitive as the labels used for direct thermal print.
- Thermal transfer printing withstands high temperatures.

The disadvantage of the thermal transfer printing method includes the following:

- It requires the added cost of using a printing ribbon.

Media (Label) Selection

There are several kinds of RFID labels. They differ by type (whether they are used for thermal transfer or direct thermal), size, and form.

As mentioned in the previous section, direct thermal labels are heat sensitive, whereas thermal transfer labels are not, but they are coated to hold the print wax and/or resin transferred from the ribbon.

TIP If you need to find out whether the label is intended for direct thermal or thermal transfer, scratch the surface of the label with your fingernail. If a black mark appears on the label, it is intended for direct thermal printing.

Labels come in various sizes; the most common are 2″ × 4″ and 4″ ×6″, but sometimes you can find 4″ × 4″ or 1″ ×4″ and other sizes. You should select the size of a label according to your requirements for the amount of information being printed on the label, the size of your product, and your choice of a tag and its antenna size and pattern. Generally, you will be able to use small labels with single dipole tags, while the dual dipole tags will require labels with a larger surface. Most companies I've worked with have an existing label requirement from their customers—there is usually some bar code (machine readable) and text (human readable) information on a standard-size label. The label manufacturers have been smart enough to understand this and make these same labels with an embedded RFID tag.

Most of the labels are supplied in the form of rolls (labels stick onto a backing and are rolled onto a core); sometimes they can be fan-fold (labels stick onto a backing and are folded zigzag into a fan). Rolls are usually placed inside the printer; however, fan-fold media can be fed to the printer through an opening in the back of the printer's body while staying in its original packaging.

TIP

If you intend to use your labels in extreme environments, mainly in extreme temperatures, make sure that you purchase labels that will withstand them. For instance, in low temperatures, the regular adhesives used on labels will not stick and you would have to find another method to ensure that the labels stay on the product. Similar problems can come up in high temperatures, when the adhesive can "melt" and stay on the label backing when you peel the label off.

Media can also be continuous (contiguous), where the labels are on an uninterrupted strip (roll) of material, or noncontinuous (noncontiguous), where a hole or a notch separates the labels.

Sometimes it can be difficult to thread the printer with the media and ribbon; therefore, in some cases, the manufacturer provides arrows on the inside of the printer's case that you can follow in order to thread the labels or ribbon correctly.

Printer Configuration and Calibration

To work properly, the installed printer has to be configured. This usually can be accomplished either directly on the printer through its front panel or through printer programming language, or remotely through middleware.

Manufacturers usually provide an option to configure their printer for printing labels and encoding RFID tags through a printer-specific programming language. For example, Zebra provides Zebra Programming Language (ZPL) and Printronix developed Printronix Programming Language (PPL). These programming languages are based on commands that are written in a text editor in a specific sequence and sent to a printer through a communication interface.

To fully set up an RFID printer, you must configure printing settings, RFID settings, and network settings. When configuring printing settings, you have to choose an appropriate print mode, media type, contrast of print and input label length, and other label positioning information.

When configuring printing and label properties, you can usually choose from default settings if you are using labels manufactured or intended for that type of printer. However, sometimes you will need to change the settings according to your application and conditions. Because the settings differ by the printer and its manufacturer, the safest way to make changes is to refer to the printer's manual.

RFID settings consist of information about the RFID tag. You have to supply the type of RFID tag (whether it is an EPC Class 0, Class 1, Class 1 Generation 2, or ISO 18000 tag part 6A or 6B) and its EPC length (64 or 96 bit) or memory length. The next setting is the inlay positioning on the label, which is important mainly if your label converter did not follow the specifications for the inlay placement given by the printer manufacturer. Another important setting is the read and write power of the printer. The recommended power is specified by the tag manufacturer. If the power is set too high, especially with small labels and inlays placed close to each other, you could read or write to neighboring tags by accident.

Communication settings include IP address, subnet mask, and default gateway. This information is important in order to communicate with your device through a network.

After the printer is configured, it is a good idea to print a configuration label. This can be done in many ways, which differ by manufacturer. The configuration label carries all the information about the printer and is useful as a record of the printer's settings for later troubleshooting. Configuration labels include not only information about the print mode, media, and sensor settings, but also network settings.

To make your job easier, most printers are able to configure themselves by calibration. There are many ways to calibrate an RFID printer, which differ by the type of printer and its manufacturer. Each type of calibration varies by the amount of time it takes to calibrate the printer, the number of labels used (they can usually be put back and used again), and its reliability. Many printers have an auto-calibration button ("Calibrate" button) on the front panel, which triggers the process of calibration when pressed. You must make sure that you calibrate the printer every time you use a new type of label and RFID inlays, especially if they are not specifically made for your type of printer.

RFID Tag Encoding

To write to tags with your RFID printer/encoder, you must make sure that your tags have encoding capability. You'll also need to know the tag's memory size. As discussed earlier in Chapter 4, "Tags," RFID tags are divided into classes. EPC Class 0 specifies that the tag is read-only; therefore, it cannot be written to. EPC Class 0+, Class 1, Class 1 Generation 2, and ISO 18000 are writable, and therefore you will be able to use an RFID printer/encoder to modify the tag's memory and encode it with information. By the end of 2006, Gen 1 tags will be obsolete and there will be no need to consider this option. What will become important are the frequency and the standard. Both Gen 2 EPC and ISO 18000 will have UHF and HF standards.

You can use the printer programming language to create your label formats. These formats will include some of the following functions:

- Set a tag type (EPC classes, ISO, and so forth)
- Read tag data
- Write tag data (a number input in hexadecimal or ASCII format)
- Print a label with data input by the user
- Print a label with data read from the tag
- Define EPC data structure
- Specify the number of read and/or write attempts to a single tag
- Verify the host computer/system
- Set RF power for reading and writing
- Set RFID tag password and other functions

You can also create label formats by using label software. Many printer manufacturers and software providers have developed easy-to-use software that will guide you through the label creation process and enable you to print and encode tags quickly and easily. This software will help you not only with basic EPC number encoding, but also with global trade item number (GTIN), serialized GTIN (SGTIN), serialized shipping container code (SSCC), and other data formats used in your supply chain. This is particularly important to the 40,000 suppliers of the DoD who do not have to pay the fees to join EPCglobal and get their numbers, but can use something called a Department of Defense address activity code (DoDAAC).

NOTE Some printers can be Extended Markup Language (XML) enabled, which increases their flexibility and interoperability with enterprise resource planning (ERP) systems. XML-enabled printers are able to print directly from common warehouse management systems (WMS), because the label formats can be directly uploaded by sending an XML data stream to a printer.

Label Applicators

Label applicators are used for automatic or semiautomatic label application to a product or packaging. They can be implemented in conjunction with RFID printers; in this system, the smart label would first be encoded and printed by the printer and then applied to a product by the label applicator. Label applicators are most suited for use with a product or packaging that does not vary in size or varies only slightly. Their advantage is their ability to apply labels at high speed with high precision.

There are several kinds of label applicators:

Automatic *Wipe-on label applicators* or *pneumatic piston label applicators* automatically place the label on a product. They are usually used on conveyors or production lines and can apply labels at high speeds.

Semiautomatic The product is manually placed in the reach of the applicator and then is automatically labeled. This type of applicator is used for short trial runs of product labeling or as a backup for automatic labeling lines.

Real World Scenario

Tag Encoding

During a slap-and-ship operation, an RFID printer was reloaded with a new roll of labels. However, initial attempts to encode the first 10 tags in the roll produced voided labels. When a local manager contacted the tag manufacturer, the manufacturer requested a swap with another roll of labels to verify whether the printer was working properly. When a new roll of labels was loaded, the machine encoded the tags correctly and did not produce any voids. As the first "problem" roll was inspected using a handheld reader, the tags were identified as being 64-bit EPC Class 1 Gen 1 tags. The reason for the voided tags was clear: a 96-bit EPC number could not be encoded into a 64-bit tag. The roll of 64-bit tags must have gotten into the batch of 96-bit tags by accident.

Handheld This type of label applicator works similarly to a pricing gun in a store and is useful for exception processing and low-volume applications.

Print-and-Apply This device includes a printer and a label applicator. After being printed (and possibly encoded, in the case of an RFID device), the label is automatically applied to a product or packaging. The applicator part of this device can be either wipe-on or pneumatic piston using compressed air or an electrical mechanism.

As mentioned, there are two main kinds of automatic label applicators: wipe-on label applicators and pneumatic piston label applicators. I bet you just can't wait to find out more about each of them, so rather than keep you in suspense I'll tell you about them now.

Wipe-on Label Applicators

Wipe-on label applicators are mostly used on a conveyor or as part of a production line, where the product or packaging moves at a constant speed and does not slow down for the label to be applied. As the item approaches the applicator, a sensor detects it and triggers the applicator to issue a label. This label is then "wiped on" the item, and a foam roller helps to press down the label to ensure its hold.

This type of label applicator can tag only items of the same size and it cannot vary the spot for the label placement. However, it can apply the label on two sides of the item as well as bend the label over an edge.

Pneumatic Piston Label Applicators

Pneumatic piston label applicators are mostly used with automated production lines because they can be applied quickly. However, some have to stop the line for a brief moment, which would be a problem when used with a common conveyor.

As the item approaches the applicator, it passes the sensor that triggers the pneumatic piston. The applicator places the label on a vacuum plate, which is then moved by the pneumatic piston to the product. The label is then pressed or blown onto this item.

Sometimes the pneumatic piston label applicator does not have to touch the product or packaging to be able to place the label on it because of its ability to use compressed air to "blow" the label onto a product. Because of its proximity sensor, which can stop the pneumatic piston according to the distance to the object, this type of applicator can label items of various sizes.

Triggering Devices

When designing an RFID network, there are times when you have to trigger the readers to read at only certain times. To reduce interference and RF noise in an environment with more than one RFID reader, you can activate the interrogation zone only when needed. There are several ways to trigger interrogations. In addition to manual triggering (rarely used, because it requires a human), timed triggering, or software triggering, a common method is to use triggering hardware, such as motion sensors.

Motion sensors can function on several principles. A common kind of motion sensor, also called "photo eye," uses an infrared or laser beam. The transmitter sends the beam across the product's path, and as the product interrupts the beam, the sensor on the other side of the path (the receiver) registers the absence of the beam and sends a signal to the interrogation zone (mostly through middleware but sometimes directly) to start interrogation in a certain time interval. This type of motion sensor often is used with intrusion alarms; in RFID systems they are often used on conveyors.

TIP

Do not forget that you need two sides in order for a photo eye sensor to work. You will need to install it on opposite sides of a conveyor belt before the interrogation zone.

Motion sensors also can work on a "radar" principle: the sensor transmits RF waves to the environment and registers the waves reflected by a passing object. You can see these sensors in stores in conjunction with automatic door openers. Proximity sensors work on a similar principle, but the reflected waves and their properties are used for calculating the object's distance from the sensor.

Feedback Devices

To ensure that appropriate actions are taken when a failure occurs in an RFID system, feedback devices are used to signal these events to responsible personnel or to a back-end system, or they can be programmed to take action. Feedback devices are also used at verification points, where they signal the validity or invalidity of a tag's function, encoding, and/or placement on the product. The most frequently used feedback devices are light stacks, sound devices, and diverters.

Light Stacks

Although you might think of a flashy light show at an old Styx concert, a light stack is a little simpler than the name might imply. It is usually a single tube with red, green, and yellow lights in it. Light stacks are often used to indicate whether the tag applied to the product or packaging functions (green for a read, red for no-read). Light stacks are used with an interrogation zone; the tag's function is verified, and the appropriate light indicates the result. There are several ways to make this work.

One method is to connect the light stack to an external I/O port through a relay circuit or a *programmable logic controller (PLC)* that can be programmed to turn on and off different lights indicating various conditions, such as reads, no-reads, read of a specific tag, and so on. PLCs also can be connected through a network and receive commands from the middleware.

Sometimes the light stack can be connected to the I/O port on the reader directly, because some readers can manage low-voltage devices without relays or PLCs and are protected from voltage spikes and ground loops.

Besides a tag read (green light) and no-read (red light or no light), light stacks can also provide other information. A red light often indicates an interrogator error, and a yellow light usually follows the booting process of the interrogator. The colors of a light stack can have different meanings, depending on the way the lights were programmed and what meaning was assigned to each color when you planned the business process change for the system.

Sound Devices

By sound, I mean noise. Beepers, buzzers, horns, or other devices producing various sound effects can be useful in environments where the interrogation zone and the light stack are out of the line of sight or as a supplement to other devices. Sound devices are not suitable for high-noise environments or places where a quiet environment is a priority. A great application for using a sound device is for asset management so that expensive items such as laptops or secure servers can be tracked through points of egress. A buzzer can be an added security device and is often coupled with a surveillance camera to track when a high-value item leaves the premises.

Diverters

Diverters, or divert gates, are used to divert a product on a conveyor or a manufacturing line based on the data read from the tag. They are also used for diverting products with nonfunctioning tags for exception processing. Divert gates have been used for a long time with barcode readers, and they work on the same principle when used with RFID systems.

A diverter is placed behind the read point and automatically routes all boxes to exception processing until a valid tag is read. Then the diverter opens and lets the valid box continue on its route. This way, all unread boxes go to exception processing, where they can be retagged, verified, and sent back on the line.

A similar principle is used for routing boxes into their appropriate dock doors. The diverter routes the boxes based on the data on the tag read by the read point. In this case, the diverter is usually managed through PLC and middleware, which indicates whether the box belongs to the particular location. This decision is made at every intersection, and boxes are routed accordingly.

NOTE Diverters work well only when the product being diverted has the same or similar RF transparency as other products on the line. Otherwise, for example, a case of water in front of a case of toilet paper on a conveyor might be read in reverse order, and the diverter would divert the wrong item. This problem can be solved by spacing the products on the conveyor and verifying that the right product is being loaded at the dock door.

Verification and Exception Handling

To make your RFID system successful and effective, it is important to make sure that the exceptions are immediately spotted and then automatically handled. How those exceptions are handled is a critical part of planning a proper RFID network. This is why the business process planning is so critical to the success of an RFID deployment.

Although the tags are tested by the manufacturer and verified by the RFID printers, that does not ensure that they will remain correctly functioning during their entire life cycle. The main reasons why the tags may stop working or cannot be read are as follows:

- Tags are damaged during the application. Reasons could be inattentive or untrained personnel, ESD, or an incorrectly set pressure on the label applicator.
- Tags are placed incorrectly on the product or packaging, and the product detunes the tag. Reasons could be personnel not following placement guidelines, a label applicator set for incorrect label placement, or the product or packaging not having been tested for best label placement.
- Tags are damaged by handling. Handling machinery can damage the tag, as can jams of boxes on the conveyor.
- Tags are incorrectly encoded, or the interrogator expects a different format or coding.

When designing your RFID system, make sure that you have sufficient verification points. Read points with feedback devices should be placed after the tag is applied to a product or packaging and before any intersection in the conveyor system. That way you can maximize the potential of your read point, not only verifying the function of the tag but also using this data for decision making, routing the box either to its destination or to exception processing.

After you choose the location of the verification points, make sure that the alerts and notifications are heard or seen. Use light stacks if you have appropriate personnel to watch them and take action, or sound devices if the verification point is out of sight. Obviously, sound devices will not be useful in high-noise environments. You can also send the alerts through the network to appropriate stations.

Make sure that all alerts are documented. The best way is to create an automated system log that captures information about what happened, the date and time, the person responsible, the problem's resolution, and other useful data. This log can be a valuable source of information for reports about your system and can provide information for managerial decisions.

Real-Time Location Systems (RTLS)

RFID technology can be used not only to identify and track single objects, but also to locate these objects within a specific area with relatively high accuracy. This can be achieved by using *real-time location systems (RTLS)*, which are based on active RFID technology.

Real World Scenario

Generation 2 Tags

In a retail distribution center, exception processing increased by 20 percent within a two-week period. The local manager cross-referenced advanced shipping notice with received goods and identified that the increase in the exception processing was due to nonfunctioning tags on products from vendor A. Vendor A started to research the malfunctioning tags but found out only that they were successfully read on departure bound to the distribution center. The distribution center contacted the RFID integrator, explained the situation, and asked them to identify the problem. The RFID integrator asked for the diverted product to be set aside. After a series of tests, the integrator found out that the tags on the diverted product were functioning, but the tag protocol was EPC Class 1 Generation 2, which had yet to be integrated into the current infrastructure of the distribution center by upgrading the reader firmware.

There are several ways of locating an item by using RTLS. One method that is currently used is triangulation (see Figure 6.1). Triangulation is based on measuring the distance between the tag and three access points (RFID interrogators), which are positioned around a specific area. In reality, there are many access points in the area that create a matrix.

When the tag sends a signal to the environment (beacons), the distance between a tag and an access point is calculated based on the time it took the signal to travel from the tag to this access point. When the distances between the tag and each of the access points are known, the area is divided into a group of triangles, and the tag's position can be calculated using trigonometry.

Of course, there is more than one way to locate the tag. Using a time response system works similarly to triangulation. The tag sends a signal to the environment, and the tag location is calculated based on the difference in time it took the signal to travel from the tag to each access point. This principle is called *differential time of arrival (DTOA)*.

FIGURE 6.1 Triangulation

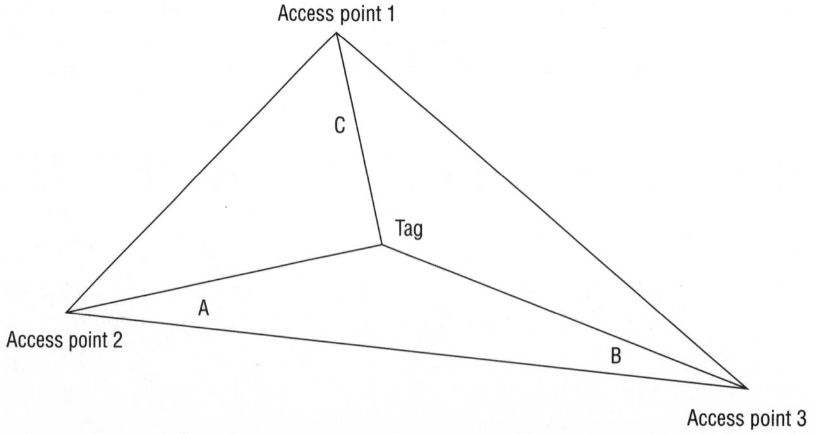

Another method of locating an item by using RTLS is based on the signal strength, or *received signal strength indication (RSSI)*. The closer the tag is to the access point, the stronger the signal that will be received by the interrogator. Because the location of the access points is known, the tagged object will be found according to the closest access point.

RTLS is often compared to a global positioning system (GPS) because of its locating capabilities. However, locating objects through GPS requires a line of sight to a satellite; therefore, it cannot be used in buildings or underground. RTLS is not restricted by satellite but uses its own access point matrix, which can be located virtually anywhere.

As with any RF-based technology, the signals can be reflected, absorbed, or distorted by various environmental conditions and RF interference, which would corrupt the distance measurements and the precision of the system. For this reason, most RTLS providers certify an accuracy of 7 to 15 feet.

Summary

In this chapter, you learned about various peripherals that can be implemented with the RFID system. Some are necessary for printing labels and encoding tags, others are used to trigger interrogation or provide feedback about the result of tag function verification.

In the first section, you learned about the function of and reason for implementation of RFID printers/encoders. RFID printers are often used for slap-and-ship or exception processing. They not only print information on the labels, but also encode and verify the embedded RFID tags. You learned guidelines for printer installation and configuration and found out about printer calibration and various ways it can be performed. Also, in order to encode the tags, you have to have the right kind. I described the two main printing methods that use different kinds of media.

Next, you learned about different kinds of label applicators and the applications they are most suitable for. The wipe-on label applicator is best for same-sized products or packaging, whereas the pneumatic piston label applicator can handle different sizes of boxes because of its proximity sensor. This type of label applicator also can apply the labels without touching the item by blowing the label on.

Following printers and label applicators, you learned about triggering devices and their importance. To reduce the RF noise in the environment as well as increase the interrogation zone efficiency, you should trigger interrogation only when needed. For this purpose, you would install motion sensors or use timed, software, or manual triggering.

After triggering devices, you learned about feedback devices. You learned that light stacks and sound devices such as buzzers and horns are used to provide an alert if the tag is not functioning. Diverters can then route each item with a nonfunctioning tag to the exception processing area, where the item can be retagged. Of course, light stacks, buzzers, and diverters can be used for other types of signaling and for routing products to their appropriate locations.

You learned that the tags can stop functioning and that is why you have to place verification points throughout your system. You must verify the tag after it is applied on the product or packaging.

The last section of this chapter was dedicated to real-time location systems, their function, and their use. You learned that to locate an item (tagged with an active tag), the system uses triangulation or signal strength measurements; the usual accuracy distance is around 7 to 15 feet.

Exam Essentials

Know how to install and configure an RFID printer. Place the printer on a solid, level surface and ensure proper ventilation and access to all buttons, ports, and cables. Connect the printer to the network through a network cable or wirelessly. Plug a supplied or manufacturer-approved power cord into the printer and into a grounded power outlet. Select the correct media for your printer and possibly a ribbon. Configure the printer for printing mode, print settings, label settings, RFID settings, and network settings. The printer can configure itself by calibration.

Explain the function of an RFID printer. An RFID printer has an integrated RFID reader board that enables this device to not only print data on a label, but also verify and encode an RFID tag. An RFID printer uses media (labels with integrated RFID inlay) and sometimes a printing ribbon.

Explain the two print modes. Thermal transfer mode uses media and a printing ribbon. The coating from the ribbon is transferred to a label by a printhead using heat. Direct thermal mode does not use a printing ribbon but it does use heat-sensitive media. The print appears on the label as the hot printhead touches the media. This type of print is not suitable for labels that will be in high-temperature environments.

Explain the function of a pneumatic piston label applicator. A vacuum plate with a label is moved by a pneumatic piston to a product. The label is then placed or blown onto the item. This type of label applicator has a proximity sensor; therefore, it is suitable for different sizes of boxes, but requires a short stop for each label to be applied.

Explain the function of a wipe-on label applicator. A label is wiped onto a product while pressed by a foam roller. This label applicator is used mainly for same-sized boxes and does not require stopping.

Explain the function of different feedback devices. Light stacks or buzzers are usually used to notify personnel as to whether the tag functions. Diverters route the product based on the information from the tag.

Know the importance of verification points in the system. The tags can be damaged or stop functioning throughout their life cycle; therefore, it is important to implement verification points mainly after the tag is applied to a product. It may be damaged by application, incorrectly encoded, or have incorrect placement on the product.

Know the principle of RTLS. Real-time location systems use active RFID technology. RTLS is based on a matrix of access points (readers) in the area and the active tag beaconing to the environment. The location of the tagged object can then be calculated by triangulation, by using time or signal strength.

Key Terms

Before you take the exam, be certain you are familiar with the following terms:

differential time of arrival (DTOA)

direct thermal

electrostatic discharge (ESD)

pneumatic piston label applicators

programmable logic controller (PLC)

real-time location systems (RTLS)

received signal strength indication (RSSI)

slap-and-ship

thermal transfer

wipe-on label applicators

Review Questions

1. Which type of label applicator would you use on a conveyor carrying high volumes of same-sized products?
   A. Automatic pneumatic piston label applicator
   B. Handheld label applicator
   C. Semiautomatic label applicator
   D. Automatic wipe-on label applicator
2. Which power cord will you purchase if your RFID printer does not come with one?
   A. Two-prong power cord, ISO certified
   B. Three-prong power cord, certified by one of the international safety organizations and approved by the manufacturer
   C. Three-prong power cord, certified by a major electrical supply store
   D. Two-prong power cord, certified by one of the international safety organizations
3. What is the name of the process in which you use the RFID printer/encoder to print and encode RFID labels that are placed only on products shipped to a certain customer?
   A. Print-and-apply
   B. Slap-and-ship
   C. Peel-and-present
   D. Print-and-slap
4. The printer continuously issues "void" labels since the beginning of the roll. What can be the problem? (Select two options.)
   A. You accidentally threaded the printer with plain labels (without RFID inlays).
   B. The tag's antenna was damaged during label transportation.
   C. You used a roll from your new label converter for the first time.
   D. The printer ran out of ribbon.
5. Which type of printing will you use for labels that will be placed on pallets that will be stored in a warehouse in Texas? This warehouse does not have temperature control.
   A. Direct thermal.
   B. Thermal transfer.
   C. Laser print.
   D. It does not matter; these methods are all equal.

6. How would you prevent electrostatic discharge (ESD)?
   A. By using proper grounding and a humidifier.
   B. ESD is not a problem.
   C. By frequently touching the problematic device with a static brush.
   D. By using a secondary ground.

7. What are the functions of the RFID printer/encoder?
   A. Tag encoding and verification and printing only human-readable information on a label
   B. Tag encoding and verification and printing any information on a label
   C. Tag encoding and verification, after the label is printed
   D. Printing information on a label, tag encoding, verification, and application on the product

8. Where would you place a light sensor to trigger the interrogation?
   A. Under the conveyor belt and before the interrogation zone
   B. Above the conveyor belt and after the interrogation zone
   C. Slightly above the conveyor belt and before the interrogation zone, on the right and left sides of the belt
   D. Slightly above the conveyor belt and before the interrogation zone, on the right

9. Which type of label applicator can place a label without touching the product or packaging?
   A. None. A label applicator always has to touch the product.
   B. Handheld label applicator.
   C. Pneumatic piston label applicator.
   D. Wipe-on label applicator.

10. You are starting a pilot project for tagging products on one of your manufacturing lines, but you are not sure of the right place to tag your product. What do you use for your test before you make a decision?
    A. Automatic label applicator
    B. Handheld label applicator
    C. Manual application of labels
    D. Semiautomatic label applicator

11. What principle do you use to calculate a tag's position in real-time location systems?
    A. Triangulation
    B. Pythagorean theorem
    C. Ampere's law
    D. Derivations

12. What type of RFID technology are real-time location systems based on?
    A. Passive RFID systems
    B. Semi-passive RFID systems
    C. Active RFID systems
    D. Active and passive RFID systems

13. What is the main advantage of RTLS (real-time location system) over GPS (global positioning system)?
    A. RTLS can be used inside or outside, GPS only inside.
    B. RTLS can be used only inside, GPS only outside.
    C. RTLS can be used inside or outside, GPS only outside.
    D. RTLS uses a satellite.

14. You need to install RFID printers/encoders in your warehouse for a slap-and-ship application, but you do not wish to run network cables. Your offices use a wireless network. Will you be able to communicate wirelessly with your RFID printers/encoders? (Select two options.)
    A. Yes, if the printer has integrated 802.11 wireless capability or through a print server.
    B. No. RFID printers/encoders can communicate only through RS-232.
    C. Yes, through an Ethernet print server.
    D. Yes, if the printer has integrated Bluetooth communication capability.

15. How do you calibrate an RFID printer?
    A. By opening and closing the printhead
    B. By turning the printer off and back on again
    C. By pressing a Calibrate button or the equivalent or through a menu on the printer's display
    D. By pressing a Feed button or the equivalent

16. How do you make sure that the boxes that are coming from your exception processing station have fully functioning tags?
    A. Tags are tested by the RFID printer; therefore, they will function.
    B. By placing an interrogation zone for verification after the box is retagged and before it leaves the exception-processing station.
    C. By placing an interrogation zone for verification before the box reaches the first intersection leading to the dock door.
    D. By testing tags before they are applied to the product.

17. How do you configure a diverter to make sure that the boxes with nonreadable tags will be routed to exception processing?

  A. Connect a motion sensor with a diverter to make sure that the diverter does not miss any boxes.

  B. Set the diverter's default position to route all boxes to exception processing. When a valid tag is read, the diverter will open and route it to its destination.

  C. Set the diverter's default position to route all boxes to their destinations; when a valid tag is not read, the diverter will open and route it to exception processing.

  D. Connect the diverter to the interrogator through a PLC.

18. What is the easiest way to find out the current settings of a printer?

  A. Print a configuration label.

  B. Look up the settings on the display on the printer's front panel.

  C. Find the settings in the manual.

  D. Figure out the settings according to printed labels.

19. What type of feedback device would you use in a noisy warehouse?

  A. Buzzer

  B. Light stack

  C. Motion sensor

  D. B and C

20. When in doubt, set the read and write power settings of the printer for the maximum. Is this statement true?

  A. Yes, maximum power will ensure reading and writing of the tag.

  B. Yes, maximum power will ensure that the tag is read or written correctly.

  C. No, it is important to follow the tag manufacturer's guidelines for reading and writing power, or the printer could read or write to a neighboring tag instead.

  D. No, it is important to follow the printer manufacturer's guidelines for reading and encoding power settings.

Answers to Review Questions

1. D. The automatic wipe-on label applicator will be the most suitable for use on a conveyor with high volumes of same-sized products. This type of applicator does not require the product to stop in order to apply the label and handles high volumes, which handheld or semiautomatic applicators usually do not. A pneumatic piston label applicator is more suitable for production lines where the product can be briefly stopped, and accommodates different sizes of products.

2. B. You should use a cord approved by the printer manufacturer. This cord will have a three-prong plug and will be certified by one of the international safety organizations.

3. B. Slap-and-ship is a process in which the labels are printed, encoded, and placed on products that are shipped only to a mandating customer. In this case, RFID is not used for the benefit of the internal business process.

4. A, C. If you accidentally use a roll of labels that does not include RFID inlays, the printer will keep looking for the inlay and will print "void" on each label if it does not find the inlay. Your new converter might not have followed the guidelines for inlay placement on the labels that are published by the printer manufacturer, and you may not have calibrated the printer for these new labels.

5. B. Thermal transfer is preferred because the labels used for this type of printing are not heat sensitive and therefore do not fade or darken when subjected to heat.

6. A. You should use proper grounding, possibly an air humidifier, and other ESD protection methods such as static mats for personnel.

7. B. An RFID printer/encoder can print any information on a label, including bar codes, and provides tag encoding and verification before the label is printed.

8. C. For the light sensor to work, it has to have a transmitter and receiver of the light beam. Therefore, both parts have to be mounted slightly above the conveyor belt, on opposite sides of the belt. The light sensor has to be mounted before the interrogation zone, because the product crosses the beam and the sensor sends a signal to the interrogator to start polling.

9. C. Some pneumatic piston label applicators provide touchless application by blowing the label onto the product or packaging.

10. D. For pilot projects and other low-volume testing projects, you should use a semiautomatic label applicator because it is a lot faster than handheld or manual tagging, but also cheaper and more flexible than a fully integrated automatic label applicator.

11. A. Triangulation is used to calculate a tag's position in RTLS.

12. C. Real-time location systems use active RFID technology, which is based on a tag that sends a signal to the environment. This signal is then received by the readers. According to the time the signal needed to travel from the tag to each reader, the tag's location can be calculated using triangulation.

13. C. RTLS can be used inside of buildings as well as outside because it does not need a line of sight to a satellite as GPS does.

14. A, D. RFID printer manufacturers usually provide a possibility of wireless communication through additional print servers enabling wireless 802.11 or Bluetooth communication. Some printers have these capabilities integrated.

15. C. A printer usually can be calibrated by pressing a Calibrate button or the equivalent, depending on the manufacturer, which is usually located on the front panel. The calibration command usually can also be located through a menu on the display. In either case, refer to the printer manual.

16. B. Tags can be damaged during application or might not function because of wrong placement on the product; therefore, you should test their function after they are applied to the box. The best way to test them is to place an interrogation zone with a light stack or buzzer that would verify the tag's function before the box leaves the exception-processing area.

17. B. The diverter has to be set to route all boxes to exception processing unless the tag is read and proved valid. If the tag is read by the interrogator, the diverter opens and lets this box continue to its destination. If the tag is not read, the diverter does not get any command, because the interrogator does not register the existence of this box and therefore cannot send a signal to the diverter to route it to exception processing.

18. A. The easiest way to find out current settings of an RFID printer is to print the configuration label, which carries information about printing settings, RFID settings, and network settings.

19. B. In a noisy environment, a buzzer would not be heard; therefore, it is more suitable to use a light stack.

20. C. It is important to follow guidelines for your RFID tag, including reading and writing power settings of your RFID printer/encoder. If the power was set too high, especially with small labels and inlays placed close to each other, you could read or write to neighboring tags by accident.

Chapter 7

Deployment and Installation

RFID+ EXAM OBJECTIVES COVERED IN THIS CHAPTER:

✓ **6.1 Given a scenario, describe hardware installation using industry standard practices**

- 6.1.1 Identify grounding considerations (e.g., lightning, ground loops, ESD)
- 6.1.2 Test installed equipment and connections (preinstall and postinstall)

✓ **6.2 Given a scenario, interpret a site diagram created by an RFID architect describing interrogation zone locations, cable drops, device-mounting locations**

It's show time *bayyyy-beeee*! The words of Dick Vitale should echo through your head before every RFID deployment. The industry is so new and exciting that each RFID deployment is like making it to the NCAA Final Four. If you're a mom-and-pop shop and pull off a great deployment, you could be the Cinderella story of the industry. If you're working for a large systems integrator or an RFID company making its living from the technology, you'd better know your stuff before you walk in the door.

CompTIA assumes most of the people being certified are likely to be the ones actually doing the hands-on work, so the exam spends a fair amount of time validating many of the principles around deployment and installation of RFID systems. This chapter will give you the key fundamentals as you learn about the following:

- Setting up a process and team structure to mange an RFID installation
- Figuring out how to perform quality control on RFID portals
- Using your site-survey and design documents for the install
- Properly configuring an RFID reader
- Working with your client to define acceptance testing protocols
- Knowing what to do with new team members

At the end of the chapter, you should have a good understanding of how the preinstallation work that you have done comes to fruition with actually setting up the readers to be installed on the premises.

NOTE This chapter has many tricks of the trade from ODIN Technologies' top engineers about what to look out for when deploying RFID systems in the real world.

Providing a Methodology for Managing an Installation

The crux of doing a great job as an RFID technician or engineer is the installation. If you are focusing your career on RFID and you are good at installing the systems and can run a project start-to-finish, you can write your ticket in the RFID industry. I have hired dozens of folks over the past few years, and for each hire I have them do a homework assignment. For an RF technician position, I usually assign a virtual RFID deployment in which I'll lay out a deployment scenario and see how that person would approach the deployment.

Every one of these assignments has some traps set for the folks who really don't know the details of RFID or who may not have that much experience. The biggest issue I have found with RF technicians is that many of them can run cable and bolt down RFID racks, but they don't have a good sense for running a project. They don't know how to make incremental steps to get to the final result—as the old saying goes, how do you eat an elephant? One bite at a time.

The steps for managing an installation methodology are as follows:

- Set up the RFID technical design team
- Create a project plan, or *plan of action and milestones (POAM)*
- *Follow a quality control (QC) process to evaluate the readers*
- Design a process to manage sub-contractors
- Pre-certify and configure the readers
- Deploy on-site

Role and Benefit of the Technical Design Review Team

Step 1 of the methodology for managing an installation is to start building the team. The Technical Design Review Team (TDRT) should serve as a checkpoint for all site *bill of materials (BOM) which is all the RFID equipment that is required for a deployment* and *deployment topology*—or where each reader is going to be installed at the physical location, designs prior to sign-off and procurement. This really needs to take place after the site analysis, after the hardware selection, and prior to installation.

Because this chapter is all about installation and Chapter 5 "Designing the RFID Network," dealt with reader selection and design, now is the time to look at putting together a project design team. The team should be made up of your company's project leader and the client company's project leader, plus facilities, IT, and RFID engineers who will be impacted by the installation of an RFID network.

A TDRT will ensure that there is a technical review and best practices consistency prior to ordering equipment and performing on-site installation. Employing RFID subject matter expertise in this way will ensure consistency across deployments and identify avoidable problems prior to on-site installation.

Role and Benefit of the Quality Assurance Team

After the TDRT is in place, you will need to make sure that work being performed is top-notch. This is where the next team is focused. The Quality Assurance (QA) Team should make sure that before any hardware is shipped to the client's site, it complies with all standards and regulations, and that it is ready to be installed and nothing is missing. Usually the QA team is made up of experienced deployment engineers who know how to run test equipment like spectrum analyzers. The QA team should make sure the following five points are covered in their process:

- Equipment receipt and assignment to installation site BOM
- FCC part-15 compliance
- RF measurement of reader performance to ensure specification conformance
- Portal preassembly and labeling of each component
- BOM consolidation and shipment

There are several benefits of having a QA team. First, testing the readers is important because much of the current RFID equipment shipped can be in violation of FCC specification. This can cause illegal deployments and less than 100 percent accurate performance.

Second, having a faulty reader show up on-site could delay installation timelines while you wait for a replacement. Considering shipping times and the time needed to discover the problem, you might have an entire engineering team standing around twiddling their fingers and waiting for a reader to be express-shipped the next day.

Third, the preconfiguration of readers and preassembly of portals based on the RF path loss contour maps completed during the site survey will significantly streamline the on-site installation process.

Finally, the association and consolidation of the orders into a single shipment will increase shipping accuracy and simplify receiving processes and time at the distribution depots.

Real World Scenario

Breaking the Law

A once high-flying RFID reader company, Applied Wireless Identifications Group (AWID) faces a very uncertain future because they not only were caught shipping RFID readers that violated FCC regulations, part 15, but also never even applied for the license to sell equipment covered by those regulations.

This puts the company and its key employees in potential legal trouble and also, any of their clients who has a reader currently deployed now has to rip out that old investment and replace it with readers that are in compliance. Knowing what is in spec and what is not can save an awful lot of time and money in the long run.

Execute with Military Precision: the POAM

My extensive work with the U.S. Department of Defense (DoD) has shown the value of having what the military—those crazy band of acronym creators—term the *plan of action and milestones, or POAM*. This is one of the most straightforward documents you could ever create, but generating one is valuable beyond most other things that you can do when getting ready for a deployment. The POAM lays down the concrete steps to successful completion of an installation. The steps can be broadly defined as follows:

1. Determine the project team.
2. Set a kick-off meeting.
3. Determine how long each facility will take to be deployed.
4. Map out interrogation zone (IZ) locations at each facility (RFID network topology).
5. Create a BOM based on the network topology.
6. Create a deployment timeline to include the following:
    - Ordering time
    - Shipping time
    - Precertification
    - Site prep
    - Installation
7. Create an acceptance testing timeline.

NOTE

The U.S. federal government gets more specific and even indicates the look of a POAM as an eight-column classification that details what weakness is being addressed by the project, who is responsible, what budget is required, and so forth. It is worth looking at for more details : `http://www.whitehouse.gov/omb/memoranda/m02-01.html`. detail

At the very least, you should take your site survey plan and either enter it into an automated program such as EasyReader, or manually sit down with your client to map out the RFID network.

The first step is to combine the site survey material, business process work, and other pertinent information to lay out the RFID network on actual blueprints or engineering drawings. This visual display should be augmented with a timeline, resource planning (often referred to as level of effort, or LOE), and dependencies to create the POAM.

Real World Scenario

To Get an A, Focus on the M

To be rated top by your clients, the best thing you can do prior to the actual deployment is to create metrics that are easily measurable. The "M" in "POAM" is for "milestones." The milestones should be determined prior to the start of the project. How those milestones are measured will be critical to ensuring that everyone is on the same page and that you and your client can determine success. As I always say, you can't manage what you can't measure.

Implementing QC Processes for RFID Systems

A challenge that we face in the nascent RFID industry is lack of quality manufacturing and assembly standards from new manufacturers. Quality control (QC) is something often passed over in favor of speed or cost. Although many see this as growing pains in the industry, those pains should not be passed on to end users. If they are, the industry will be slower to adopt it and reported results will be skewed because of poor equipment.

As an implementer of RFID technology, you hold responsibility to make sure that you perform every deployment to the best of your ability, particularly if you are carrying a CompTIA RFID+ certification with you. There are two simple but very effective processes that you can execute to make sure that the overall quality of the deployment is top notch:

Create a Complete Bill of Materials The project management document—whether it's in Excel, Project, or EasyReader—should have a dedicated section to track the BOM. Each standard piece of equipment and application (dock door, conveyor, printer stations) should have a dedicated list of materials such as *Programmable Logic Controller (PLC)* which controls devices attached by the reader like light stacks and directional gates, connectors, cables, and other ancillary products. Making sure that all of these items are associated with the reader's IP address is the easiest way to keep from losing the associated items. Figure 7.1 shows EasyReader's primary BOM tracking screen. Note that the reader and antennas are all associated with one primary IP address. Those actual pieces of hardware will also have that IP address affixed to the outside for easy verification.

FIGURE 7.1 BOM tracking via IP address in EasyReader

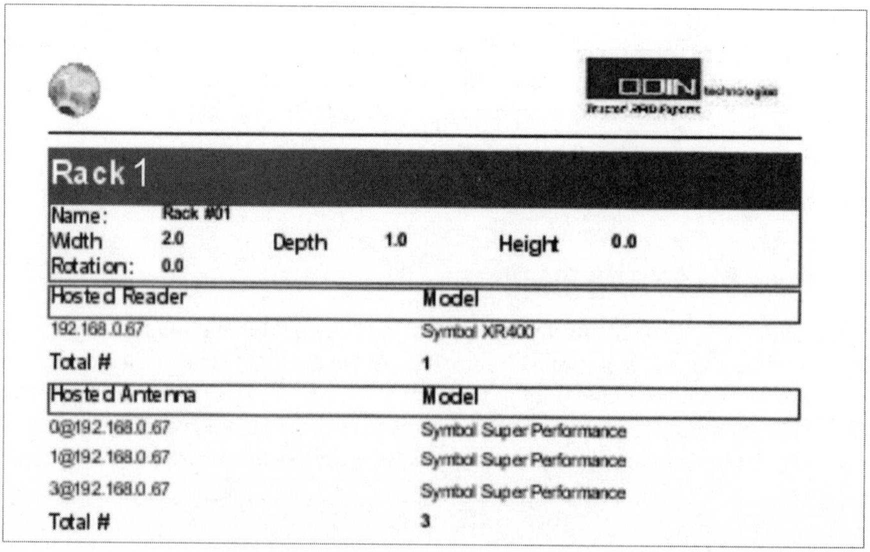

Test Readers for Compliance and Performance Testing the readers is the key first step to making sure you don't waste time, money, or effort in the on-site deployment. Remember, the more work you can do in a controlled, clean, quiet lab environment, the better. The following process has been proven over hundreds of reader deployments all across the globe. If you can use this type of process to get ready for the actual on-site deployment, you will be well prepared to succeed.

The first step toward configuring an RFID system is to set up a software tool (such as ODIN's EasyReader or even a hand-built Excel spreadsheet) to track the configuration of each RFID portal. If you don't know where each component is and where is has to go, you'll find out when you arrive on-site that pieces are missing or components are faulty.

As you prepare to test and configure the reader for predeployment, it is most helpful to set up a repeatable, measurable methodology to help the deployment scale. What we have found most effective is to set up an assembly-line-like process using long tables so that tests and configurations are set up right next to each other, as shown in Figure 7.2.

There are five key steps to pre-kitting of the readers. They are:

1. Assign all subcomponents—light stack, antennas, uninterruptible power supply, and so forth—to each portal. This means having numbers and an identification system for your portal or associating each peripheral and required component to a specific reader. That way, when everything gets tested, it can be put together.

FIGURE 7.2 The testing and certification setup for RFID readers

2. Record serial numbers for reader, printer, and PLC into a spreadsheet or EasyReader so that each serial number is mapped to a physical location on the site. Each location should have a specific reader and system setup.
3. Assign a virtual IP address to each hardware device in the spreadsheet or EasyReader. This step makes it a lot easier for the network folks at the client site. Before you get on-site, ask the network guy for a block of virtual IP addresses that you can preload onto each reader. Just make sure that you keep track of each reader and its location to make sure that you are not confusing readers by IP address.
4. Test each reader and associate the results with the specific device and serial number either in the spreadsheet or your software program. Testing the reader requires the following tests:
   - Record conducted power output measurements at each reader port. To do this, you need to attach either a power meter or a spectrum analyzer to each port and turn on the reader to full power. You also need to set a threshold for failure—usually a variance of 5 percent is acceptable. So for a UHF reader, we would look for an average of 1 watt in the United States. If it goes to 1.05 or down to 0.95, that is acceptable, but beyond that would cause the reader to be failed because it does not meet FCC compliance. Knowing the regional regulations is critical to understanding the testing requirements.
   - If power exceeds 1 watt of conducted power, mark the reader noncompliant with FCC specs and return the reader to the manufacturer.
   - Conduct a basic functionality check.
   - Configure the IP address on the reader based on an EasyReader or Excel spreadsheet assignment.
5. After the reader is tested, the next step is to configure the reader based on the site survey and analysis. If you have planned correctly, you should know which reader is going to a dock door, which reader is going to a conveyor, and so forth. At this point you need to start planning for shipment and making sure that the right hardware gets to the right location. This is usually where we create an IP address label and affix it to the reader's exterior.

The associated peripherals need to be set up, tested, and associated with a location in your spreadsheet or in EasyReader. The next logical item to test out and make sure it meets the needs of the particular location is the antennas. For each antenna, you have to make sure that you have adequate cable and that you bundle with the antennas any connectors needed to attach the antennas and cable together. Keep in mind that if you have a mono-static antenna, you need only one cable, and if you have a bi-static antenna, you need two cables for every antenna going with the reader.

The *light stack* is a critical piece of equipment that marries the business process and the workers interfacing with the RFID system, with the technology. The challenge is that most light stacks (the red, yellow, green indicator lights to signal people about an RFID read) are not Plug and Play with an RFID reader. Therefore you need to use some sort of controlling box. This is usually a PLC box. To communicate with the box, you'll need to connect through *Telnet* (the protocol for remotely accessing a device over the network) into the PLC and configure the box according to your business process specifications.

TIP When you connect through Telnet into the PLC to configure it for the light stack, make sure you issue an Activate Light command for all three colors in the light stack. To keep your items straight, create an ID tag for the light stack that associates the PLC with the light stack and the reader.

There are two other pieces of hardware that will need to be tracked and prepped prior to being shipped out the door: the printer and any handheld units that you have slated for deployment. The preconfiguration testing for both of those items is quite similar: turn them on, write or read a tag, and power them down.

By following the processes I've outlined for testing and certifying hardware, you will be ready to ship out all your equipment and organize your team on-site.

Getting the Team Ready On-site

I remember the first big client engagement we did at ODIN Technologies. It was exciting because of the real-world scope, and the tension was heightened because it was a classified engagement within the federal government. What I wasn't ready for were all the details involved with getting on-site: when and where we had access, who would bring in what, where things would be shipped, and what seemed like 100 other little details. The project was a big success, despite its multi-frequency, multi-protocol, multi-vendor complexity. Looking back on that blessed day several years ago, I can easily see how much room for improvement there was and how many things we learned.

What I'll share with you now are some of the lessons I've learned over the years in doing scores of projects all around the world.

Logistics and Access Management

When you put together your POAM, you need to add in some assumptions—for example, when you can get on-site, who will be arriving, and how long they will stay. This of course is critical on classified facilities, but it is becoming standard practice even in many global corporations operating in this world of heightened security. Logistics and access management are components that many teams do not stress. This ends up causing full team delays that are completely avoidable, and there is nothing worse than having half a dozen guys standing around unproductive for a couple of hours because there are access or logistics problems.

The key is to communicate the logistics are regarding the people and products that need to be in place to execute the necessary tasks. This includes site access, bill of materials delivery, and travel plans. The flow of information goes through the project management office (PMO) to the deployment team, and to on-site point of contacts.

For each site visit—whether for site survey, site prep, or deployment—the PMO office should contact the on-site facilities person and coordinate schedule. The PMO office should follow up with a detailed e-mail that gives the timeline for arrival on-site and shares contact information with all parties involved (particularly if there are subcontractors).

Communications

Even the smartest engineers and best equipment can create a failed RFID deployment if the communication strategy is weak. Specifically as an RFID+ engineer, you will need to know about project management and planning for deployments, but doing it right requires having a solid process in place for communication. It is easy to spend a lot of time talking with your client point of contact, but what about the subcontractors who might be putting in electrical outlets, installing bollards, or running Cat 6 cable? These too often go overlooked in the initial project planning and then that omission creates a cascading problem once on-site.

One of the most critical aspects of any subcontracting plan is the communications plan. To aid in communication in the project, you should create a means of simple communication, such as a secure Web-based portal where the team can come together to share knowledge and to access information relevant to the project. This is a good model to follow. There are also a number of tools and techniques that you can apply to ensure a smooth and predictable flow of information that helps keep the project on track. Standard project management and program management models such as the Microsoft Excel- or Project-based POAM and the EasyReader bill of materials can both be easily shared. Training RFID project team members as Six Sigma trainees or in PMI's Project Management Professional program also helps.

A well-defined and established communication plan is critical to managing multiple tasks and subcontractors in a project of this size. You need to create a plan that takes into account all of the key project participants and tasks and use tools to ensure that the overall program stays on track.

NOTE

At ODIN, we differentiate between the content being communicated, the mechanism for communication, the tools for managing content, and the timing of communication. These factors represent the "what," "how," "where" and "when" of effective communication.

There are four key content areas that will be critical for communication for any successful RFID project:

- Project status
- Execution coordination
- Procedure
- Artifacts

We will look at these in the following sections.

Project Status Information

Project status information is general information that is relevant to all parties engaged in the project. Information elements of project status include the following:

- Activity definition and tracking
- Issue tracking

- Weekly project status summaries
- Deliverable tracking
- Team contact information

Although many project participants contribute to this content, it is the responsibility of the PMO to maintain and communicate to all parties involved. This is particularly important for scope change or timeline adjustments.

Execution Coordination Information

Execution coordination is the next critical area of control around communication. With multiple teams and large amounts of equipment shipping to different sites, it becomes even more essential to have detailed coordination pertaining to the logistics of the people and equipment, the access to the facilities, and the deployment specification itself. If any of the execution coordination is misaligned, it can add significant extra travel costs and project delays, so this information must be tracked carefully.

The distribution of execution coordination communications will be based on the events that are taking place. For example, people and equipment logistics information should be posted to the secure project portal I mentioned earlier. It can then be pushed out to the teams at a site level on various sites. Access to the facility will be provided to each team member individually to ensure that they know exactly where they are going, whom they need to meet with, and what kind of security paperwork they may need in order to get access to a site, or where prepackaged equipment needs to be delivered and staged, if that is different from the original delivery spot.

Procedural Information

The more secure and larger the company that you are dealing with, the more likely they will require you to adhere to strict procedural standards. General procedure information should be distributed to team members when they first start the project. As part of the on-boarding process, creating a method for training will give information and documentation that can be referred to at a later date. This ensures that new and existing team members will have the tools they need to work effectively within the team.

Of course, as the project grows and new people are added, you should make sure to set up training meetings to introduce the members to the teams, the project methodologies and best practices, and management processes that will be employed. The PMO will maintain procedural information to ensure consistency and make the content available as needed throughout the project.

Project Artifacts Information

Finally, a number of artifacts are generated both in the process of a deployment as well as in deliverables for a deployment. An *artifact* is simply a document or deliverable that is specific to the client. The artifacts are generated on an event basis and may be either simple work-in-process (WIP) artifacts that are made available for the team's use or deliverables that are submitted in fulfillment of required work products. Most of the project artifacts will be developed by the deployment teams and will be used by the teams that are responsible for troubleshooting and maintenance of the RFID network.

Subcontractor Management

Earlier in the chapter, I mentioned subcontractor management as being one of the biggest overlooked facets of a deployment. It's important to ensure that subcontractors are providing the best possible value by checking and measuring performance against defined goals and metrics. There are two pillars to the management of subcontractors:

- On-boarding and checkpointing
- Quality and conformance control

Each pillar plays an important role when dealing with a diverse team that is composed of different companies and multiple stakeholders.

On-boarding and Checkpointing

The on-boarding process begins with initiation and training of the staff that will be joining the team. The goal is to make sure that any members new to the team are fully aware of how you will operate and know the rules of engagement for the project. Each integrator or engineering shop has their own way of doing things, and each project manager may have strengths and weaknesses. Making sure you are aware of those before you manage a subcontractor or look for a subcontractor who can augment the weaknesses is paramount to a successful relationship. On-boarding is usually a three- or four-day process when getting a subcontractor up to speed on how you do RFID.

After the subcontractor is trained, you should create checkpoint reviews after the first site survey and deployment. The checkpoints ensure that the subcontractor is reviewed for performance outside of the site-by-site compliance, and it provides an opportunity to provide feedback from both the subcontractor and from your team. This is why strong project management can have such a positive impact on an RFID deployment's success.

Quality and Conformance Control

Throughout an RFID project, you have to make sure that there are processes in place to confirm that each task and milestone is completed with the level of quality necessary for the deployment and that each subcontractor is executing in conformance to the specifications. There are three key tools you can use to track quality and conformance:

Infrastructure Analysis Checklist This details all of the elements involved in each deployment. The checklist should go through quality checks on electrical, site prep, network, debris removal, protection placement, and all of the other key elements that go into analyzing and deploying a site.

Quality Assurance Reviews This should be conducted to make sure that each item on the checklist is being executed up to the level that is required and that the equipment functions as expected. These reviews are conducted both randomly and at scheduled intervals. By using this dual approach, quality consistency is assured.

Quality Management Plan This is owned by the PMO. The plan is then tracked during the weekly reviews. The quality management plan includes an overall plan, the tasks to execute the plan, audits and reports that come out of the deployment teams and the Technical Design Review Team, and metrics that are used to measure and report quality.

Installing an RFID System

Although it may seem like there is a lot leading up to the actual on-site deployment of an RFID network, the up-front work can really pay off when you are on-site. My father used to say, "Measure twice and cut once." This is from a guy who had a circular saw that for at least 15 years never made it out of the box. Nonetheless, his advice has stuck with me.

The work getting the site analysis, creating a POAM, and putting communications standards in place will all meld together to make sure that deployment goes quickly and without surprises. The following sections will give you the step by step process to install the RFID network.

Marrying Design Documents with Installation

The site analysis and design document are your blueprints to start building your RFID network. Ideally, you should use a tool such as Microsoft Visio to put together the design of each portal location so that you and anyone else on the installation team knows what the final installation will look like.

Take a look at Figure 7.3 for an average dock door layout.

FIGURE 7.3 Visio diagram of an average dock door

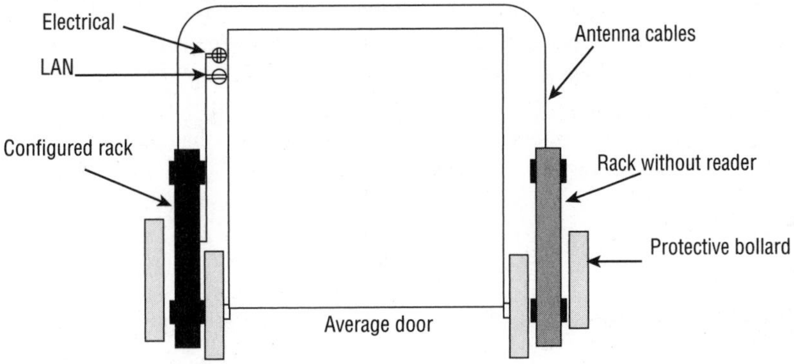

It is always a good idea to get on-site a day or two before the actual equipment arrives. Bring your blueprints or your deployment software and make sure all the portal locations that you laid out in the site survey have everything they need for proper installation of the portals. The big things to look for are as follows:

1. Proper electric circuits dedicated to the RFID reader
2. Adequate grounding for electric outlets
3. Local area network (LAN) connection punch-down
4. Live LAN connection or WiFi connection
5. Clear, nonobstructed installation space

WARNING

A *ground loop* is caused by an unexpected current that flows in a conductor and connects two points that are technically at the same potential, but are actually at different potentials. Because the potentials are different, this causes one of the points to be out of balance and usually results in some circuitry being overloaded and burnt out.

Securing Electrical and LAN Connections

Refer back to Figure 7.3 and you'll notice that there is a clear representation for the electrical and LAN connections. After the site survey, you should have a good idea of where each dedicated 110 V circuit for the RFID reader needs to be to make the deployment successful. If you can standardize the location and create a very clear layout, similar to Figure 7.3, you will save a lot of time, money, and headaches.

The diagram of the portal layout should be distributed to the site electrician who can then know exactly where to put the electrical or LAN connections. The first thing you do when you get on-site is to make sure that these are in the proper location and are functioning properly. Testing power is easy: plug something in and turn it on, or use a circuit tester. The LAN requires a little help from a network analyzer or special LAN connection testing device. Either way, make sure you test connectivity as one of the first things when you get on-site.

Different objects can possess a property known as electric charge, often manifested as electrostatic discharge (ESD). What happens at the time of discharge is that an electrical field exerts a force on charged objects, accelerating them in the direction of the force. This happens, for example, when you drag your feet across the carpet in the dry winter months and then touch your cubicle mate's earlobe with your fingertip. This force has the same direction as the electrical field vector (pointing your finger), and its magnitude is given by the size of the charge multiplied by the magnitude of the electrical field (how much you scuff your feet). Touching the unsuspecting earlobe results in discharge. You need to make sure that you don't discharge any current on a tag or reader, rather on a grounding device or ground strip.

Preparing for Disaster

Most people deploying RFID racks never give thought to where they are being installed. The same can be said for the folks designing the racks that hold readers and antennas. Two critical things to keep in mind are the weather just outside the dock door and the infrastructure supporting the facility.

The weather pertains directly to wind or rain impacting the reader or antennas or lightning affecting the facility. A properly designed and installed RFID rack should have a flange of heavy gauge steel welded to the bottom of the rack, which can be bolted into a concrete floor. This should be immediately bolted to the floor in its proper location.

The next order of business is to cover all the fragile contents of the RFID rack such as reader, antenna, PLC, light indicator boxes, and wiring. This is best accomplished with material such as Lexan, which does not affect the RF radiation pattern emanating from an antenna. Although the rack should also be vented to allow for escape of the limited amount of heat created by the reader, more important is that the entire enclosure be covered so that dust from the warehouse environment does not enter the fragile inside of an RFID reader. Figure 7.4 shows the setup of ODIN's hardware-neutral RFID rack with one of the Lexan covers off the side.

The other likely problem to be caused by nature is a power outage. If you look at the rack in Figure 7.4, which is ready to be shipped to the client's premises, you'll notice a cardboard box in the bottom. Inside there is an *uninterruptible power supply (UPS)*, which provides protection from power spikes, ground loops, and brownouts. A simple UPS that can keep the reader running for 20–30 minutes will ensure that configuration files are not lost, and data is not missed in the event of a power hit. The other component of this system is making sure the portal is properly grounded in case there is a lightning strike that is looking for a place to ground out.

Performing Reader Optimization Analysis and Configuration

System installation accuracy is critical to meeting client objectives. You can ensure that the RFID reader configurations are accurate for all instances by measuring the RF performance physics, in other words how do the various radio frequency waves behave as they propagate through out a facility.

FIGURE 7.4 RFID rack with side cover removed

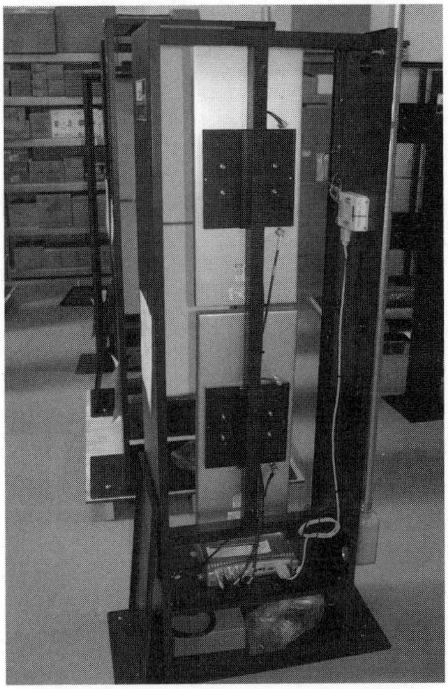

There are a several tests that help you optimize an RFID portal, namely critical boundary, RF radiation, power levels, and other settings crucial to achieving 100 percent read rate. In addition to achieving 100% read rate, it is important to remember you are trying to do just the opposite of setting up a WiFi point (which tries to flood as much area with a signal) you are trying to limit the broadcast area so you don't create any *ghost reads*, which are reads that aren't actually taking place at the portal you are testing. This gets down to limiting interference in the multi-reader environment. ODIN technologies offers an automated services delivery software called EasyReader which analysis and final configuration specification is automatically recorded and can then generate "as-deployed" configuration reports. If you don't have a access to EasyReader what you want to maker sure you do is follow a process and document all the steps in that process.

The process should be:

1. Install and connect to the reader.
2. Set the power level for each antenna for 100% read success of your product.
3. Layout a boundary where you do not want reads to take place, the critical boundary.
4. Reset the power down to a level that does not give reads outside the boundary.
5. Using a spectrum analyzer measure the level of power at various points inside that interrogation zone.
6. Record the settings and levels for the configuration database (Microsoft Excel works well for this).
7. Many companies new to RFID will configure using a trial-and-error approach. This is a recipe for disaster and lengthy deployments. Using a set process or an automated services delivery tool is the right way to ensure repeatability and accuracy.

Working off the Site Assessment

The site assessment will allow you to determine the maximum number of configurations. So, for instance, you should be able to come up with two or three baseline configurations such as a standard dock door or a personnel door. You can preconfigure your readers with that setup based on where they belong. This is also why having that IP address for each reader and each location is so critical, so you can preload the configuration.

Here are the typical steps for configuring a reader:

Step 1: Connect antennas to the reader. If it is a bi-static antenna, make sure that you connect the transmit (Tx) on the reader to the transmit on the antenna, and the receive port on the reader (Rx) to the receive port on the antenna. (The ports on the antenna are not usually dedicated to transmitting and receiving; this is determined by the connection to the reader ports.)

WARNING Do not power on the reader without a proper antenna connection or other form of protection on the antenna ports (*terminators*). Doing so could overload the reader and fry the unit.

Step 2: Power up the reader. Most readers have a green power light indicating that the reader is turned on. Usually during the bootup cycle, the green light will flash. Before you proceed, make sure the green light is steady. If it continues to flash after power up, there is likely a firmware problem and the unit will need to be checked for its firmware version or replaced.

Step 3: Set up the direct network connection. This is usually referred to as a crossover. The crossover allows you to communicate to the reader directly from a laptop.

NOTE Some PCs or laptops perform the conversion by themselves so that you will not even need the crossover cable, but a regular Cat 5 or 6 will do.

Make sure you keep in mind that a regular *Cat 5 or 6 cable (the type of cable that is used to communicate over a local area network)* is different from a crossover cable.

To set up the network connection, follow these steps:

1. Connect the Cat 5 crossover cable to the reader and to the host PC or laptop.
2. Configure the network interface on the host PC (in this case, Windows2000 or XP most likely) per the manufacturer's instructions.
3. Access the Control Panel via the Start menu.
4. Access network and Internet connections via the Control Panel.
5. Select the Local Area Connection for the hard-cabled RJ-45 network connection.
6. Select Properties for the connection.
7. Set the IP address and subnet mask. Usually you would use a virtual IP such as the following:
   - IP address: 192.168.127.10
   - Subnet mask: 255.255.255.0
8. Check the network configuration and connectivity to the reader.
9. Select Run from the Start menu.
10. Type **`cmd`** and select OK.
11. Type **`ipconfig /all`** at the command line and press Enter on the keyboard.
12. Verify the correct IP address and subnet mask in the output.
13. Check connectivity to the reader with the `ping` command. Type **`ping 192.168.127.254`** and press Enter on the keyboard. Verify reply from 192.168.127.254 in the output.

The reader is now properly configured and can likely communicate to the network. At this point, you can open up either your deployment software such as EasyReader, which can be started on most major reader manufacturers, or you can start the manufacturer's built-in configuration tool.

FIGURE 7.5 A Properly Connected RFID Reader

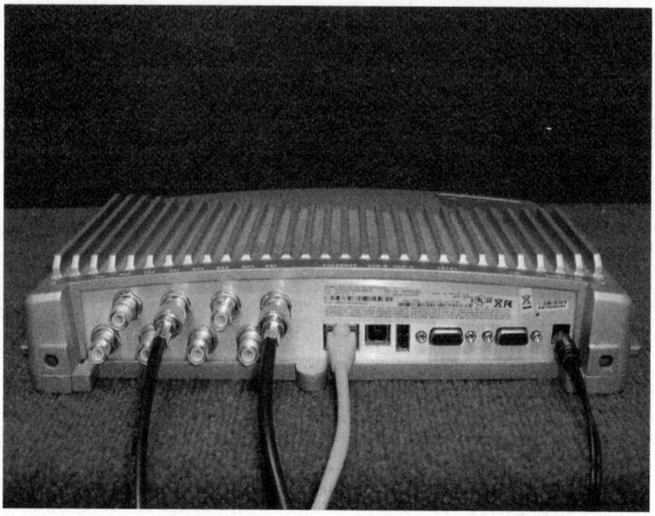

The first configuration step is the grandaddy of them all: setting the power level. The best way to do this is to get the reader set up and configured properly in its rack and make sure you are set up with either a laptop or host computer to talk to and control the reader. You should also take a product that is indicative of the products going through the portal and make sure it has an average tag on it (see Chapter 4, "Tags" for how to select an average tag).

Real World Scenario

Want a Reader with That Fry

Back in the early days of RFID, there was a reader called the Mercury II that did not have any sort of power-overload protection. Back then, readers were several thousand dollars each. At the time, I was hiring a new engineer about every month.

It was no surprise that each month we'd get one of these Mercury II readers that just stopped working. It turned out that someone was either powering them up with no antennas attached or was changing antennas with the power on. It didn't take long for us to learn not to power up without antennas on, or for the reader company to add power-overload protection to the reader or at least a 50-ohm terminator to screw on the port when the reader was shipped. There is also the concept of ESD which can fry a reader or tag as well. Electrostatic potential is the ability of a stored charge to essentially zap an electric charge from one point to another based on electrostatic discharge (ESD).

At this point, set the product in the middle of the IZ and start up the reader at the lowest power level. Slowly increase the reader's power until you are able to get a consistent read from the tag. You may want to move the product to several locations in the IZ where you would like to receive the signal from the tag. Make sure you try different box orientations as well, if the boxes are likely to come through the IZ in various directions.

After you have established a lower limit of the read rate, you can look for cross talk and ghost reads. *Cross talk* occurs when a reader in a dock door that is not receivng any items picks up reads from adjacent or nearby doors. The best way to limit cross talk is to take that same "average" product case and put it on the outer edge of the IZ, where you want to make sure it wouldn't be read. Then, turn up the power until you find that you are able to read the tag even at that outer edge. This will establish your *critical boundary*.

NOTE

The critical boundary is the outer edge of the IZ, where you do not want to read any tags. This is important to determine. In fact, it's critical, because you may have a forklift with tag items driving by, or a printer printing RFID tags, or something similar, and you wouldn't want to pick up those stray tags.

After the power levels have been properly set, you are 50 percent of the way to a properly configured RFID reader. The next most common configuration parameter is the antenna configuration. The antenna configuration changes how the antennas each sequence. For instance, if you are at a dock door with four antennas, you can change the way that each antenna cycles in the read order; in other words, if you number the antennas 1, 2, 3, and 4, you can have the reader poll twice on one side of the dock door, so the reader would broadcast from antennas 1 and 2, and then 1 and 2 again before going to 3 and 4. You want to use this antenna configuration to make up for issues that you may have found in your site survey. If one side of the IZ has some equipment that you know is going to reduce the overall effectiveness, you may want to cycle twice on the "weak" side for every time you cycle on the "strong" side.

WARNING

There are some systems still being used that require reading Generation 1 of the EPC protocol and Generation 2 that necessitates the reader be set to poll both of those protocols. The industry has come a long way over the past couple of years when it comes to creating one interoperable system, so hopefully this will not be an issue in the future.

Unfortunately, the reader companies vary so widely in their configuration processes and protocols that it's impossible to go through each one. There are simple readers such as Conveyor that allow you to choose a configuration and then walk away from a setup system. There are other extremes—for example, a reader such as the Symbol XR series, which has 120 configuration parameters.

Fortunately, there are programs, such as ODIN Technologies' EasyReader, that provide a drag-and-drop interface to configure and tune the readers without having to learn every one of those 120 commands. EasyReader allows you to use a patent-pending portal probe to talk to the reader and automatically tune and configure a reader, and to create a critical boundary and develop real-world RF coverage maps. This software tool makes precise tuning and 100 percent read rates a snap. Figure 7.6 shows an RF coverage map within a designated critical boundary.

The final step of getting a portal completely installed and tested is to make sure that the portal is protected from operator error. The biggest culprit of damaged portals is the forklift driver who has slightly poor judgment. Whacking a reader with a forklift blade, bashing it with a skid, or grinding it with a wheel is a sure way to ruin an expensive investment. The easy solution to protecting the fully deployed RFID portal is to set up a bollard that can withstand a bump or bash from a forklift or other moving vehicle. Figure 7.7 shows a double bollard setup providing ultimate protection of the black portal racks behind the bollards. Some will use a single bollard in front of the rack, but a forklift driver taking a sharp turn can take out the edge of an RFID rack. If I can, I always try to install two bollards at the front of an interrogation zone.

It's ideal if you can install the bollards before you start the testing and tuning because of their metallic nature. You may have to adjust power, angle the antennas, or compensate for any change in the RF field due to the bollards.

Real World Scenario

Reading at the In-bound Doors

One thing that works well if you are trying to read items coming in from trucks at a dock door is to slightly angle the antennas toward the inside of the truck, at a 15- to 20-degree angle. It starts the signal propagating a little ahead of when the tag gets in the center of the interrogation zone to get a response. This is why we made our RFID racks at ODIN with swiveling antenna mounts, to make sure you could angle the antennas to shape the field.

FIGURE 7.6 Critical boundary in EasyReader

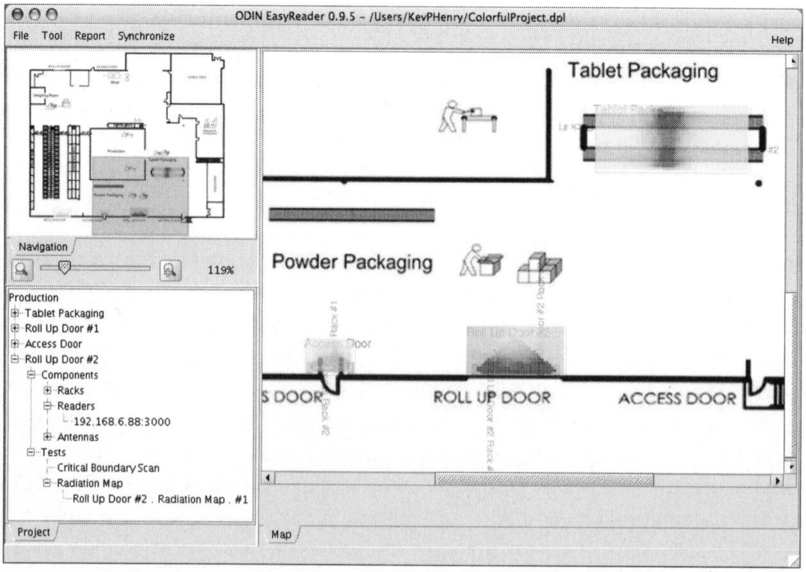

FIGURE 7.7 Protective bollards in front of an RFID portal

After you have the reader set up, configured, and tuned properly, it's time to prove it. The best thing you can do for a client relationship is to set up the metrics in advance. Let's say they want to read 20 cases on a pallet at an average rate of 98 percent success rate. Get that acceptance testing protocol (ATP) determined before you get on-site and start work. Decide how many tests you will perform and what happens if you are or are not successful.

If your ATP requires you to read 20 tags, make sure those tags are tested first. For information on testing tags, refer to Chapter 4. The tags need to be "average" performing tags, not too sensitive or poor receptors. You want average tags that will represent the typical quality likely to go through the IZ. Acceptance testing and configuration can also be refined after several months of collecting statistics and data about how well each portal is performing. Sometimes, particularly if there are items of different composition being tagged, the readers will need to be adjusted slightly for optimal results.

Real World Scenario

It's All in the Numbers

One of the largest computer manufacturers in the United States hired ODIN Technologies to optimize their RFID network by using our testing tools and scientific methods. Given their more than 250 read points and massive volumes, getting the client from a 98 percent read rate to over a 99 percent read rate could mean millions of dollars for them in return. Following well-proven methodologies, our team was able to optimize the system and get great results for our clients based on the metrics we all agreed on before even starting work.

Leverage CompTIA Training Experience and Verification

Several training companies, such as RFID4U and OTA Training, have RFID training classes to prep for the test. In addition to prepping for the test, you'll learn many of the basics of the RFID systems. One of the best parts of these courses is the actual hands-on training. There will be a time when you can play with the readers, learn how to configure them, try to talk with them, and test out some of the software packages that work with the readers. Clearly, the more often you have a chance to use the readers and set them up in various environments, the more you'll be comfortable with how to configure, tune, and test the final IZ. The folks at CompTIA are a great resource for making recommendations for books and training courses. And don't forget their website: `www.comptia.org`.

Summary

In this chapter, you finally learned how to install the RFID readers. Although this may seem like the first step in setting up a system, this chapter should have shown you that it really comes after an awful lot of planning and coordinating, physics and testing. Finally, you can get to the stage where the system goes live with an actual installation.

The first section focused more than you might have expected on proper project management. I spent a lot of time, and hopefully you learned a lot, because this is one of the biggest causes of failure for an RFID deployment. Just as you are spending a lot of time preparing for the CompTIA RFID+ exam, you should also spend a lot of time preparing for the RFID deployment. Understanding who does what, when they need to be there, and how all the gear you need gets where it is going is critical to your long-term success. As a soon-to-be RFID+ certified professional, you need to make sure that you enter the RFID world fully prepared.

Next you learned about getting the gear ready to ship. There are a number of tests and steps you learned to take to make sure that everything going out the door is in good working order and kept together as a complete package. It's a waste of time and money to have all but one small piece on-site when you start deploying systems.

You also learned how to take a site survey document and a design document and create the actual on-site build of an interrogation zone. Each IZ should have been clearly mapped out and there should be no surprises as to what goes where.

The really fun part came in the next section, when you learned how to talk to a reader and set it up for initial configuration as well as about what could go wrong. The CompTIA exam will definitely ask you about the electrical, grounding, and lightning-related questions, so it's important to understand some of these concepts. The key concepts you learned were setting power levels, turning on readers, and reading a reference tag in the right areas. Equally important was understanding how to make sure you don't read a tag where you didn't want one read.

The installation section focused on protecting the portal from harm's way. You saw what a bollard looks like and learned the difference between a single bollard and dual bollard setup.

Finally, you learned what happens after installation—the acceptance testing. The important thing that you learned here was that defined metrics will help you claim success and make your client happy.

Exam Essentials

Know how to install and configure an RFID reader. Make sure the reader has either antennas or a load terminator attached to each port to keep the reader from being overloaded and causing an internal short. After the antennas are attached, attach the power supply and turn on the reader. After the reader is on and the green light is steady, you can attach a crossover cable and start communicating with the reader.

Explain the function of a UPS. A well-planned RFID portal will have an uninterruptible power supply, or UPS, built into the system between the reader and the external power source. The reader is susceptible to power spikes caused by such things as lightning strikes or generator variations. The UPS also helps keep data that may be in the random access memory and not yet pushed up to the application from being lost and can make sure your configuration is not wiped out.

Describe electrostatic potential. Electrostatic potential is the ability of a stored charge to essentially zap an electric charge from one point to another based on electrostatic discharge (ESD). The reader designers usually account for this by grounding inside the reader, so it is not a significant concern when deploying readers in a typical warehouse situation. There are times, however, in a manufacturing environment, or when custom building a reader system outside a case, that you should keep in mind the potential for ESD.

Explain the value of the site assessment document. The site assessment document tells you what systems go where, where electrical outlets and circuits are needed, where the local area network cable needs to be, and other predeployment essentials. It will also help you create an association between a reader and a specific geographical location. This will allow you to create an IP address for all the components of the IZ.

Tell why it is important to create a bill of materials (BOM). The BOM ensures that when you arrive on-site, you will not be missing equipment required to effectively put together the interrogation zone. It also helps you order the correct amount of equipment for each portal from the various manufacturers.

Know the value of putting an IP address on a reader. An Internet Protocol, or IP, address is required to allow a reader to talk to the greater local area network (LAN). In order for any data to get beyond the reader to where it is actionable by an ERP system, it has to be routed up through the network and needs to know where it came from based on its IP address. The IP address has a secondary function of allowing you to associate other components to the reader, so that in preconfiguration and certification all the correct parts can be associated with the reader. When you go to ship all the devices and the reader, you can make sure that all the right parts go to the right places.

Key Terms

Before you take the exam, be certain you are familiar with the following terms:

artifact

bill of materials (BOM)

boundary

Cat 5 or 6 cable

critical

Cross talk

deployment topology

ghost reads

ground loop

light stack

plan of action and milestones (POAM)

plan of action and milestones, or POAM

PLC) which controls devices attached by the reader like light stacks and directional gates

Programmable Logic Controller

Telnet

terminators

uninterruptible power supply (UPS)

Review Questions

1. What is the first step in certifying hardware prior to an actual deployment?
   A. Assign all subcomponents to each portal, rack, or reader.
   B. Call the FCC and have their representative come on-site to supervise the installation.
   C. Attach the antennas to readers.
   D. Make sure that the readers and antennas have all functions as specified by the manufacturers.
2. What do you need to get from the network staff prior to installing RFID readers on-site at a client's facility?
   A. Permission to sniff packets on the job
   B. A block of IP addresses to assign to the readers
   C. DHCP-enabled network
   D. All network cables that you need
3. What is the best way to track which reader goes to which location as part of predeployment certification?
   A. Writing an IP address on a label attached to a reader and making sure the IP address is correlated to a location in your project plan
   B. Assigning names to readers and making sure you remember them
   C. Writing reader serial numbers into your project plan
   D. Color-coding the readers and appropriate zones in your project plan
4. What is an important test for light stacks?
   A. That they flash three times
   B. That each color illuminates correctly
   C. That a green light always signifies a successful read
   D. That a red light always signifies an error
5. Name the most important facet to being ready on-site for an installation.
   A. Dedicated electrical circuit for the reader
   B. LAN connection
   C. Adequate grounding
   D. All of the above

6. When does a ground loop occur?
   - A. When you repeatedly somersault on the floor
   - B. When two devices are connected to the same network
   - C. When two points have different electrical potentials and receive an unexpected current flow between them
   - D. When two devices are connected to the same power plug

7. What is an artifact?
   - A. A little-known bit of information about a painting
   - B. A document of information regarding something specific about the RFID network
   - C. A document about the RFID project funding
   - D. A piece of hardware

8. Why should you install an uninterruptible power supply (UPS) in each RFID portal you deploy?
   - A. To prevent potential lost data
   - B. To protect the reader from damage
   - C. To make it brown in color
   - D. A, B

9. What is the first step to setting up and configuring a reader?
   - A. Plug in the power supply and boot up.
   - B. Plug in the antennas to their respective ports.
   - C. Plug in a Cat 5 cable to the Ethernet port.
   - D. Plug in an RS-232 cable to the back of the reader and your laptop or host PC.

10. Outside the critical boundary you should be able to do which of the following?
    - A. Read a tag
    - B. Write a tag
    - C. Not read a tag
    - D. Jump wicked high

11. When in doubt, set the read and write power settings of the reader for the maximum. Is this statement true?
    - A. Yes, maximum power will ensure reading and writing of the tag.
    - B. Yes, maximum power will ensure that the tag is read or written correctly.
    - C. No, it is important to test and find out the appropriate power settings to prevent interference and reading tags that shouldn't be read.
    - D. No, it is important to follow the manufacturer's guidelines for power settings.

12. How do you check a reader's connectivity to a network?
    A. Using a `ping` command
    B. Checking if all lights on a reader are on
    C. Using a Select command
    D. All of the above

13. How many cables do you need for bi-static and mono-static antennas?
    A. Two cables for a mono-static antenna, and one for bi-static
    B. One cable for a mono-static antenna, and two for bi-static
    C. One cable for both a mono-static antenna and bi-static
    D. Two cables for both a mono-static antenna bi-static

14. If you are plugging two antennas into a reader and you have two ports left without antennas, do you need to do anything special with them?
    A. No.
    B. Connect dummy antennas into the unused ports.
    C. Use an overload protection or terminators.
    D. Use plastic caps for the unused ports.

15. When preparing for an installation, what is an important part of the process?
    A. Obtain appropriate permits to access the facility.
    B. Hire only CompTIA-certified installers.
    C. Ask the network people to tell you which IP addresses are already taken.
    D. Make sure that your equipment for use in Europe is FCC certified.

16. When you hire a new installer, what is the essential part of the process?
    A. Making sure the installer has done at least a dozen installations
    B. Training the installer on the way you do RFID installations
    C. Making sure the installer has electrical certifications
    D. Making sure the installer is CompTIA certified

17. Which are the most common reasons for damages to your readers? (Select two options.)
    A. Hit by a forklift
    B. Hit by a person
    C. Electrostatic discharge
    D. Wrong configuration

18. How do you protect a reader and antennas at the dock door from being hit by a forklift?
    A. Using color drawings on the floor to show "no access" zone
    B. Using one or two bollards in front of the RFID stand
    C. Using a plastic screen in front of the RFID portal
    D. Talking to forklift drivers about driving carefully

19. When installing your RFID system outside, what do you need to protect it from besides rain and snow? (Select two options.)
    A. Low humidity
    B. Lightning
    C. Extreme temperatures
    D. Electrical potential

20. What is important to establish before you are testing the equipment and system performance?
    A. Performance metrics
    B. If the tag gets read or not
    C. Customer trust
    D. Installer trust

Answers to Review Questions

1. A. As a first step to prepare your hardware for a deployment, you must assign all subcomponents (light stack, antennas, UPS, and so forth) to each portal. This means having numbers and an identification system for your portal or associating each peripheral and required component to a specific reader. That way, when everything is tested, it can be put together.

2. B. When prepping your hardware for an installation and before you get on-site, ask the network staff for a block of virtual IP addresses that you can preload onto each reader. Just make sure that you keep track of each reader and where it goes so you are not confusing readers by IP address.

3. A. The best way to track which reader goes where is to write an IP address on a label that you will attach to a reader and make sure the IP address is correlated to a location in your project plan. Using an IP address is a lot better than using serial numbers or other coding because if you have to switch readers, you can still configure them with the given IP address without changing your project plan.

4. B. When testing light stacks, make sure that each color correctly signifies the condition you set it for.

5. D. To power the reader and protect it from electrical damage, you need to have a dedicated electrical circuit and adequate grounding. The reader also has to communicate with a back-end system; therefore, a LAN or other network connection is necessary.

6. C. A ground loop occurs when two points have different electrical potentials and receive an unexpected current flow between them. A ground loop can easily damage electrical devices. To prevent ground loops, you have to ground your devices properly, but make sure that you do not use secondary grounding because it may also result in a ground loop.

7. B. An artifact is a document carrying information regarding something specific about the RFID network or a deliverable. The artifacts are generated on an event basis and may be either simple work-in-process (WIP) artifacts that are made available for the team's use or deliverables that are submitted in fulfillment of required work products.

8. D. A UPS is an essential device that will keep the readers running in case of a power failure and also protect them against unexpected power spikes.

9. B. When you are setting up and configuring a reader, the first thing you have to do is to connect the antennas into appropriate antenna ports on the readers. After that you can plug in the network cables and power supply, and boot up a reader.

10. C. The critical boundary is the outer edge of the IZ, where you do not want to read any tags. This is important to determine. In fact, it's critical so that you can avoid picking up a stray tag (for example, if a forklift with tag items is driving by or if a printer is printing RFID tags).

11. C. Appropriate power settings of the reader have to be determined based on establishing the antenna pattern and the interrogation zone dimensions. You want to adjust the power to cover your interrogation zone but not to interfere with adjacent interrogation zones and read tags that do not belong to the interrogation zone.

12. A. To make sure that the reader communicates with a network, you should ping it with its IP address. If it replies, this will mean that it will communicate with a network.

13. B. A mono-static antenna needs only one cable. This cable will go to a Tx/Rx port in a mono-static reader. A bi-static antenna always needs two cables. One will go to a transmitting (Tx) port and the other to a receiving (Rx) port in a bi-static reader.

14. C. Most of the readers have built-in overload protection in antenna ports, in case they are not used for connecting the antennas. However, in the past, readers required protective terminators to be placed onto unused antenna ports. Today this is used only with a very few readers; therefore, make sure you read the manual.

15. A. To start the installation, you will need appropriate permits for you and your team to access the facility, and permits for bringing equipment in and work on-site. If you do not obtain necessary permits, you will delay your installation and have your team standing by.

16. B. To have a successful team for your installation, you should not skip the training of the hired installers. Everyone performs the installations differently, and the installers should understand not only how to bolt and plug in but also the reason behind the configurations. This will save you a lot of time troubleshooting and re-explaining things on-site.

17. A, C. In a warehouse environment, various vehicles could accidentally hit the equipment and cause damage to your readers and antennas. One of the hidden causes of damages can be ESD.

18. B. To prevent your equipment from being hit by a forklift, you should install one or two bollards near the dock door and in front of the RFID equipment.

19. B, C. You should always protect your equipment from extreme temperatures, regardless of where it is installed. When installing equipment inside, you have to worry about lightning protection of the building. When installing the equipment outside, you should use lightning suppressors or protectors to prevent damage in case of a lightning strike in the area. This is particularly important in geographical areas that are prone to lightning.

20. A. After you have the reader set up, configured, and tuned properly, you must prove that it works as it should. The best thing you can do for your client relationship is to set up the performance metrics in advance. Let's say your client wants to read 20 cases on a pallet at a 98 percent success rate on average. Get that acceptance testing determined before you get on-site and start work. Decide how many tests you will perform and what happens if you are or are not successful.

Chapter 8

Troubleshooting and Optimizing an RFID Network

RFID+ EXAM OBJECTIVES COVERED IN THIS CHAPTER:

✓ **2.1 Given a scenario, troubleshoot RF interrogation zones (e.g., root-cause analysis)**

- 2.1.1 Analyze less-than-required read rate
    - 2.1.1.1 Identify improperly tagged items
- 2.1.2 Diagnose hardware
    - 2.1.2.1 Recognize need for firmware upgrades
- 2.1.3 Equipment replacement procedures (e.g., antenna, cable, interrogator)

✓ **2.2 Identify reasons for tag failure**

- 2.2.1 Failed tag management
- 2.2.2 ESD issues

✓ **2.3 Given a scenario, contrast actual tag data to expected tag data**

RFID is not a Plug and Play technology, yet. One of the issues the industry has faced is slower-than-anticipated adoption of the technology. The blame for this can be put on the shoulders of hardware manufacturers and integrators. The hardware manufacturers try to sell a complicated piece of equipment (an RFID reader) as a simple box that end users can "buy, bolt down, and boot up." Unfortunately, end users and new integrators have taken the reader salespeople at their word and did just that—buy, bolt, and boot. Then they discovered the stark reality of 60 percent read rates. Before they had a chance to fix the problem, the press latched on to the read rates being a lot lower than expected. This had many end users saying the technology "wasn't ready for prime time," which slowed its adoption.

All of this could have been prevented if there were people who knew how to deploy these complex machines by using a proven process or best-of-breed tools. This chapter will show you how to solve problems that may have come from someone attempting to "buy, bolt, and boot." You can also use this chapter for the second step in an RFID deployment, the optimizing and tuning of an RFID network.

Being able to correctly determine the causes of poor performance and mitigate those issues is what can take you from a good-enough RFID technician to a rock star in the fastest growing industry today.

This chapter will help you understand what factors can make or break an RFID deployment with the various readers and how their components can affect functionality. You'll also learn the details of tuning a reader and of course the antennas that are attached to that reader. The next ingredient in the mix is the tag that is being read—you'll see various ways for identifying the problems with a tag and determining whether you are using subperforming tags. Of course, after you have looked at all the individual components of a reader network, you'll need to make sure that the environmental issues are not causing performance degradation.

Then we'll get a little dirt under our fingernails by actually trying to solve some real-world RFID problems. You will get to review a case study of performance issues and then be given the right steps to troubleshoot and optimize that RFID network.

The last part of this chapter will cover the use of specialized infrastructure software and tools to make your life easier and your RFID setup more accurate. You will get an introduction to the various software programs, and learn about how to use them in a deployment or troubleshooting scenario.

Understanding RFID Performance Drivers

Troubleshooting a faulty RFID portal or a poorly performing reader will require you to become the Sherlock Holmes of RFID. You'll need to have a basic understanding of what could go wrong with the various components of an RFID system to qualify as a supersleuth. There is a saying pilots use to determine whether they have their head in the right place while they are flying: "Being ahead of the airplane." This means always anticipating what needs to happen to make a desired change, or how the pilot would react when a certain event happens—for example, an engine falling off. The same attitude can help an RFID technician as you go about initially deploying an RFID network, and it can really come in handy when you need to determine what is causing problems with the interrogation zone. If you are ahead of the RFID system, you are always thinking about what might go wrong and how to deal with it. With that in mind, I'm going to review the basics of the interrogation zone in terms of what could go wrong.

Reader Functionality

The reader controls the foundation of the interrogation zone. Remember that the power level is the biggest variable in how an RFID reader performs. Don't get hung up on power, though; many other components depend on the reader, from retry rates to antenna cycling order. A lot of people also tend to overlook the fact that the reader has to send its data someplace to be effective. The communication method can be broken when the reader is working perfectly, and thus give the impression that everything is broken.

The RFID industry is relatively new; consequently, manufacturing consistency and quality are all over the map. One thing we discovered at ODIN Technologies, doing thousands of tests before deploying readers from all the major manufacturers, is that there is a significant variability in the power output at each port. The Federal Communications Commission (FCC) allows 1 watt of effective radiated power (ERP) for UHF RFID in the United States with at least 50 channels hopping. Some reader manufacturers interpret this FCC rule as being the power level after it's attached to the reader, so they account for cable loss (more on that later) and check power at the antenna. Almost all the reader manufacturers have variability in power output at each port, and some ports just plain don't work. Remember that power is the big daddy of the interrogation zone. If you want to read at a farther distance, you need more power; conversely, if you don't want to read at another location, such as a dock door adjacent to the interrogation zone you're working on, power needs to be contained.

Another interesting consideration is operating temperature of the reader. This is a double-edged sword like many other components of RFID—if the reader is too hot, the performance drops off precipitously, and if it is too cold, the performance will be subpar. This should also be an important consideration when setting up your RFID system, and another thing to look at when you're troubleshooting.

TIP

As you become more and more involved in the RFID world, one of the best things you can do is keep a journal. When you go on-site, if you are doing tag testing, or if you are prebuilding an RFID rack, you should write down metrics. The metrics can provide key insights into being successful going forward. Some of the metrics you should track when you are keeping a journal are the length of time that a particular action took, the issues you ran into, the temperature when you deployed, and the humidity. If you are a big quantitative analysis (QA) fan, you can dump all of this data into a spreadsheet and figure out what levers really move performance and pricing.

Antenna Options

Antennas are how the reader gets its signal out to the tags coming through the interrogation zone. The antenna is responsible for shaping the RF pattern, and can be wildly variable depending on the need. Think of an RFID antenna as you'd think of a cutting instrument—one requirement may call for a Swiss Army knife, another may call for a meat cleaver, and still another for a chain saw. To make matters worse, if the blade is dull (even if it is the right kind for the job), it will not work well. Antennas can create various shapes or radiation patterns and be sending a suboptimal amount of power to the tag. The antenna can take a perfect RF signal that would ideally provide a great read back from the tag, and if the antenna is improperly tuned or is the wrong design, it can distort that perfect reader signal to the point where nothing will be read.

Tag Impact

The tag is the third critical aspect in the RFID system. It's important to remember that for a passive ultra-high-frequency (UHF) RFID tag in the United States, the antenna is specifically tuned with a resonant frequency around 915 MHz, and designed to cover a broad band of communication. Because the passive tags are so sensitive, they can easily be detuned by material in close proximity to the tag. This means that metal inside a box, liquid in a container, and other objects hidden inside a box being tagged can change the nature of how the tag is likely to communicate with a reader. The RFID reader and antenna can be putting out just the right amount of RF energy in just the right form, but a bad tag will keep you from getting any accurate read results. The largest two variables in tag performance are manufacturing quality and trial-and-error placement. Other factors that can have an impact on performance are environmental issues such as humidity or damage from a direct blow.

Other frequencies are equally important to know about—13.56 MHz or high frequency is very common, particularly at the item level in pharmaceuticals. Also, 433 MHz is very common for active tags worldwide because the U.S. Department of Defense has standardized an active tag from Lockheed Martin (formerly Savi Technology). The active tag can be *the* critical factor if there is a battery failure. Active tags do not function without a battery on board. The battery life is driven by how often the tag is broadcasting its signal.

Middleware

In truth, middleware cannot by itself affect the performance of an RFID interrogation zone. However, what it can do is change the setting of the RFID reader, which in turn can wreak havoc on the well-tuned RFID reader that you spent hours getting right. To make sure that you are not setting yourself up for certain disaster, it's critical to know what functionality the middleware controls and how it speaks to the reader. Some middleware can control only one or two parameters of a reader, such as power level or retry rate, when in fact a reader may have a dozen or more different parameters that can be finely tuned. From a communication perspective, it is important to find out whether a reader is constantly sending information to the middleware or if the middleware is asking for information only at certain instances. Finally, you need to determine how much filtering is being done at the reader level so you know how hard the middleware server is going to have to work.

NOTE Don't confuse the firmware with the middleware. The *firmware* sits natively on every reader and needs to be changed if you are upgrading a reader to read different tags—for instance, changing from *Generation 1* to *Generation 2*, which affects whether or not they can read the latest version of tags.

Determining Possible Causes of Problems

Like the star pupil that you are, I bet you are already ahead of the game—you're thinking to yourself about all the possible scenarios of what can cause bad things to happen to good readers. You might think about how the antennas could have been dropped during shipping, the cable could be kinked, or the reader placement could be causing overheating. If you have been playing with RFID long enough, you might be catching on to some of the patterns in deployments. Although that is the right way to start thinking about being ahead of the reader, what you really need is a process. The process has to focus on two critical factors of diagnosis:

- The surrounding environment
- The RFID system

The RFID system has everything to do with what is happening with tags, readers, and antennas. There is a logical sequence you should follow to perform a proper diagnosis, which I'll get to in a minute. The surrounding environment is the other factor that should have been looked at very closely during installation. Either may have changed after the RFID system was installed or was not properly evaluated in the first place.

What is the ideal process for diagnosis? It has to start with gathering metrics and defining the test scenarios. I always say you can't manage what you can't measure. So for the first step, find the reader site(s) that you are going to test and gather some meaningful data around how they are performing today. Depending on your time frame, you should do this over the course of a week or two, and try to get at least several hundred data points so that you will have a sample of data that is representative of the entire population. This is creating a starting level or *baseline* performance that can be used to assess the impact of individual changes on performance and offer insight into the most effective test sequence.

The next step after creating the baseline is to determine whether there is any potential ambient electromagnetic noise (AEN) by following the procedure for a full Faraday cycle analysis, as outlined in Chapter 3, "Site Analysis." If you see any interference in or around the frequency you are operating within, you know you have a potential cause of your problem. It's important to note that even if you are operating in the 902–928 MHz range and you spot some AEN at 900 MHz, if the wattage is sufficient, that signal outside the 902 range can bleed over and cause interferences at the low end of your useful range (for example, 902, 903, or 904 MHz).

The next step in the physical analysis is to measure the actual reader topology. You need to document and understand where the antennas are placed in relation to where the tag is to be read. Taking measurements should also include how long the cable is between the antenna and the reader, because the longer the cable, the more loss is incurred as the signal travels from the reader to the antenna. You'll also need to understand where the tag falls within the interrogation zone and how much variability there is in where the tag falls compared to the antennas.

These three steps give you critical information needed to make changes within the surrounding environment that can have a significant improvement on system performance. This is particularly true if you are dealing with a situation that includes a conveyor or shelf reader. The reason is RF localization—you would likely be looking to read in a very small area; this means that power levels are much lower and the "sweet spot" of the interrogation zone is much smaller. Therefore, measuring the specific physical area is critical, both where the tag comes through the zone and where the coverage of the antenna is.

While you are doing an analysis of the environment, you can start to look at issues with the actual equipment as well. The first place to begin is with the reader. One of the biggest areas of variation are the reader ports. Sometimes the connections are not welded securely, other times the reader quality check was not performed thoroughly, and other times there may just be damage during use. You'll be the first one to determine how consistent the power output of the reader is across each port. You will need a very accurate spectrum analyzer hooked up to each port, and set the reader to broadcast at full power. With your spectrum analyzer, track and record the power out of each port and see what kind of variation you have.

The next step is to investigate the cable leading to the antenna. Cable that connects RFID readers to antennas comes in all different shapes and sizes. There are several factors that can cause loss over antenna cables:

- Amount of insulation on the cable (thickness)
- Length of the cable
- Number of connections on the cable
- Radius of bends as the cable is routed from reader to antenna
- Type of connector used

A basic investigation of the cabling can reveal some interesting information. Make sure you take the time to look for cuts, scrapes, bends, and connections because those things all induce loss or noise.

FIGURE 8.1 The process flow of troubleshooting an RFID system

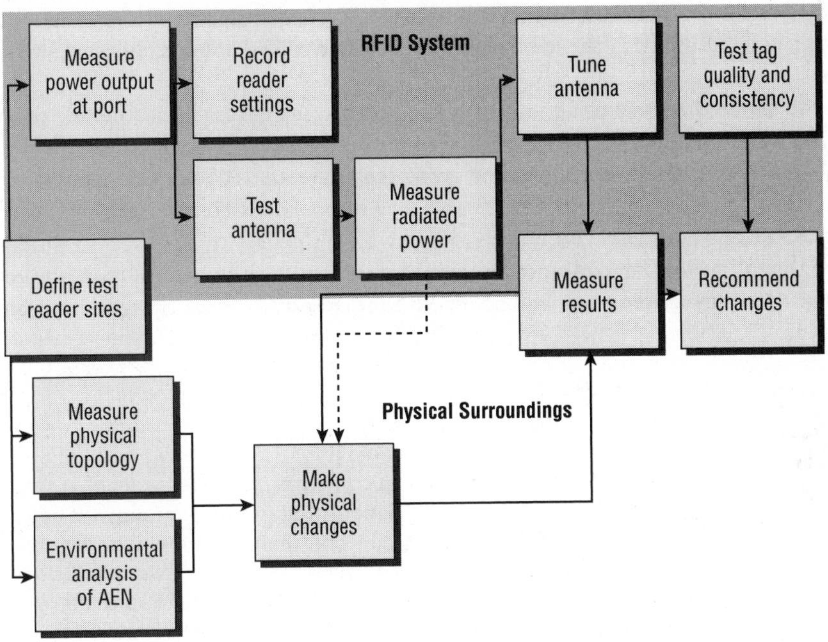

It may be more helpful to look at troubleshooting as a flow of closely related steps. If you look at Figure 8.1, you'll see the two specific areas (the RFID system and the physical environment) and the steps that you need to take to investigate each one in greater detail.

As you can see from the flow chart, it takes about a dozen tests to do a good job evaluating a poor RFID system. Now I'll take you through the details of each one of those tests and teach you specifically how to conduct each one from start to finish.

Environmental Interferences

This is the easiest of all the tests because you should already be familiar with site surveys, full Faraday cycle analysis, and path loss contour mapping. If you're not, you need to go back and review Chapter 3 to learn how to set up a spectrum analyzer for the proper protocol.

NOTE If you want more detail, you can purchase a copy of my other book, *RFID For Dummies* (Wiley Publishing, 2005).

A simplified version of a full Faraday cycle analysis would entail setting up a spectrum analyzer to investigate what is happening near the area under investigation. If you do it initially with the reader functioning, you should set your spectrum analyzer to Max Hold and watch the signal as it frequency hops pseudo-randomly through the entire band. In just a few minutes, the entire 902–928 MHz band should be filled with the exact same signal power. This is a great chance to see whether the reader is broadcasting outside the 902–928 MHz band and to make sure that each channel is outputting the same power level. After you've investigated that, shut off the reader.

If you set up the spectrum analyzer while the power light is on the outside of the reader and you don't see anything, you may have already found your issue. The first thing you should try to do if the power light is on is to *ping* the reader. You can do that by connecting the reader to a laptop via an Ethernet cable or a serial cable. To connect using a serial cable you need a cable with DB9 connectors and you have to know the COM port number on the laptop that allows you to configure the COM port. It is very important that you know what baud rate settings are required to connect with the reader, so check the reader manual before using the serial port.

TIP

To ping a reader, you need to know the reader's IP address and have an Ethernet cable (a crossover cable or use a switch with a regular Ethernet cable) and a laptop or desktop computer. It's as easy as plugging the computer into the reader and clicking the Start button, followed by Run, and then typing **cmd**. This gives you a command window where you will likely see `C:\Documents and Settings\Administrator>_`. Just type the word **`ping`** followed by a space and the reader's IP address. If you get a response indicating "request timed out," the reader is not communicating with the outside world.

As you by now realize, troubleshooting is slightly different from the initial site survey because you'll want to make sure that you are capturing your reader's RF output as well. The specifics of the reader are going to be addressed later in the "Reader Settings" section, but you need to know that the reader is functioning first. First set up a spectrum analyzer and signal generator as you would to create a path loss contour map (PLCM). The difference when using the PLCM for troubleshooting is that the antennas are already set up and mounted where they will be. So rather than have the outside antennas on a tripod, they will be attached to the dock door, conveyor, or other location—in other words, you'll be using the actual antenna from the interrogation zones.

The process to use PLCM for troubleshooting is as follows:

1. Turn on the spectrum analyzer as you would to create a normal PLCM, with the center frequency set at 915 MHz if you're testing UHF, or 13.56 MHz if you're testing high frequency (HF). Set the span appropriately.
2. Verify that there is no external noise generating a signal to the spectrum analyzer.
3. Unplug the first reader antenna from the reader (which should be turned off) and plug it into the spectrum analyzer.

4. Set up a signal generator as directed in the PLCM method and attach it to a ground plane at the same location you would ideally like to read a tag.
5. Set the signal generator to broadcast a signal at the desired frequency—UHF or HF. If it's UHF, you will want to test across the frequency band, at the very least at 902, 915, and 928 MHz.
6. Leaving the signal generator to broadcast at a constant power level, test all the antennas attached to the reader as they are mounted.
7. Gather all the input data across the full frequency span for each antenna that is used in the interrogation zone and input the average power into an Excel spreadsheet.

Armed with the performance data from each individual antenna, you can look at how they are performing relative to each other and determine whether there are any glaring issues—usually this will be seen as nulls or null spots within the interrogation zone.

The next step is to leave the spectrum analyzer set up in that same location and test through the reader's frequency band again. This will quickly identify whether other readers are on and operating at a powerful-enough level to interfere with the interrogation zone under test. You may pick up other readers or other devices. Figure 8.2 shows a screen from a spectrum analyzer showing several eruptions of RF interference that need investigating. If you do pick up interference locally, your poor read rates could be caused by standing wave or multi-path issues. (See "Surfing a Standing Wave.")

FIGURE 8.2 Spectrum analyzer showing points of potential interference

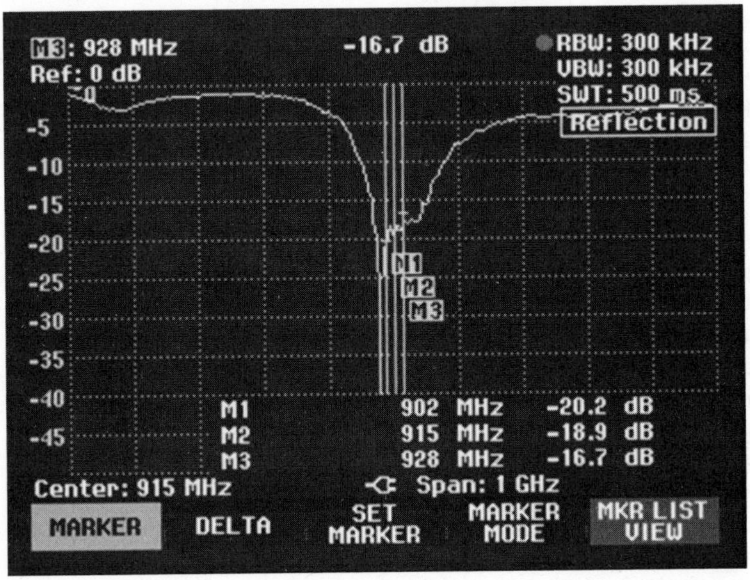

Surfing a Standing Wave

Because radio frequency communication travels over electric or magnetic waves, it has a consistent, predictable waveform, or pattern. For instance, a UHF wavelength at 915 MHz is about 33 cm. That means that from start to finish, a full wave takes just over a foot. A *standing wave* is caused when a wave that starts in one direction is heading toward a wave from the opposite direction, and those waves started 15.6 cm out of phase from each other—a half a wavelength apart. This is also referred to as a *multi-path* issue. When the waves eventually meet, they cancel each other out and there no longer is any RF energy to read a tag.

Standing waves most often happen when multiple readers are set up in close proximity to each other, because there are so many RF waves being produced at usually a very high power. The second cause of standing waves is a highly reflective environment, so that waves might bounce off metallic surfaces and come back to create standing waves. Combine the two causes—multiple readers set up in a metallic environment—and you've got RFID Armageddon!

Antenna Tuning

The antenna is to the RFID network what the tires are to a car. If the reader has the best engine, is running high-octane gas, and has bald tires, you'll never get the benefit of using that great engine because the tires will keep slipping when you hit the gas. An antenna has the same issues—you might have a great reader and ideal configuration, but if your antenna is poorly tuned, you may never get good results. The only way to do a specific and isolated analysis on an antenna is to use a spectrum analyzer equipped with a *voltage standing wave ratio (VSWR)* bridge. The VSWR bridge will allow you to tune an antenna properly for whatever resonant frequency you are looking to read across. You can also compare the performance across the antenna. The best way to do this is to save the VSWR measurements, like the ones in Figure 8.3.

The deeper the trough, the more power will be available to power the tag and get a response back. Look at Figure 8.3, a set of real-world test results from an ODIN Technologies deployment team that was brought in to fix an RFID system that was poorly performing in a manufacturing line. Scenario A was the original result, which is tuned close to the resonant frequency (in this case 13.56 MHz) but is not very deep, so the read performance is mediocre at best. Scenario B is another faulty antenna that has a much deeper response (the trough goes all the way down to the bottom of the screen), but the resonant frequency is significantly off of 13.56 MHz and the result is no read rates. Finally, scenario C is an ODIN-tuned antenna that has a resonant frequency spot on to 13.56 MHz and a nice deep trough. This resulted in 100 percent read rates in the manufacturing line.

HF is very different from UHF in terms of working in the field environment. HF works on the principle of inductive coupling. The bad news is that most HF antennas straight out of the box are tuned to read in free air at that 13.56 MHz. The resonant frequency can easily be changed, usually by just turning a screw on the antenna. This allows you to account for any detuning of the antenna that might happen because of a close proximity to steel, aluminum, or other metal surfaces.

FIGURE 8.3 Antenna performance

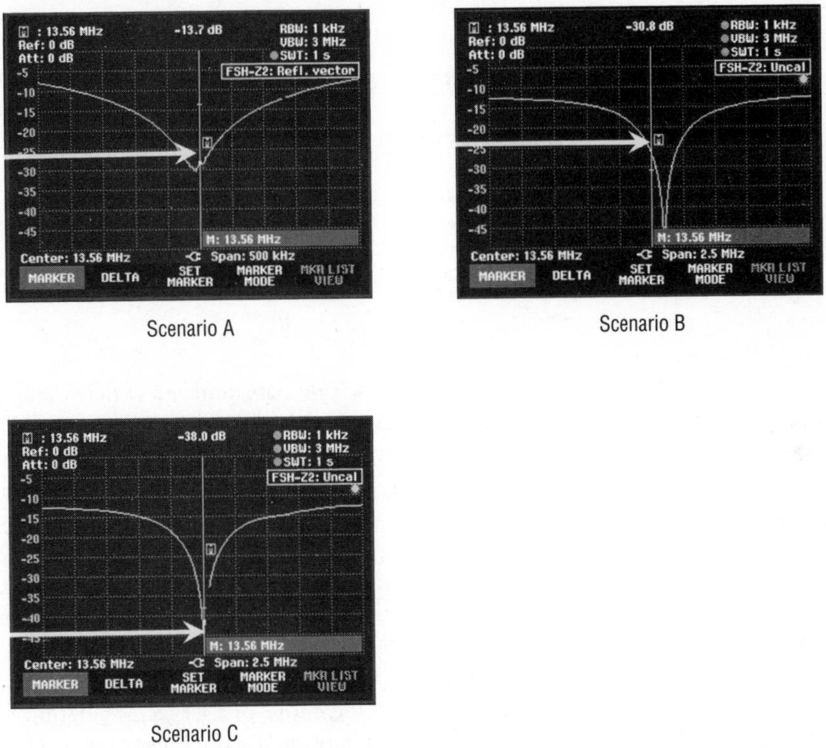

TIP

Cables can contribute as much to poor performance as the antenna. The industry typically ships out *LMR*-240 with a reader. If you are running to the other side of a dock door, using LMR-240 across a span of 25 or 30 feet can mean that the power getting to your antenna might be cut in half, particularly if there are connectors and elbow attachments. Consider shortening the length of the run or using a lower-loss antenna cable such as LMR-400. Another cause of loss in signal is using connectors that are not soldered to the coax cable. Make sure that for maximum efficiency soldered connections are what connect the core and the connector.

Tag Quality

The good news from a troubleshooting perspective is that tags can have a huge impact on the performance of the RFID network, and can be easily measured using the physics of science—not trial and error. The bad news is, if you don't have control over what tags come into the

RFID network that you are troubleshooting, the tag can be your biggest headache. Aside from the obvious problems of a tag being damaged because of how it was applied or how it was handled before storage, the biggest issues with tags are where and at what orientation they are put on an object.

A number of factors impact a tag's performance. Figure 8.4 summarizes these influences.

FIGURE 8.4 Performance factors of a tag

The best way to determine whether the tags are the cause of a problem with read rates is to get some high-quality tags, test for an average-performing tag, and run a known "average" performing tag through the interrogation zone on empty cardboard boxes with the tags exactly parallel to the interrogation zone antenna. If you consistently get read rates that are above 99 percent, your tag is unlikely to be the problem.

A common problem is that tags are stored improperly or put onto the cases with too much force. The tags might have been written to without issue, but then been damaged enough to stop working once applied. It's always a good idea to test actual tags that are in the supply chain to see how effectively they are being read.

Just to refresh your memory on testing your tags, take a look at Chapter 4, "Tags." Make sure that you use a sample of 10–12 tags that are indicative of a larger population of tags to find one that is an *average tag*. This is why it's so important to test with average tags—tags that require the same minimum effective power to get a response. Using a tool such as ODIN's EasyTag is the best way to determine—by using science, not trial and error—what the proper location and the optimal tag is for a specific product. Tools such as EasyTag also give users a measurement of minimum effective power (MEP), which is the de facto standard for tag testing, so that different tags can be measured using MEP as a way of comparing performance with a similar metric no matter where the tags are being tested.

WARNING Electrostatic discharge (ESD) can, although rarely, damage RFID tags. ESD occurs when, because of an excess of electric charge, electric current suddenly flows on a path from where it is stored on an electrically insulated object to an object at a different electrical potential such as a ground—which is what an RFID tag can act like.

The last thing to investigate on the tags is the data stored on the tag. If the tags are coming off a printer/encoder or being prewritten, it is possible they have the wrong data or the incorrect data construct. Some tags can be "put to sleep" by using special commands or even made entirely inoperable. It is possible that bad tags aren't really bad but have been written with an improper command.

Reader Settings

Before you even start to troubleshoot an individual reader, you need to take five simple steps:

1. Reboot the reader.
2. Verify that the reader has the latest available firmware on it.
3. Verify that the reader is communicating to the outside world.
4. Visually inspect the cables and connections.
5. Verify that the antenna configuration is in the proper mode (either multi-static or bi-static).

If you complete these five simple steps and still have not identified a simple solution, you have to put on your physics hat and start using your science training and RFID tools such as a spectrum analyzer and signal generator to find the problems.

The granddaddy of reader settings is ERP. Different readers have different power settings, but the biggest single mistake that novice RFID technicians make is to set the reader on full power. This will work if there is only a single reader set up in an area without much interference, but introduce another reader or two and some reflective material, and full power is a recipe for disaster. The problem with using full power is that you are likely to get ghost reads and to pick up tags that are coming in through other dock doors, or worse yet that are sitting on a spool inside an RFID printer. At ODIN Technologies we have deployed hundreds of readers across the globe, using HF, UHF, and other technologies, and we have found that very seldom is putting a reader on full power the best way to start setting up a reader.

Start out the investigation of your reader by checking the power setting. Use the operating manual to determine what the power levels are and how much control your reader gives you. Then set the reader at its lowest level and begin your testing. To test the right setting, you can use a very scientific method with the spectrum analyzer and 1/4-wave dipole antenna in the middle of the interrogation zone and track the power being broadcast at each channel in the frequency of the reader. This should result in a very even power level on your spectrum analyzer showing that each channel puts out the same power level.

The next step to investigate is the reader temperature. Two scenarios need to be investigated. First, is the reader being left on for too long, causing the temperature to get too hot inside the reader? Second, is the reader turning on only for the read event, via an I/O, so it is not effectively warmed up? Either issue can cause poor read results.

After the obvious power settings and reader temperature reviews, you'll need to break out the operating manual and look at what features you have available to you for tuning the reader. Depending on the reader, you may have preset configurations that would be best used for a conveyor or a dock door, which can be changed for better performance. The better readers will have many parameters that can be changed one at a time to see whether that improves performance. These settings can include parameters such as protocol setting; reading Gen 1 Class 1, Class 0, Gen 2 Class 1, or all three; retry rates; antenna sequencing; listen-before-talk; dense reader mode; and many other specific tuning parameters.

If you've exhausted all of these possibilities and still are not getting adequate results, it's time to call the reader manufacturers and find out whether there are any known problems or changes required. It is not uncommon for your problem to be the same one faced by many other people, and changing firmware or performing a specialized test may reveal whether the problems you are having are something the reader manufacturer has seen before.

WARNING

The wrong firmware can make a good reader fail miserably. Firmware is the reader's driving software. It tells components such as the antennas, the DSP chip, the processor chip, and the communication devices how to behave, when to act, and what to do. Firmware is the nerve center of an RFID reader.

Physical Layout

The physical layout works hand in hand with the business process. If the reader is set up properly and reading when you go through the testing protocol outlined in the preceding section, you might have a problem with the business process.

The physical layout and business process can interrupt the read success in various ways. For example, a forklift may pick up a case of goods with the RFID tags or pallet tag oriented against the forklift blades and body. The metal against the tag would prevent any RF energy from getting into or backscattered back from the tags on that side of the pallet. The two simple ways to solve a problem like this are to train the end users not to slide the pallet directly up against the forklift, or to put in place a spacer so that the skid cannot slide directly against the forklift. Either is a simple solution, but the problem can be identified only by actually observing the process that happens during the normal day-to-day business operations.

Optimizing Large-Scale Deployments

In RFID networks, there is strength in numbers. The best way to optimize a large-scale deployment is to look at the common configurations and start collecting performance data on those various scenarios.

Even after years of deploying the most complex RFID networks in the world, I have found that there are usually four or five basic reader configurations that are indicative of everything you will deploy. Keeping data on what the various configurations are and how they perform is the key to optimizing large-scale deployments. This is something that we used to do manually at ODIN, but now have automated tools to do. If you are building your own RFID network, it's something you can easily track by using Microsoft Access or even Excel. Think of your RFID deployment as a football team. There are probably 25 specialty positions that a typical professional football team may define, but at the end of the day it comes down to three or four key functions—really big guys who need to stop other people, lightning fast guys with good hands, a guy who can throw something, plus the occasional guy who can kick that same thing. Now Bill Belichick of the World Champion New England Patriots probably has 200 pages detailing a left inside guard vs. a right defensive tackle, but at the end of the day the requirements can be sorted out into those four functions.

RFID networks should be sorted out by base configurations. The most common ones are standard dock doors, conveyors, personnel doors, and stretch-wrap machines. Keep track of how each one of those are configured and set up. If you have 30 or 40 dock doors set up, even though there may be some differences, you should have a very high correlation as to how each one of those readers performs. You can use configuration changes to determine the optimization of a particular portal class. You can do this by creating a baseline performance for each interrogation zone type, and experimenting with new configurations and hardware by comparing with the existing performance. Just remember to test to statistical significance with the reader under test, so the data are meaningful.

The other way of optimizing a large-scale RFID deployment is to look at dependencies in the business process and set performance standards based on those dependencies. Think of a typical distribution center as an example. After items go through a dock door read zone, they usually are loaded onto a conveyor and pass another read zone, and then are often run through a sorting system read zone. Each one of these interrogation zones should have a very similar read rate of the same tag numbers. There should be a high correlation of specific tags in this business process flow. If there isn't—if one particular interrogation zone is significantly lower than the others in that same work flow—there is an opportunity to optimize that performance.

Describing a Troubleshooting Protocol

For CompTIA's RFID+ exam, you'll need to know what actions to take for troubleshooting, such as rebooting the machine, checking firmware versions, and inspecting cables. If you are interested in taking it a step further, you'll need to figure out a plan to do your own root-cause analysis. This section is going to walk you through a methodology for finding the problem with a faulty RFID network or system. (The section purposely does not spend much time on handheld readers because I've found that problems with handheld read rate and performance are going to be there when the handheld is initially deployed. If there is not an issue right from the start with a handheld, then it is likely to be a straight warranty issue that needs to be worked out with the manufacturer.) As you deploy these systems, there is no reason for you to hesitate to pick up the phone and call the hardware manufacturer. Many of the reader manufacturers, particularly the ones with well-established support networks such as Intermec, Zebra Technologies, Paxar, and Symbol Technologies, have a great support network of people to field calls relating to any issues with their products.

RFID Rescue

One of the country's largest producers of electronics equipment had installed over 250 readers in an east coast manufacturing facility. They had their conveyor vendor do the install and had read rates varying from 70% to 99.99%, but needed all readers to be consistent. When they hired us it was clear the conveyor company had only used a trial and error methodology for installation. Following ODIN's step by step troubleshooting protocol we were able to identify the primary issues and re-tune the readers to be providing greater than 99% read reliability.

Understanding the Steps to Isolate a Problem

Root-cause analysis begins with defining all the variables. This process will be specific to your problem, the hardware, the frequency under test, and the environment. For each particular problem, you should define a series of steps that will change one variable at a time to determine the effect on performance. Although this seems easy in theory, in practice it can be a lot more challenging.

The first step to isolate the problem is to effectively document the business process and record the entire system component by component, then test each one of those components one at a time. This is known as the *variable isolation approach*. It's tempting to overlook details in this part of the analysis. You may be tempted to put down something like the following:

1. Symbol XR-400 reader
2. Symbol general purpose antenna and cable

when what really should be listed is this:

1. Symbol XR-400 reader
2. Firmware version 8.2 with six subfiles
3. LMR-400 cable, 16′ long
4. Reverse XYZ connector
5. P-23 power supply
6. APC UPS back-up, 7550
7. ODIN universal rack for single side
8. Symbol light indicator box (LIB)
9. Thompson tri-lite lightstack, 12 V
10. Acme EPC sec middleware, version 2.3.2

As you can see, taking what could have been described with 2–3 items and expanding it into 10 gives a lot more detail and provides more single, discreet points of investigation.

Using a Variable Isolation Approach to Fix the Problem

You've probably heard the old adage, "If it ain't broke, don't fix it." Well, the big question in RFID is to find out what is or isn't broken. The key is to isolate each single variable at a time; that's why you went to the trouble of identifying and defining all the key variables in the previous step. It doesn't do any good to take out the nonworking system and just replace it because you won't learn what caused the problem, and can't do anything to keep it from happening again. Look at every diagnosis as an opportunity to learn for a future deployment project.

Isolating each variable in the system may require test equipment that is very specific to RFID, such as a spectrum analyzer, a VSWR bridge, a network analyzer, and a signal generator. These tools can allow you to take out one component—such as a length of cable—and test it against other similar items from a reference model system.

It is critical to keep in mind that something as simple as removing a type of connector can reduce the loss enough to make a difference in read rates. With that in mind, methodically going through your list of system components one at a time is the only way to find the root cause of the problem.

Containing Radiation

RFID readers, particularly UHF in the United States, radiate a significant amount of energy from their antennas. This can help you read items that absorb a lot of energy, and help you read at long distances (up to 10 meters). Like everything with RFID, that performance comes at a price. The trade-off comes when you have multiple readers set up in close proximity to each other. Usually a key business process requirement is that an RFID reader reads only the items coming through the portal where the reader is mounted. So if you have 10 dock doors, each with a reader, you want the reader at dock door 1 reading only items that come through dock door 1, not reading items that come through dock doors 2 and 3. The problem that you face when a reader reads beyond the desired boundary is a problem of RF containment.

There are two simple ways to determine the proper RFID settings. One takes a while and is manual; the other is industry best practice and is automated.

The manual method entails taking an average-performing tag from your tag testing, placing it on a cardboard box with similar contents of your typical case, and setting the case on a tripod or stool the same height as the products that come through the dock door. This is your test case. Next you take a roll of tape or can of spray paint and mark out on the floor where you want your boundary of reads to be. Using the reader's demonstration software and the test case, move the case around the outside of that boundary marker on the floor and turn down the power level on the reader until you are unable to read the test case. After you've made it around the entire boundary layer, bring the case back to the middle of the interrogation zone with the power at the lowest setting used on the outside and make sure you can still read it effectively in the middle of the interrogation zone.

The second method uses a configuration and deployment tool called EasyReader. This tool is the industry best practice, and allows the user to take a portal probe (which acts like a virtual tag) and employ the software to tune the reader at the critical boundary. ODIN Technologies developed this software after hours and hours of using the manual method and found that the accuracy is increased while the time to configure properly is significantly decreased. The software allows the portal probe to give enough information back to automatically configure the reader. I'll talk about the software in greater detail in the sidebar on the next page.

TIP If you do not want to go through extensive testing or buy a software tool such as EasyReader, you can configure most readers and middleware to work only when there is something inside the interrogation zone. A simple motion sensor triggering the Read command will make sure that the reader is reading only when there's something in the zone. This doesn't mean that the same reader won't read adjacent dock doors or have poor performance because it's not warmed up, but it's an easy way to play the odds of reading only in a single zone.

Software to Keep You from Getting into Trouble, or to Get You out of Trouble

After deploying dozens of readers the "old-fashioned way" by using a spectrum analyzer to test power consistency, tapping out critical boundary layers, and attaching signal generators to the portal antennas, it was clear that the manual method would not scale to meet the needs of the industry. That's when ODIN Technologies began looking for an automated way of doing it. Originally, as with many software programs, we started trying to do one or two things automatically—record read success rate, measure performance from each antenna, and other time-consuming tasks. Pretty soon we had a group of products that could be put together to make up a software suite that would make the deployment of large, complex RFID networks more scalable, accurate, and faster. That's when EasyReader was created.

EasyReader provides a simple drag-and-drop interface that allows some of the more-complex and time-consuming tasks to be fully automated. Based on hundreds of deployments using EasyReader, we were able to reduce deployment time from six to eight hours per portal to less than 90 minutes.

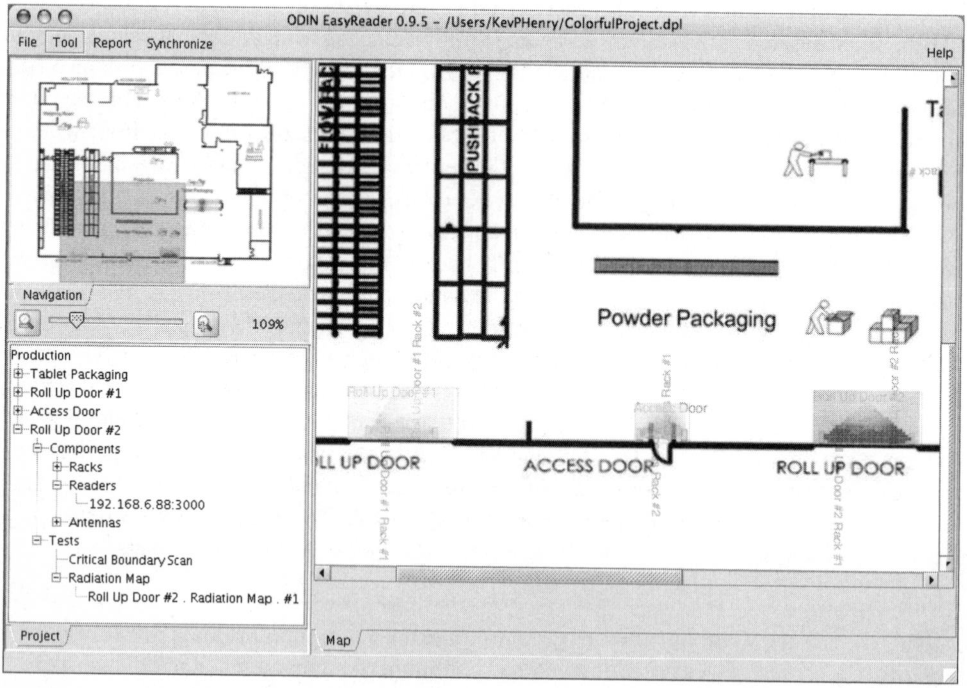

EasyReader can be used in the initial setup of an RFID network or can be used as a troubleshooting tool for a poorly functioning interrogation zone. The figure above shows what EasyReader looks like. The upper-left corner is the blueprint of the entire facility, or the engineering drawings; the lower-left corner is the individual component description (such as antenna or reader); and the large screen on the right is the workspace where you can drag and drop to add new portals, create bills of materials so you don't forget any components, and go through a detailed configuration and testing process. You should pay particular attention to the shaded areas around the various read points, this gives an actual look at the *radiation containment*. You can tell exactly where the RF energy propagates to. This patented technology is a huge help in initial deployments as well as troubleshooting.

The last step in any troubleshooting scenario is to document the steps you took and the results from the various tests. With EasyReader you can do this automatically, and the configurations and test results are stored for other people to review. This is particularly important if a problem arises again and you are not the one troubleshooting. A smart service technician is going to look back at the last trouble ticket or service documentation and see what the issue was. That's the place to start in investigating a problem with the same reader.

The last method of containing radiation is to use metallic or synthetic material to block radio waves from going outside a certain area. This is commonly referred to as shielding and can be done anywhere you want to try and block off direct RFI signals. The problem is that RF waves bounce up down and sideways and therefore can work around a single piece of shielding.

Summary

This chapter gave you a solid overview of the challenging process of troubleshooting an RFID interrogation zone. You may have set up the reader yourself and are trying to find out why it doesn't work right, or you may have been called in to clean up someone else's mess. Either way, you have to follow a process to get to the root cause of the problem.

The first step is understanding what affects the performance of an RFID system. You learned that there are several dependencies that can affect read rate:

- Tags
- Readers
- Antennas
- Middleware
- Business processes

Next you looked at specific issues within an interrogation zone that may be caused by the zone's individual components. You learned some of the specific details of those subcomponents and how to investigate parts that might fail.

Finally I showed you a software tool that automates much of the deployment and troubleshooting. You saw how to set up a process for isolating variables and then test for a root-cause analysis. This is time-consuming and can be facilitated by an automated program. A repeatable process is also something that should be created as a standard protocol for testing poorly performing systems, gathering data on those systems, and creating a strategy to optimize them.

Exam Essentials

Explain the key drivers of an RFID system. The RFID system and its performance can be attributed to tags, readers, antennas, and the software controlling the devices which is called middleware. Each of the core components has the capability to totally disrupt the performance of an RFID system.

Describe the function of firmware. Firmware is the specialized device software that controls what happens inside the readers and with the antennas. Depending on the reader, the firmware can have some filter functionality that limits the amount of traffic required to go over the network.

Describe a basic troubleshooting protocol. A basic troubleshooting protocol identifies all the variables that have the potential to impact the performance and stability of a system. The variables should be identified down to the lowest possible level. After the variables are identified, they should be tested one at a time to determine whether any one specific variable is the root cause of the problem.

Illustrate business processes having an impact on read rates. The way that you do things when RFID readers are around can be as important as how the readers are set up. Business processes determine how things are done. These processes need to be considered when setting up an interrogation zone so you can make sure that a person, vehicle, or material-handling machine does not interfere with the RFID reader's ability to send a signal to the tag and receive a signal back. Standing in front of the antennas that are attached to a reader can create an impenetrable barrier to reads, so know where workers can and can't be is a key part of mapping the business processes.

Determine how cabling affects an interrogation zone. Cabling comes in varying levels of insulation to protect from signal loss and noise. The industry standard is LMR-240. This size is effective for distances under 25 feet from the antenna to the reader. The more connectors that are attached to any cable, the more loss that is likely to occur as the signal travels from the reader to the antenna.

Verify that a reader is communicating data to the outside world. Connecting an interrogator to a laptop and then pinging the reader to make sure it is communicating to the outside world is essential to troubleshooting a communications problem. Most readers are deployed with a fixed IP address (not DHCP), which are IP addresses from a specific subnet (normally starting with 10. or 168.). You need to know the IP address before you can ping it.

Define a standing wave. A standing wave from tag to interrogation antenna is a wave in which the distribution of field strength (always a null) is formed by the superposition of two waves propagating in opposite directions. Because it is a null, there is no power to read the tag. This is also called a multi-path effect.

Key Terms

Before you take the exam, be certain you are familiar with the following terms:

average tag

baseline

firmware

Generation 1

Generation 2

LMR

multi-path

ping

radiation containment

standing wave

variable isolation approach

voltage standing wave ratio (VSWR)

Review Questions

1. A customer calls you up and tells you that their RFID portal has stopped reading tags completely. What is the first thing you should do when you get on-site?

   A. Call the reader manufacturer for help.

   B. Install the newest firmware.

   C. Set up a signal generator with a frequency equal to the center frequency of the interrogator and attach the reader's antenna to the signal generator.

   D. Reboot the reader.

2. What is the best kind of cable to use for a dock door that is 15″ to the center of the door from one side, if you are installing a reader on one side and antennas on both sides?

   A. LMR-240

   B. LMR-400

   C. PJS007

   D. It does not matter; the cable is irrelevant.

3. What type of software is required to change if you are going from reading one protocol to another, such as ISO to EPC, or Gen 1 to Gen 2?

   A. Firmware

   B. Middleware

   C. Shareware

   D. Edgeware

4. A UHF tag was applied to a corrugated cardboard box and was read successfully when shipped. The box was transported by sea. The tag was well protected from any damage. On receiving the box, the tag did not read. What can be a probable cause for the failure?

   A. Tag was damaged

   B. Humidity

   C. Product inside the box

   D. Wrong tag for destination country frequency

5. What accessory used with the spectrum analyzer helps determine the performance of an antenna?

   A. Reader

   B. Tag

   C. VSWR bridge

   D. Tuning fork

6. A particular read zone did not have optimal performance. You tested the cable and noticed one of the following. Please indicate the reason that can lead to the poor reads.

   A. The cable was kinked.

   B. The cable was red in color.

   C. There was dust on cable.

   D. The cable used was LMR-400.

7. You are attempting to write to tags with a newly installed reader; however, the process is constantly failing. What is the most likely problem?

   A. The tags are all damaged.

   B. The network connection is damaged.

   C. The reader is improperly configured.

   D. The reader antenna is improperly installed.

8. You are reading tags on pallets of oatmeal in an interrogation zone but some of the tags do not get read. You find out that you are usually missing tags in a similar spot. What can be the problem?

   A. Oatmeal is RF-unfriendly material.

   B. Tags were not read in one spot because of a hole or null in antenna coverage.

   C. Oatmeal causes multi-path reflections.

   D. Your reader is improperly configured.

9. You found out that in a particular interrogation zone, the UHF tags were not read at random times during the day, in periods varying from 1 to 10 minutes. What could have been the problem?

   A. Damaged tags were applied to products.

   B. The reading was triggered at incorrect times.

   C. A nearby airport was broadcasting communication signals at 1000 MHz with power many times what an RFID reader broadcasts.

   D. Warehouse workers were using microwave ovens in the reader proximity.

10. How do you prevent reader interference from adjacent dock door interrogation zones? (Select two options.)

    A. Using time synchronization

    B. Using shielding

    C. Using anticollision

    D. By proper antenna tuning

11. When you are trying to connect the reader to your laptop via a serial port, which of the following will be required?
    A. Serial cable
    B. Knowing the COM port number on the laptop
    C. Baud rate setting
    D. All of the above

12. You are on a client site, trying to troubleshoot poor read rates. After some analysis, you come to a conclusion that tags may be the reason for the poor reads. You are equipped with only a reader, an antenna, a measuring tape, and a laptop. How can you evaluate the performance of 100 tags? (Select two options.)
    A. Perform distance testing on the 100 tags.
    B. Call the tag manufacturer.
    C. Vary reader power and obtain minimum effective power (MEP).
    D. Order new tags.

13. Which of the following can result in power loss? (Select two options.)
    A. Long cable lengths
    B. Connectors
    C. A vacuum
    D. Nitrogen

14. An HF RFID system is deployed in a conveyor system in a manufacturing plant. The system is surrounded by a lot of metal. The read performance is poor. How can you improve the performance?
    A. Use a VSWR bridge to tune the antenna back to 13.56 MHz.
    B. Provide shielding.
    C. Use a UHF system.
    D. Nothing can be done.

15. From the following list, select the options that can introduce noise in a UHF RFID system.
    A. Adjacent readers
    B. Antenna cables having damaged insulation
    C. Wireless handheld system operating at 915 MHz
    D. All of the above

16. You need to buy cables for deploying a UHF RFID system. What type of coax cable and RF connector connection (joint) method should you opt for?

A. The core of the coax cable should be soldered to the connector.

B. The core of the coax cable should be crimped to the connector.

C. The core of the coax cable should be wrapped around the connector.

D. The core of the coax cable automatically connects to the RF connectors.

17. What is the best method for troubleshooting an RFID handheld device?

A. Take the cover off and investigate the connections from the antenna to the CPU.

B. Replace the battery and fully charge.

C. Hold a tag in front of the reader and measure the distance away it will read.

D. Call the manufacturer.

18. You are receiving shipping containers in the European Union, where ETSI is the governing body. What is the first thing to check if you are not reading the active 433 MHz tag that is attached to each container? (Select two options.)

A. Use a VSWR bridge to test the reader's antenna for a resonant frequency of 433 MHz.

B. Check the battery of the active tag.

C. Make sure your reader is also 433 MHz.

D. Nothing can be done.

19. A UHF RFID system is deployed in a data center to track servers coming and going through the door. The software attached to the portal and four antennas (two on each side) have stopped giving information on whether the server is coming into or out of the data center. What could be wrong?

A. The antennas on one side of the door have stopped functioning.

B. A firmware upgrade may have changed the configuration.

C. Installing new middleware may have changed the reader's configuration.

D. All of the above.

20. An HF RFID system is deployed on a shelf in a hospital pharmacy. Recently the shelves were replaced and the system stopped working. What can you do to remedy the problem?

A. Use a VSWR bridge to tune the antenna back to 13.56 MHz.

B. Increase the power output in effective radiated power (ERP).

C. Check the data being written to each tag.

D. Switch out the reader.

Answers to Review Questions

1. D. The first thing you should do is to reboot the reader. Readers are small computers, without the keyboard, video, and mouse, so occasionally they will lock up when things go wrong. The simplest first step after you've checked to see whether the power is on is to reboot the reader and see whether that fixes the problem.

2. B. Because the dock door has to be 30″ wide (15″ to the center from one side, times two), that run is likely to cause excessive loss over LMR-240. Therefore, the correct choice is to use LMR-400, which will have less loss because of increased insulation.

3. A. Firmware is the software that sits on the reader and controls what it can or can't do. Allowing it to read one type of tag and not another is part of its functionality. Middleware accepts read data from an interrogator and creates business logic or actionable items from the RFID data. The only time middleware can affect an interrogation zone is when the middleware is programmed to change the reader settings.

4. B or D. Corrugated cardboard boxes have a high affinity to store humidity. The box was transported by sea, so the box must have absorbed humidity, which can detune the tag. (Moisture is RF unfriendly at UHF.) The tag could also be read by a different protocol reader, for instance a proprietary system might be trying to read an ISO tag.

5. C. The VSWR bridge along with the spectrum analyzer helps determine the performance of an antenna. The larger the dip in the VSWR graph, the less loss exhibited by the antenna, and hence the better performance it will have.

6. A. A kinked cable can introduce high losses resulting in less power for the tag to operate. This can lead to poor read rates.

7. C. In this case, the reader is improperly configured, and most likely the air interface protocol and data protocol of the reader and the tag do not match.

8. B. Multi-path interference or imperfections in antennas can cause holes in RF coverage in the interrogation zones. The unread tags in the same spot were most likely falling into the hole in the antenna field. This could be solved by overlapping fields as well as by moving the tagged objects.

9. C. Completing the full Faraday cycle analysis will show things on the periphery of the frequency, and also show the power level. Having something close to one of the end frequencies (either 902 or 928 in the USA) can bleed over into the range used.

10. B, D. To prevent interference from adjacent interrogation zones, you may need to use proper shielding and adjust the power going to the antenna. This will prevent interference by containing the RF fields within their own interrogation zones.

11. D. To achieve serial connectivity between the reader and the laptop, it is essential that you have a serial cable with DB9 connectors and know the COM port number on the laptop, so you can configure the COM port. It is very important that you know what baud rate settings are required to connect with the reader. This information can be obtained from the reader manual.

12. A, C. By determining a set distance where some tags for the batch respond and some don't, you can find superior, average, and under-performing tags. You can also find the superior, average, and under-performing tags by varying the reader power and keeping each tag from the batch at a set distance. By reducing the power below a certain value, tags will stop responding, allowing you to determine the MEP value for each tag and sort them as superior, average, and under-performing.

13. A, B. In an RFID system setup, longer cable lengths and connectors add to power loss. In cables, the loss is due to impurities in conductors and leakage. In connectors, losses are due to contact resistance and leakage.

14. A. The high amount of metal surrounding the conveyor system detunes the antenna. By using a VSWR bridge and tuning screwdriver, you can tune (change the inductance and capacitance) the system to operate at 13.56 MHz.

15. D. Adjacent readers can be the biggest source of interference or noise; a reader that is noisy can easily kill a tag response, resulting in poor read rates. Cables that have a damaged insulation can directly add noise to the center conductor carrying the signal of interest. Just like the adjacent readers, the wireless handheld systems can also act as noise sources.

16. A. The soldering approach provides the best connectivity in terms of both electrical and mechanical connectivity. Crimped connections result in mechanically weak joints. Wrapped connectors are difficult to use as RF connectors; also, wrapping the thick coax core conductor can result in higher resistance at the point of contacts, resulting in heat, which results in oxidation.

17. D. RFID handhelds usually work out of the box, and you know the performance you are getting. If there is a problem, it's usually due to the handheld being dropped or damaged, and is best dealt with by the manufacturer.

18. B, C. The battery tag is the first thing to check; it could have failed for a number of reasons, but an active tag without a battery will not read. The other issue is that the reader may be for a passive RFID tag for 968 MHz, and you are trying to read an active tag. Although this last point may seem obvious, you'd be surprised at the number of times it happens.

19. D. The combination of middleware, firmware, and reader settings can create a number of issues. If something is working well and there is any change to the system, then it will be highly likely that one of the "soft" components of the RFID network has caused the problem.

20. A. The shelves that were swapped out were likely metal shelves instead of wood, or perhaps the reader was tuned for metal shelves but wood shelves were installed. A simple check is to see whether the antenna has been detuned because of the change in material.

Chapter 9

Standards and Regulations

RFID+ EXAM OBJECTIVES COVERED IN THIS CHAPTER:

✓ **3.1 Given a scenario, map user requirements to standards**

- 3.1.1 Regulations, standards that impact the design of a particular RFID solution

✓ **3.2 Identify the differences between air interface protocols and tag data formats**

✓ **3.3 Recognize regulatory requirements globally and by region (keep at high level, not specific requirements—may use scenarios)**

✓ **3.4 Recognize safety regulations/issues regarding human exposure**

If your idea of a standard is a type of poodle, you might not be RFID technician material. To speed end-user adoption and make sure that people across the globe are speaking the same language, RFID, as with many other industries, follows standards and regulations created by international, regional, national, and local authorities. Standards that apply to RFID are usually regulations that were created for other RF-emitting devices or data-capture technologies and were amended or changed to provide specifications for RFID applications. Many organizations base their standards on current uses of the technology as well as best practices and leave space for future inventions and expansions. These standards also ensure that the RFID applications do not restrict operation of other systems and are not safety hazards.

In this chapter, you will learn about the international, regional, and national standards organizations and regulatory authorities, as well as industry groups and their efforts to standardize and regulate RFID technology. I must warn you though: there are many acronyms in this chapter!

First, you will learn about the International Organization for Standardization (ISO) and the International Electrotechnical Commission (IEC). There you go—the acronyms are taking over already. These two organizations joined in an effort to provide technical standards for information technology including RFID, and they developed many data standards and air interface protocols specifically for RFID technology.

Next, you will find out about the frequencies around the world that were allocated by the International Telecommunication Union (ITU) and discover which countries belong to which of the three regions the ITU established. You will also learn about other functions the ITU performs.

Last but not least of the main group of international standardization organizations is the Universal Postal Union (UPU), which regulates everything related to postal communication and services. The UPU also developed standards for RFID. These standards were presented to the ISO and were used as the basis for some of the ISO/IEC RFID standards.

You will also learn about regional organizations. You will see that there are many organizations in Europe, such as the European Committee for Standardization (CEN), the European Committee for Electrotechnical Standardization (CENELEC), the European Conference of Postal and Telecommunications Administrations (CEPT) including the Electronic Communications Committee (ECC) and the European Radiocommunications Office (ERO), and the European Telecommunications Standards Institute (ETSI). In the United States, the main organizations are the Federal Communications Commission (FCC) and the American National Standards Institute (ANSI). In China, RFID is regulated by the Standardization Administration of China (SAC), and in Hong Kong by the Office of the Telecommunications Authority (OFTA). In Japan, RFID is regulated by the Ministry of Public Management, Home Affairs,

Posts, and Telecommunications (MPHPT). You will also learn about various limits for transmitted power posed by these organizations.

Next, you will learn about individual organizations and groups that are more focused on the automatic identification and data capture (AIDC) and the RFID industry, such as GS1, EPCglobal, and AIM Global. You will also recognize different EPC formats and learn their specifics.

Finally, you will also discover various safety regulations, which apply to personnel safety and radiation exposure safety of humans as well as devices. You will find out which organizations publish standards related to worker safety and which organizations take care of human exposure limits to RF and other radiation, as well as guidelines for safe power output and proximity to Hazards of Electromagnetic Radiation to Ordnance (HERO) Unsafe devices. (More on HERO later in this chapter.)

I told you, many acronyms! You will find out more about them in the following text.

International Standardization Organizations

The main international organizations that create and publish technical standards and specifications are the ISO and IEC. Other important international organizations are the ITU, which governs telecommunication and radiocommunication around the world, and the UPU, which governs postal communication including digital services and mail tracking. These organizations develop global standards and guidelines that are related to the RFID systems.

International Organization for Standardization (ISO)

The ISO develops technical standards and specifications for various products, services, processes, materials, and systems. The ISO has also developed standards for goods conformity assessment and managerial and organizational practices for industrial and business organizations as well as governments and other regulatory bodies.

ISO standards help with the efficiency, safety, and environmental impact of the development, manufacturing, and supply of products and services. These standards provide the technical basis for governments to create regulations around health, safety, and environmental issues. The ISO's general goal is to safeguard consumers and users of products and services.

The ISO regulates all areas except the parts associated with electricity, electronics, and related technologies, which are governed by the IEC. The ISO and IEC came together, creating the Joint Technical Committee for Information Technology (JTC1).

Table 9.1 describes the most important standards related to RFID systems developed by the ISO (in cooperation with the IEC).

TABLE 9.1 ISO/IEC Standards Related to RFID

Standard	Description
ISO/IEC 10373	Identification cards—test methods
ISO 10374	Freight containers—automatic identification (RF automatic identification)
ISO 11784 ISO11785	Animal tracking standards including RFID identification codes for animals and means for animal data communication
ISO 14223	Radio frequency identification of animals—advanced transponders
ISO/IEC 14443	Proximity cards—guidelines for RF power, signal interface, transmission protocol, and physical characteristics
ISO 14814	Road transport and traffic telematics—automatic vehicle and equipment identification—reference architecture and terminology
ISO/IEC 15434	Syntax for high-capacity automatic data capture (ADC) media
ISO/IEC 15459-1	Unique identifiers—Part 1: Unique identifiers for transport units
ISO/IEC 15459-4	Unique identifiers—Part 4: Unique identifiers for supply-chain management
ISO/IEC 15693	Vicinity cards—air interface, initialization, anticollision, transmission protocol, and physical characteristics
ISO/IEC 15961	RFID for item management—Data protocol: application interface
ISO/IEC 15962	RFID for item management—Data protocol: data-encoding rules and logical memory functions
ISO/IEC 15963	RFID for item management—unique identification of RF tags
ISO 1736X series	Series related to shipping container applications of RFID
ISO/DIS 17363	Supply-chain applications of RFID—freight containers
ISO/DIS 17364	Supply-chain applications of RFID—returnable transport items

TABLE 9.1 ISO/IEC Standards Related to RFID *(continued)*

Standard	Description
ISO/DIS 17365	Supply-chain applications of RFID—transport units
ISO/DIS 17366	Supply-chain applications of RFID—product packaging
ISO/DIS 17367	Supply-chain applications of RFID—product tagging
ISO/IEC 18000 series	RFID for item management: applies to air interface management
ISO/IEC 18000-1	Reference architecture and definition of parameters to be standardized
ISO/IEC 18000-2	Parameters for air interface communications below 135 kHz
ISO/IEC 18000-3	Parameters for air interface communications at 13.56 MHz
ISO/IEC 18000-4	Parameters for air interface communications at 2.45 GHz
ISO/IEC 18000-5	Parameters for air interface communications at 5.8 GHz (this part has been withdrawn)
ISO/IEC 18000-6 (A, B and C)	Parameters for air interface communications at 860 to 960 MHz (EPC Class 1 Generation 2—18000 Part 6C)
ISO/IEC 18000-7	Parameters for active air interface communications at 433 MHz
ISO 18185	Freight containers—electronic seals
ISO/IEC 19762-3	Automatic identification and data capture (AIDC) techniques—harmonized vocabulary—Part 3: Radio frequency identification (RFID)
ISO 21007	Gas cylinders—identification and marking using RFID
ISO/IEC 22536	Telecommunications and information exchange between systems—near-field communication interface and protocol (NFCIP-1)—RF interface test methods
ISO/IEC 24730	Real-time locating systems (RTLS)

Note that the ISO specifies not only *data protocols,* but also *air interface protocols.* What is the difference? A tag data format/data protocol specifies the size and structure of the tag memory, tag data formatting and length, and the means of storing, accessing, and transferring information. A tag data standard is, for example, EPC Class 1 Generation 1 or ISO 15962.

The air interface protocol defines the rules of communication between tags and interrogators. The air interface protocol includes rules for encoding, modulation, and anticollision, as well as for reading and writing to a tag and other operations. The protocol usually does not define the tag architecture or encoding capacity of the tag. An example of an air interface protocol is the ISO 18000 Part 6A.

A standard that describes both the tag data format and air interface protocol is the EPC Generation 2/ISO 18000 Part 6C.

International Electrotechnical Commission (IEC)

The IEC prepares and publishes standards for all electro-related technologies including electronics, magnetic and electromagnetic devices, electroacoustics, multimedia, telecommunication, and energy production and distribution, as well as related areas including terminology and symbols, electromagnetic compatibility, measurement and performance, dependability, design and development, safety, and environmental effects. Standards developed by the IEC are used as a basis for national standards development and as a reference for international contracts. As I mentioned earlier, the IEC produces standards in cooperation with the ISO.

The IEC also produces conformity assessment and certification schemes in order to reassure the end user that the products meet minimum quality standards (which are high). The schemes are operated by the following organizations:

- IEC System for Conformity Testing and Certification of Electrical Equipment (IECEE)
- IEC Quality Assessment System for Electronic Components (IECQ)
- IEC Scheme for Certification to Standards Relating to Equipment for Use in Explosive Atmospheres (IECEx scheme)

International Telecommunication Union (ITU)

The ITU is a specialized agency of the United Nations and has 190 member countries, as well as an additional number of sector members and associates. The goal of this organization is to govern and improve international telecommunication technology and radiocommunication-based systems by producing standards and recommendations, assigning radio frequencies, managing the radio spectrum, and developing partnerships between governments and private industries to help improve the telecommunication infrastructure in underdeveloped countries.

The ITU is divided into three main sectors:

- ITU-D (Telecommunication Development)
- ITU-R (Radiocommunication)
- ITU-T (Telecommunication Standardization)

The sector that is related to RFID is the Radiocommunication sector. The ITU-R determines the technical characteristics and operational procedures for various wireless technologies and services. This sector also manages the radio-frequency spectrum and assigns the frequencies to various technologies and purposes.

You were probably wondering why certain frequency bands are used for RFID and not others and why some regions (Europe, for instance) have to fight hard to get a reasonable chunk of the frequency so that the RFID systems can be implemented and efficiently used. The ITU-R's system is behind the reason. The frequency spectrum between 9 kHz and 400 GHz has been divided into 1,265,000 terrestrial frequency assignments, 87,096 assignments servicing 590 satellite networks, and another 46,179 assignments related to 3,163 satellite earth stations. So now you can see that RFID cannot choose its frequency bands but has to fit in with wireless and cellular networks, satellites, television and radio broadcasting, and other radio-based systems.

For the purpose of frequency assignment and management, the ITU divides the world into three main regions:

Region 1 Includes Europe, Africa, the Middle East west of the Persian Gulf (including Iraq), and the former Soviet Union

Region 2 Includes North and South America

Region 3 Consists of Asia (excluding the former Soviet Union) and the Middle East east of the Persian Gulf, including Iran, Australia, and Oceania

Universal Postal Union (UPU)

The UPU is the main organization overseeing postal services around the world. It participates in the development of quality, universal, efficient, and accessible postal services for people around the globe by guaranteeing the free circulation of postal items, promoting standards adoption and the application of technology, and addressing customer needs.

The UPU has also developed standards related to RFID technology. It has produced the working draft standards listed in Table 9.2, which were eventually presented to the ISO to provide some information and basis for ISO RFID standards development.

TABLE 9.2 UPU Standards Related to RFID

Standard	Description
S20-3	Identification and marking using radio frequency identification technology: Reference architecture and terminology
S21-2	Data presentation in ASN.1
S22-3	Identification and marking using radio frequency identification technology: System requirements and test procedures
S23a-2	Radio frequency identification (RFID) and radio data capture (RDC) systems—air interfaces: Communications and interfaces Part A: Definitions of parameters to be standardized

TABLE 9.2 UPU Standards Related to RFID *(continued)*

Standard	Description
S23b-1	Radio frequency identification (RFID) and radio data capture (RDC) systems—air interfaces: Communications and Interfaces Part B: Parameter values for 5.8 GHz RFID systems
S23c-1	Radio frequency identification (RFID) and radio data capture (RDC) systems—air interfaces: Communications and interfaces Part C: Parameter values for 2.45 GHz narrow band RFID systems
S23g-1	Radio frequency identification (RFID) and radio data capture (RDC) systems—air interfaces: Communications and interfaces Part G: Parameter values for 13.56 MHz band RFID systems

Standardization and Regulatory Organizations by Region

Several organizations develop standards and regulations with jurisdiction over certain regions, such as Europe. There are also national standardization and regulatory organizations that usually closely cooperate with the regional and international organizations and adopt the rules specified by these authorities.

Europe

The main standardization organizations in Europe that produce standards related to RFID systems are as follows:

- European Committee for Standardization (CEN)
- European Committee for Electrotechnical Standardization (CENELEC)
- European Conference of Postal and Telecommunications Administrations (CEPT)
- European Telecommunications Standards Institute (ETSI)

We will look at them in more detail in the following sections.

European Committee for Standardization (CEN)

CEN is an organization contributing to the objectives of the European Union and European Economic Area with voluntary technical standards promoting free trade, worker and consumer safety, interoperability of networks, environmental protection, and other areas.

European Committee for Electrotechnical Standardization (CENELEC)

CENELEC prepares voluntary electrotechnical standards that help develop the Single European Market/European Economic Area for electrical and electronic goods and services. CENELEC consists of the national electrotechnical committees of 29 European countries and affiliates. CENELEC produces directives with assessments and limits for radio frequency emissions, such as the following:

- Assessment of electronic and electrical equipment related to human exposure restrictions for electromagnetic fields (0–300 GHz)
- Information technology equipment—Radio disturbance characteristics—Limits and methods of measurement
- Electromagnetic compatibility (EMC)—Part 6-4: Generic standards—Emission standard for industrial environments
- Electromagnetic compatibility (EMC)—Part 6-3: Generic standards—Emission standard for residential, commercial, and light-industrial environments
- Limits for harmonic current emissions, and other emission and exposure limits

European Conference of Postal and Telecommunications Administrations (CEPT)

CEPT includes the following organizations:

- Electronic Communications Committee (ECC)
- European Radiocommunications Office (ERO), which supports ECC
- European Postal Committee (CERP), which takes care of the postal communications

NOTE

CERP translates into "Comité Européen des Régulateurs Postaux."

The ECC's main function is the development of radiocommunications policies, primarily regarding frequency coordination, allocation, and utilization. The ECC publishes "ECC decisions," which are then presented to the governments of each European country. These decisions can be accepted and implemented or not, depending on the country's choice.

The ECC's decisions and recommendations are published by the ERO, whose functions besides supporting the ECC are to provide consultations on frequency spectrum issues, work with national frequency spectrum management authorities, identify and promote best practices in national numbering schemes, and generally provide expertise and advice to the ECC in the radio and telecommunications fields.

ECC decisions related to RFID include documents regarding nonspecific short-range devices:

ERC/DEC(01)01 ERC decision of March 12, 2001, on harmonized frequencies, technical characteristics, and exemption from individual licensing of nonspecific short-range devices operating in the frequency bands 6765–6795 kHz and 13.553–13.567 MHz.

ERC/DEC(01)04 ERC decision of March 12, 2001, on harmonized frequencies, technical characteristics, and exemption from individual licensing of nonspecific short-range devices operating in the frequency bands 868.0–868.6 MHz, 868.7–869.2 MHz, 869.4–869.65 MHz, and 869.7–870.0 MHz.

ERC/DEC(01)05 ERC decision of March 12, 2001, on harmonized frequencies, technical characteristics, and exemption from individual licensing of nonspecific short-range devices operating in the frequency band 2400–2483.5 MHz.

ERC/DEC(01)06 ERC decision of March 12, 2001, on harmonized frequencies, technical characteristics, and exemption from individual licensing of nonspecific short-range devices operating in the frequency band 5725–5875 MHz.

European Telecommunications Standards Institute (ETSI)

ETSI is an organization spun off from CEPT and is officially recognized by the European Commission as an authority that produces standards for information and communication technologies (ICT) within Europe. These standards include telecommunications as well as Internet, broadcasting, and related areas.

ETSI describes operation of RFID systems in the following standards:

EN 300 220 Electromagnetic compatibility and radio spectrum matters (ERM); short-range devices (SRDs); radio equipment to be used in the 25–1,000 MHz frequency range with power levels ranging up to 500 mW.

> This UHF regulation allows a maximum reader-transmitted power of 500 mW in a band of 250 kHz at 869.4–869.65 MHz.
>
> The UHF band is limited in power, bandwidth, and duty cycle when compared to the United States.
>
> Readers are required to either use listen-before-talk (LBT) or transmit in duty cycles, which limit them to operate in only a short period within each hour (for less then 10 percent of the time within 869.4–869.65 MHz at 500 mW).

EN 302 208 Electromagnetic compatibility and radio spectrum matters (ERM); radio frequency identification equipment operating in the band 865–868 MHz with power levels up to 2 W. This is a new standard, which creates better conditions for adoption and implementation of RFID in the UHF band in Europe.

> The UHF band got an addition of 3 MHz, 865–868 MHz, which was divided into three sub-bands. For 865–865.6 MHz the allowed transmitted power is up to 0.1 W (ERP); for 865.6–867.6 MHz it is up to 2 W (ERP); and for 867.6–868 MHz it is up to 0.5 W (ERP).

NOTE The allowed power in Europe is provided in effective radiated power (ERP). If you convert it to effective isotropically radiated power (EIRP), you will get about 3.26 W EIRP, which is very close to the allowed power in the United States, although the frequency band is still a lot smaller (only 2 MHz in Europe as opposed to 26 MHz in the United States.)

This regulation does not require operation in duty cycles, but requires using LBT and triggered interrogation in order to reduce interference.

North America

In North America, the main regulatory authorities specifying functions and restrictions for communication technologies are the FCC and ANSI.

Federal Communications Commission (FCC)

The FCC is an independent agency of the U.S. government that regulates interstate and international communications via radio, television, wire, satellite, and cable, including telephone, telegraph, and cellular networks. The FCC's jurisdiction covers the 50 states, the District of Columbia, and U.S. territories.

FCC Part 15 specifies regulations under which an intentional, unintentional, or incidental radiator may be operated without an individual license. It also contains the technical specifications, administrative requirements, and other conditions relating to the marketing of devices regulated by Part 15. If the operation of the radiator is not in accordance with the regulations, it has to be licensed or you could be fined for every day of using such a radiator.

Section 15.225 specifies the operation within the band 13.110–14.010 MHz, which applies to the HF frequency of 13.56 MHz used for RFID systems.

Section 15.240 regulates the operation in the band 433.5–434.5 MHz, which is used for UHF active tags.

Section 15.247 defines the operation within the bands 902–928 MHz, 2400–2483.5 MHz, and 5725–5850 MHz (UHF and microwave frequency). Radiators have to employ frequency hopping or digital modulation.

Real World Scenario

Differences between American and European installations

Once, I had to put together a collection of RFID equipment (readers, antennas, and printers) for a training session taking place in Europe. Although I had enough RFID devices on hand in the United States, I had to do research and purchase new devices that would comply with European standards. I had to make sure not only that this equipment was ETSI compliant (which is not always the case), but also that it had correct power supplies and plugs for the country where the training was taking place. As you may know, in Europe the electrical sockets are not "one size fits all" and it is useful to have a converter or a correct plug for your device. Also, do not forget that although the United States uses 110 V power, Europe usually runs at 220–240 V.

Rules for systems operating at 902–928 MHz using frequency hopping are as follows:

- If the 20 dB bandwidth of the hopping channel is less than 250 kHz, the system should hop across at least 50 channels, with the average time in one channel not exceeding 0.4 seconds within a 20-second period. Such a system can transmit up to 1 W.
- If the 20 dB bandwidth of the hopping channel is 250 kHz or greater, the system should hop across at least 25 channels, with the average time spent in one channel not exceeding 0.4 seconds within a 10-second period. The maximum allowed 20 dB bandwidth of the hopping channel is 500 kHz. If the system employs between 25 and 49 hopping channels, it can transmit up to 0.25 W.

Rules for systems operating at 2400–2483.5 MHz using frequency hopping are as follows:

- Systems should hop across at least 15 channels, with average occupancy time less than 0.4 seconds within a period equal to 0.4 number of hopping channels.
- If the systems hop across at least 75 nonoverlapping channels, the allowed transmitted power is up to 1 W. If they hop across fewer channels, the allowed power is 0.125 W.

Rules for systems using digital modulation at 902–928 MHz, 2400–2483.5 MHz, and 5725–5850 MHz bands are as follows:

- The minimum 6 dB bandwidth has to be at least 500 kHz.
- The allowed transmitted power is up to 1 W.

The FCC specifies that the output power limits are based on antennas with directional gains under 6 dBi. If an antenna has higher gain than 6 dBi, the power output has to be reduced in order to stay within the transmitted power limits. As you recall, I explained the reason for this in Chapter 1 on physics (yes, those crazy calculations). There are exceptions to this rule for systems operating at 2400–2483.5 MHz and 5725–5850 MHz when these systems are used for fixed, point-to-point operations.

NOTE One watt of the interrogator output power with a 6 dBi antenna means that the EIRP of this system is 4 watts.

The FCC also publishes limits for radio frequency radiation exposure (Section 1.1310) related to occupational as well as general public exposure.

American National Standards Institute (ANSI)

Another important standards organization in the United States is ANSI. This institute develops voluntary consensus-based standards and recommendations for various regulatory organizations and industries.

One ANSI technical standard related to RFID systems is ANSI INCITS 256, which defines RFID devices that are operating without restrictions on available international frequency bands at power levels that do not require a license. This standard intends to promote interoperability and compatibility between RFID devices by defining a common API and limited Physical and Data-Link layer options. It also supports item management applications and provides flexibility in the physical layer definitions.

ANSI also developed recommendations for radiation exposure that were used by the FCC for its Section 1.1310 standard.

Asia

In Asia, every country has its own administration and regulations, and the frequencies used differ from country to country. I will go through some of the countries that you are most likely to encounter in worldwide trade.

In China, the main standards authority is the Standardization Administration of China (SAC); this organization issues standards and regulations for RFID systems. China has not fully developed its RFID standards yet, and so far has assigned the temporary frequency band of 917–922 MHz for RFID and requires a temporary license.

Hong Kong (under China's special administration) has its own regulation agency, the Office of the Telecommunications Authority (OFTA). Hong Kong has established two frequency bands for UHF RFID operation, 865–868 MHz and/or 920–925 MHz. OFTA also creates the requirements for electrical safety, radiation protection, and technical requirements for operation in these bands. RFID equipment should operate on a "no-interference, no-protection basis," and the manufacturers and suppliers of RFID systems should consider the interference due to using frequencies that may be shared with other technologies.

Japan has had a hard time selecting the frequency band for RFID because of its high population density and number of RF-emitting devices. Finally, the frequency band of 952–954 MHz was made available for UHF RFID systems. These do not need a license, but have to be registered. RFID in Japan is regulated by the Ministry of Public Management, Home Affairs, Posts, and Telecommunications (MPHPT).

Pan-industry Organizations

Pan-industry organizations are member based and create specifications and recommendations for groups of industries and users. These standards are usually voluntary, and only after being ratified by an international standardization organization such as the ISO do they become standards for everyone.

GS1

GS1 is a global voluntary standards organization that manages the GS1 system and the global standards management process (GSMP). The GS1 system develops standards for bar codes, EDI transactions sets, XML schemas, and other supply-chain solutions that help to increase the efficiency of business (for instance, traceability for tracking in the food supply chain and patient safety in the healthcare supply chain).

GS1 took over the legacies of EAN International and the Uniform Code Council (UCC), including their member base, and now maintains the largest item identification system in the world and "the most implemented supply-chain standards system in the world."

GS1 works through its 104 international member organizations, including GS1 Australia, GS1 United Kingdom, GS1 Brazil, GS1 Canada, and the like. In the United States, the GS1 works through the GS1 U.S.

The GS1 system is divided into four main areas based on GS1 identification keys:

GS1 BarCodes Consists of global data and application standards for bar codes.

GS1 eCom Comprises global standards for electronic business messaging between trading partners. This area is based on GS1 EANCOM and GS1 XML.

GS1 EPCglobal Includes a global standards system combining RFID, existing communication network infrastructure, and the electronic product code (EPC) to provide automatic identification and item tracking throughout the supply chain, including improved efficiency and supply-chain visibility.

GS1 GDSN Enables trading partners to have the same item data in their systems at the same time. A key component of the GDSN network is the global product classification (GPC).

EPCglobal

EPCglobal is an organization that develops industry standards and specifications for the EPC to support and promote the use of RFID in supply-chain applications. Its primary goal is to increase supply-chain efficiency and visibility and support high-quality information flow between trading partners.

EPCglobal's goal is to support and commercialize the EPCglobal Network developed by the Auto-ID Center at the Massachusetts Institute of Technology (MIT). The Auto-ID Center ended its administrative functions in 2003, and its research has been continuing under the Auto-ID Labs.

EPCglobal developed the specifications for the EPC Generation 1 and Generation 2 tags. The EPC Gen 2 specification is being ratified by the ISO to become ISO/IEC 18000 Part 6C, and will function as a unified global standard for UHF tags. Gen 2 specifies not only the data format, but also the air interface protocol.

EPCglobal has established a standard format for the EPC number, which consists of the EPC identifier that uniquely identifies an individual item, and a filter value that supports effective reading of the EPC tag. The EPC number itself does not carry any information except for the unique number, which has to be matched to a database to retrieve any information associated with this number.

NOTE A new version of the EPC standard was published in March 2006 and related to EPC Gen 2 tags. Although it maintains compatibility with the previous version 1.1 for EPC Gen 1 tags, some changes were made, such as abandoning the rules for tiered headers (which became a fixed 8-bit length with provision for future extensions); deprecation of 64-bit encodings; preference for EPC encodings to fit the structure of Gen 2 tags; changes related to extending the number of bits used for SGTIN, SGLN, GRAI, and GIAI; and changes in the alpha-numeric serial number encoding.

Every EPC number includes a *header* (fixed 8-bit length), which carries the information about the encoding scheme used; this scheme determines the type, length, and structure of the EPC. The header is then followed by the unique EPC identifier and a filter value. EPC supports several encoding schemes:

- *General Identifier (GID)* GID-96.
- *SGTIN* and *GTIN* (Serialized EAN.UCC Global Trade Item Number: SGTIN-96 SGTIN-198).
- *SSCC* (EAN.UCC Serial Shipping Container Code: SSCC-96).
- *GLN* (EAN.UCC Global Location Number: SGLN-96, SGLN-195).
- *GRAI* (EAN.UCC Global Returnable Asset Identifier: GRAI-96, GRAI-170).
- *GIAI* (EAN.UCC Global Individual Asset Identifier: GIAI-96, GIAI-202).
- *DOD Construct* (DoD-96). This identifier is defined by the U.S. DoD and may be used to encode a 96-bit Class 1 tag that is being shipped to the U.S. DoD, if the supplier has a Commercial and Government Entity (CAGE) code.

The General Identifier (GID) consists of four components:

- A header (8 bits), which has the same function for all EPC numbers. The GID header is 0011 0101. (You have to remember this number for the exam ... just kidding!)
- A *general manager number* (28 bits), which identifies the organizational entity or company. This number is assigned by EPCglobal and is unique for each entity.
- An *object class* (24 bits), which identifies a type or class of the item. It has to be unique within the general manager number domain. An object class can be a stock-keeping unit (SKU) or a related code, and it is assigned by the company.
- A *serial number* (36 bits), which is a unique number identifying a single item. The number has to be unique within the object class, and it is assigned by the company.

The Serialized Global Trade Item Number (SGTIN) is based on the GTIN. The GTIN is just like the barcode universal product code (UPC) that is on everything you buy. The UPC identifies the company and the item, but is not unique to that particular product. The SGTIN adds a serial number to the GTIN so every item is uniquely identified. The SGTIN consists of the following:

- A header (8 bits)
- A *filter value* (3 bits), which is used for fast filtering and preselection of defined logistic types.
- A *partition* (3 bits), which indicates the point where the company prefix and the item reference are divided, because their length is not fixed.
- A company prefix (20–40 bits), which is assigned by GS1 to the company/organization.
- An item reference (4–24 bits), which is assigned by the company to a particular object class. In order to encode the item reference to a tag, the indicator digit from the GTIN is combined with the item reference digits into a single integer.
- A serial number (38 bits in SGTIN-96, up to 140 bits for SGTIN-198), which is assigned by the company to an individual item. This number is the part that turns the GTIN into the SGTIN.

The Serialized Shipping Container Code (SSCC) uniquely identifies a shipping container, including its contents. The SSCC includes the following:

- A header (8 bits)
- A filter value (3 bits) and partition (3 bits)
- A company prefix (20–40 bits), which is assigned by GS1 to a company.
- A serial reference (18–38 bits), which is assigned uniquely by the company to a specific shipping unit. To encode the serial reference to a tag, the serial reference digits have to be combined with the extension digit into a single integer.

NOTE In SSCC-96, 24 bits are unallocated and unused.

Because the certification is vendor-neutral, it also does not go too deep into EPC data formats. However, if you are interested, you can find more details and description of the remaining EPC numbers at `http://www.epcglobalinc.org/standards_technology/Ratified%20Spec%20March%208%202006.pdf`.

AIM Global

AIM Global is a global trade association with over 900 members in 43 countries. Its main goal is to support and promote the use of *automatic identification and data collection (AIDC)* technologies and services around the world. Members of AIM Global are companies involved in RFID, bar code, card technologies, biometrics, and *electronic article surveillance (EAS)*.

AIM Global produces reports such as AIM Global Technical Report: RFID for Food Animal Identification in North America, specifications such as Proposed Guidelines for the Use of RFID-Enabled Labels in Military Logistics: Recommendations for Revision of MIL-STD-129, or bases for standards that are being published by ANSI.

Safety Regulations

Although you may not realize it, you will also have to know and abide by the safety regulations posed by various agencies when designing and implementing an RFID system. There are three main groups of safety concerns. First is the safety of personnel when installing and working with equipment, especially electrical equipment. Second is human exposure to radio frequency and electromagnetic fields (also commonly called electromagnetic radiation, or EMR). Third is the safety of other equipment or products when exposed to EMR.

Personnel Safety

When designing and installing an RFID system, you must make sure that not only is your equipment safe and protected from damage, but also, more importantly, that your or your customer's personnel have a safe working environment.

TIP Although you may love your interrogators to death, always remember that personnel safety is the main priority!

There are many organizations publishing safety laws, recommendations, and best practices. In the United States, the organization ensuring the safety and health of workers is the Occupational Safety and Health Administration (OSHA) under the U.S. Department of Labor. Every warehouse, plant, or company has its own safety manager or officer, who is responsible for its safe working environment. However, it does not mean that you are not also responsible! You must make sure that you know the OSHA safety regulations related to any facility where you are implementing your system and that your employees or contractors have gone through the OSHA or other required safety training.

There are a few things that you need to watch for:

- You cannot install or leave any equipment in a place where it could obstruct the access to any safety equipment, such as fire extinguishers, drinking fountains, or fans, or block access to exit doors.
- Make sure that your equipment, mounting, and cables do not cause a trip hazard.
- When installing equipment far from the ground (for instance, by the warehouse ceiling) you must use a ladder, a scissor lift, and/or a safety harness to prevent falling.
- When installing electrical equipment, do not forget proper grounding and safety practices published by the U.S. National Electrical Manufacturers Association (NEMA).

For electrical work such as running electrical lines or adding additional circuits, I recommend hiring a certified electrician, or if possible use the facility's electrician. It is always a good idea to cooperate with the technicians or electricians who are employed or contracted by the facility, because they already know the space and possible issues as well as regulations they have to comply with.

NOTE NEMA also provides ratings of enclosures. These ratings determine the use of the NEMA enclosure, and how much protection it provides and what conditions it can withstand. You will need to use NEMA enclosures when installing interrogators in order to protect them from extreme temperatures, liquids, humidity, and other conditions.

When working with electrical equipment and electricity in general, you should know the standards published by the U.S. National Fire Protection Association (NFPA), which develops fire, electrical, and building safety codes. The NFPA's standards include the National Electrical Code (NEC), which describes specifications for electrical equipment and parts, as well as markings for hazardous products (NEC 500 and NEC 505). Other markings you may see on electrical products include UL or ULC. UL stands for Underwriters Laboratories (C for Canada), and this mark signifies that the product or device has been tested and approved by this organization and it is safe to use. In Europe, you may see the CE mark, which is the equivalent to the U.S. UL mark.

To learn about safety requirements outside the United States, you may want to check with the European Agency for Safety and Health at Work, which is the European equivalent of OSHA; the International Commission on Occupational Health (ICOH); the International Labour Organization (ILO); and the World Health Organization (WHO).

Human Exposure to Radiation

Because exposure to radiation can be harmful to humans, there are regulations that set limits on the allowable amount of human exposure to radiation from various sources, including radiation from electromagnetic fields.

The International Commission on Non-ionizing Radiation Protection (ICNIRP), which is allied with the WHO, publishes guidelines for human exposure to electromagnetic fields. Its guidelines were adopted by the EU and some world administrations.

ICNIRP specifies that low frequencies under 10 MHz can have effects on the central nervous system because of electric current flow in the human body. The exposure to low frequencies cannot be time-averaged. Frequencies above 100 kHz, on the other hand, can have a warming effect on the human body. (You do know how the microwave oven works, right?) Exposure to high frequencies can be time-averaged. However, do not get too worried. These effects are related to strong magnetic and electric fields and high radiated power.

The U.S. military specifies (complying with ANSI/IEEE) that the safe dosimetric parameter for exposure to RF fields is 0.4 watts per kilogram (W/kg) for controlled exposure and 0.08 W/kg for uncontrolled exposure. This ensures at least a safety factor of 10 below the body-specific absorption rate, which is 4 W/kg.

Let's say that you weigh 90 kg (200 pounds). Your safe uncontrolled exposure could be up to 7.2 watts ($90 \text{ kg} \times 0.08 \text{ W/kg} = 7.2 \text{ W}$). You know that the maximum allowed radiated power from RFID systems in the United States is 4 watts, which is the power you would be exposed to if you stood right in front of the antenna. (If you weighed at least 50 kg, which is about 110 pounds, you would still be safe.)

The FCC publishes exposure limits in its Section 1.1310 that are based on the guidelines of the National Council on Radiation Protection and Measurements (NCRP) and ANSI. The limits are divided into limits for occupational and therefore controlled exposure, and limits for the general public, which means uncontrolled exposure. Generally, the recommended safe distance from RFID antennas emitting allowed EIRP for prolonged periods of time is 9 inches (about 27 cm).

Device Exposure to Radiation

When working with hazardous materials or explosives, you have to follow an extra set of rules. The military has always led in the development of such standards, and currently follows the *Hazards of Electromagnetic Radiation to Ordnance (HERO)* and Hazards of Electromagnetic Radiation to Fuel (HERF) standards.

HERO specifies the measures of electro-explosive devices' (EEDs) susceptibility:

- Maximum no-fire current (MNFC), which is measured in milliamperes (mA). MNFC is the largest current that can be induced in the EED and does not initiate a detonation.
- Maximum no-fire power (MNFP), which is measured in milliwatts (mW). MNFP is the highest power that can be absorbed by the EED without detonation.

HERO specifies three categories of EEDs:

HERO Safe Such a device cannot be initiated by electromagnetic radiation, and no protection is necessary.

HERO Susceptible Such a device could potentially be initiated by electromagnetic radiation. The sensitivity of this device is no less than 2.25 W MNFP and 340 mA MNFC.

HERO Unsafe The device has to be considered Unsafe if the environment cannot be sufficiently analyzed and the device cannot be determined HERO Safe or Susceptible. Protective measures for the worst possible scenario have to be taken. A device is also considered Unsafe if it withstands less than 2.25W MNFP and 340 mA MNFC, with the worst-case susceptibility of 85 mA MNFC and 54 mW MNFP.

TIP

If you are using active tags to tag explosives or EEDs, you should use a tag with maximum transmitted power under 54 mW, or 0.5 W to be on the safe side.

Summary

In this chapter, you learned about the international, regional, and national standards organizations and regulatory authorities, as well as pan-industry organizations. You read about their efforts to standardize and regulate RFID technology and support and promote the use of this technology throughout various industries and supply chains.

In the first section, you learned about standards developed by the ISO and IEC. (I hope that you remember what those acronyms stand for!) These two organizations formed the Joint Technical Committee 1 to provide technical standards for various areas of information technology, including RFID. The ISO and IEC developed many data standards and air interface protocols for RFID, and you certainly should remember at least ISO/IEC 18000 Parts 1–7, where Part 6 (A, B, and C) is related to UHF.

Next, you found out that the frequencies around the world were allocated by the ITU and that the world is divided into three regions. Region 1 consists of Europe, Africa, part of the Middle East, and the former Soviet Union; Region 2 includes the Americas; and Region 3 includes the rest of the world. The ITU also has other functions such as governing and improving telecommunications and radiocommunications around the world, publishing standards and recommendations, and other activities.

In the next section, you learned about the UPU, which regulates postal communications and services. The UPU also has developed standards for RFID that were presented to the ISO and were used as a basis for some of the ISO/IEC RFID standards.

Following the international organizations, you discovered many regional organizations. In Europe, there are organizations such as CEN, CENELEC, CEPT (including ECC and ERO), and ETSI. ETSI is the authority that regulates RFID systems including communication and allowed transmitted power. In the United States, the main organizations are the FCC and ANSI. The FCC specifies the operations of RFID systems and limits for transmitted power.

You also learned that in China, RFID is regulated by the SAC, which has assigned a temporary frequency band for UHF. In Hong Kong, RFID is regulated by the OFTA, and in Japan it is regulated by the MPHPT. You also learned that the frequencies used around the world for RFID applications differ and that these organizations pose different limits on transmitted power.

In the next section, you learned about various organizations and groups that are focused on the AIDC and RFID industry, such as GS1, EPCglobal, and AIM Global. The EAN.UCC became GS1, which now standardizes and manages barcode systems as well as an EPC numbering system for RFID. You also recognized different EPC formats and learned about the specifics of different types such as GID, SGTIN, SSCC, GIAI, GRAI, GLN, and the DoD Construct.

At the end of this chapter, you also discovered various safety regulations regarding personnel safety and radiation exposure safety for humans and devices. You learned about organizations that publish standards related to workers' safety, such as OSHA, ICOH, ILO, and WHO, and organizations that produce codes for the safety of electrical equipment and buildings, such as NEMA, NFTA, and UL. Some authorities take care of human exposure limits to RF and other radiation, such as the FCC, ANSI, the military through HERO, and so on. Finally, you discovered the ratings of explosives and the power limits to prevent possible detonation.

Exam Essentials

Recognize international and regional standards and regulatory organizations. The main international standards organizations are the ISO and IEC, which develop standards that are the basis for regional as well as national standards and requirements. The ISO and IEC develop standards for air interface as well as data standards for RFID. In Europe, the main organizations standardizing and regulating RFID are ECC, ERO (under CEPT), and ETSI; in the United States, they are the FCC and ANSI.

Know the ISO air interface standards for RFID. The main standard specifying RFID air interface is ISO/IEC 18000. Part 1 specifies general requirements; Part 2 applies to frequencies less than 135 kHz; Part 3 applies to HF frequency at 13.56 MHz; Part 4 specifies the 2.45 GHz frequency; Part 5 specifies the 5.8 GHz frequency (which was withdrawn); Part 6 applies to UHF and has sections A, B, and C (Gen 2); and Part 7 applies to active tags at 433 MHz.

Recognize the ITU regions. There are three ITU regions. Region 1 consists of Europe, Africa, the former Soviet Union, and the Middle East including Iraq. Region 2 consists of North and South America. Region 3 consists of Asia (without the former Soviet Union), the Middle East from Iran to the east, Australia, and Oceania.

Know the maximum allowed transmitted power limits in the United States and Europe. The maximum allowed transmitted power in the United States is 1 W, up to 4 W with gained antenna, therefore 4 W EIRP. Readers must employ frequency hopping or digital modulation. Maximum antenna gain can be 6 dBi. In Europe, the maximum ERP is 2 W (which is approximately 3.26 W EIRP). Readers must employ frequency hopping and LBT. Previous regulations required also using duty cycles.

Identify the differences between air interface protocols and tag data formats. Tag data format/data protocol specifies the size and structure of the tag memory, tag data formatting and length, and the means of storing, accessing, and transferring information. Examples of tag data standards are EPC Class 1 Generation 1 or ISO 15962. The air interface protocol defines the rules of communication between tags and interrogators. The air interface protocol includes rules for encoding, modulation, anticollision, and reading and writing to a tag as well as other operations. An example of an air interface protocol is the ISO 18000 Part 6A. A standard that describes both tag data format and air interface protocol is the EPC Generation 2/ISO 18000 Part 6C.

Recognize the structure of basic EPC tag data format. The general identifier (GID) consists of a header, which specifies the type, length, and structure of the EPC number; a manager number, which identifies the company; an object class, which identifies the type or class of the item; and a serial number that identifies the single item.

Recognize the effects of human exposure to electromagnetic fields and RF radiation. Low frequencies (under 10 MHz) can affect the central nervous system. These effects cannot be time-averaged. High frequencies (above 100 kHz) can cause warming of the body. These effects can be time-averaged. These effects are usually related to exposure to high-power radiators that emit a lot more power than what is allowed by the standard limits mandated by regulatory authorities.

Key Terms

Before you take the exam, be certain you are familiar with the following terms:

- air interface protocols
- automatic identification and data capture (AIDC)
- data protocols
- DOD construct
- electronic article surveillance (EAS)
- filter value
- general identifier (GID)
- general manager number
- Global Individual Asset Identifier (GIAI)
- Global Location Number (GLN)
- Global Returnable Asset Identifier (GRAI)
- Global Trade Item Number (GTIN)
- Hazards of Electromagnetic Radiation to Ordnance (HERO)
- header
- object class
- partition
- serial number
- Serialized Global Trade Item Number (SGTIN)
- Serial Shipping Container Code (SSCC)

Review Questions

1. What does the air interface protocol specify?
   - **A.** Tag memory size
   - **B.** Way of communicating between tags and readers
   - **C.** Maximum allowed transmitted power
   - **D.** Dense reader mode

2. Which standard applies to active RFID tags?
   - **A.** EPC Generation 2
   - **B.** ISO/IEC 18000 Part 3
   - **C.** ISO/IEC 18000 Part 7
   - **D.** ANSI INCITS 256

3. Which organization allocates and manages global frequencies?
   - **A.** ISO (International Organization for Standardization)
   - **B.** IEC (International Electrotechnical Commission)
   - **C.** ITU (International Telecommunication Union)
   - **D.** EPCglobal

4. What is the function of the header in an EPC tag data format?
   - **A.** Determines the type, length, and structure of the EPC
   - **B.** Carries the EPC number
   - **C.** Determines rewritability of the tag
   - **D.** Carries the memory passwords

5. What is the maximum allowed transmitted power (ERP) in Europe under ETSI 302 208?
   - **A.** 0.5 W
   - **B.** 1 W
   - **C.** 2 W
   - **D.** 4 W

6. Which standard specifies the operation in the UHF band including the limits on transmitted power in the United States?
   - **A.** FCC Part 15
   - **B.** ISO/IEC 18000 Part 6
   - **C.** FCC Part 13
   - **D.** ANSI INCITS 256

7. What is the worst-case susceptibility of explosive devices that you have to be aware of?
   - **A.** 95 mA and 69 mW
   - **B.** 350 mA and 2.3 W
   - **C.** 35 mA and 0.3 mW
   - **D.** 85 mA and 54 mW
8. What standard does the ISO ratification of the EPC Generation 2 protocol create?
   - **A.** ISO/IEC 18000 Part 6C
   - **B.** ISO/IEC 18000 Part 8
   - **C.** ISO/IEC 19000 Part 1
   - **D.** FCC Part 15.103
9. Which organization regulates RFID in China (mainland)?
   - **A.** OFTA (Office of the Telecommunications Authority)
   - **B.** SAC (Standardization Administration of China)
   - **C.** MPHPT (Ministry of Public Management, Home Affairs, Posts and Telecommunications)
   - **D.** OSHA (Occupational Safety and Health Administration)
10. What has to be your primary concern when installing an RFID portal?
    - **A.** That the portal achieves high read rates
    - **B.** That the portal does not obstruct exit doors
    - **C.** That the personnel will see the light stack
    - **D.** That the portal doesn't cause RF interference
11. What type of enclosure would you use to protect your interrogators from harsh conditions?
    - **A.** ISO-certified enclosure
    - **B.** Any available watertight enclosure
    - **C.** NEMA enclosure
    - **D.** Any available airtight enclosure
12. What country uses a UHF band that is very different from the band used in the United States or Europe?
    - **A.** Brazil
    - **B.** Japan
    - **C.** Australia
    - **D.** Mexico

13. What types of standards does the GS1 create?
    A. Voluntary, international, barcode, and RFID standards
    B. International enforced standards
    C. Voluntary barcode standards in Europe
    D. Enforced RFID standards in the United States
14. What are the parts of an EPC GID (General Identifier)? (Select three options.)
    A. Manager number
    B. Partition
    C. Filter value
    D. Serial number
    E. Object class
15. According to the FCC, what is a safe distance for a human to be from an antenna for prolonged periods of time?
    A. 5 inches
    B. 9 inches
    C. 18 inches
    D. 25 inches
16. Which standard includes the military specifications for hazards of exposure to electromagnetic radiation?
    A. FCC Part 15
    B. HERO (Hazards of Electromagnetic Radiation to Ordnance)
    C. WHO (World Health Organization) Recommendation
    D. ANSI INCITS 256
17. What effects can low-frequency radiation in high powers have on the human body?
    A. No effects. Only high frequencies have negative effects on the human body.
    B. Warming of the body.
    C. Effects on the central nervous system.
    D. Effects on reproductive organs.
18. What effects can high-frequency radiation in high powers have on the human body?
    A. Warming of the body.
    B. Effects on reproductive organs.
    C. Effects on the central nervous system.
    D. No effects. Only low frequencies have effects on the human body.

19. What techniques does the FCC require for transmissions in UHF and microwave bands? (Select two options.)

A. Frequency hopping

B. Digital modulation

C. Triggered interrogation

D. Duty cycles

20. How does the GS1 work?

A. Through local governments

B. Through its member organizations

C. Through the press

D. Through industry councils and trade groups

Answers to Review Questions

1. B. The air interface protocol defines the rules of communication between tags and interrogators. It includes rules for encoding, modulation, anticollision, and reading and writing to a tag, as well as other operations. The protocol usually does not define the tag architecture or tag memory size.

2. C. ISO/IEC 18000 Part 7 specifies the air interface protocol for active tags operating at 433 MHz.

3. C. Global frequencies are allocated and managed by the ITU, which assigns the frequencies to various regions, technologies, and purposes.

4. A. The header in an EPC number has the same function for all types of EPC formats—it carries information about the encoding format of the rest of the number. It determines the type, length, and structure of the encoded EPC number.

5. C. Under the new ETSI regulation 302 208, the maximum allowed transmitted power is 2 W in a band of 865.6–867.6 MHz.

6. A. FCC Part 15 specifies the conditions for an intentional, unintentional, or incidental radiator to be operated without an individual license. It also contains the technical specifications, administrative requirements, and conditions relating to the marketing of devices regulated by Part 15.

7. D. A device is considered Unsafe if it withstands less than 2.25 W MNFP and 340 mA MNFC, but the worst-case susceptibility is 85 mA MNFC and 54 mW MNFP. The highest protective measures must be employed.

8. A. When ratified by the ISO, the EPC Generation 2 protocol will become ISO/IEC 18000 Part 6C. Parts 6A and 6B are already established UHF ISO tag protocols.

9. B. The SAC regulates RFID in mainland China, while the OFTA regulates RFID in China's special administrative area of Hong Kong. MPHPT regulates RFID in Japan. OSHA is a safety agency of the U.S. government.

10. B. When installing any equipment, you have to make sure that you do not obstruct any exit doors or safety devices such as fire extinguishers, drinking fountains, or fire hydrants.

11. C. When choosing an enclosure to protect your interrogators, you should use an enclosure certified by NEMA (National Electrical Manufacturers Association). These enclosures are rated according to the protection they provide. This way you will ensure that the enclosure will appropriately protect your equipment and personnel and avoid failures of noncertified products.

12. B. Japan uses a band of 952–954 MHz, which is quite different from 865–868 MHz in Europe and 902–928 MHz in the United States. This may cause problems in international supply chains; however, this issue can be made less problematic by using tags that can operate on all three frequencies (see Chapter 4, "Tags").

13. A. The GS1 creates voluntary international standards for bar codes, EDI transactions sets, XML schemas, RFID, and other supply chain solutions.

14. A, D, E. An EPC GID consists of a header; a manager number, which carries the company reference; an object class, which describes the group of the item; and a serial number. Partition and filter values are present in other types of EPC formats such as SGTIN and SSCC.

15. B. The recommended distance for prolonged human exposure to radiation from an RFID antenna is 9 inches.

16. B. The military publishes the Hazards of Electromagnetic Radiation to Ordnance in order to specify the limits for exposure of military personnel as well as electronic devices to electromagnetic radiation.

17. C. Low frequencies under 10 MHz can have adverse effects on the central nervous system. These effects cannot be time-averaged.

18. A. When the human body is exposed to strong high-frequency (above 100 kHz) radiation, it tends to start warming up. You can relate this to the microwave oven principle.

19. A, B. The FCC requires interrogators to employ frequency hopping or digital modulation when transmitting in the UHF and microwave frequency bands. Triggered interrogation and duty cycles are required in Europe by the ETSI.

20. B. The GS1 works through 104 member organizations around the world. It now maintains the largest item identification system in the world and "the most implemented supply-chain standards system in the world."

Appendix A

Vendors and Links

So why bother with this appendix when the topic of vendors and other resources is not on the exam? I am hoping that you will use this book even after you successfully pass the exam, and that it will become a good tool for your future RFID endeavors. To succeed, you may need some advice regarding where to turn to get your readers, tags, and printers, as well as useful links that provide reliable information about who is who and what is going on in the RFID industry. Using the Internet is the easiest and the most comprehensive way to find educational resources about the RFID technology itself and its innovations and applications.

RFID Vendors

In this appendix, I will show you some of the largest RFID equipment vendors and solution providers, tell you what products and solutions they offer, and disclose a little bit of information about them that you will not find in their marketing slicks. The lists are in alphabetical order so that nobody gets angry. (Well, those who didn't make it onto these pages probably will anyway.)

Alien Technology

Alien Technology Corporation

18220 Butterfield Blvd., Morgan Hill, CA 95037

Website: `www.alientechnology.com`

Phone: 1-408-782-3900

Alien Technology is a major manufacturer of passive UHF RFID readers and tags. Besides readers intended for use in the United States, Alien also offers readers that comply with European standards. Using its patented manufacturing technology, Fluidic Self Assembly (FSA), Alien is capable of producing passive EPC tags in large quantities relatively quickly. Its tags used to employ only a single dipole antenna, which posed problems with orientation sensitivity; however, currently it also provides orientation-insensitive tags ("omni-squiggle"). Alien also offers battery-assisted tags and readers, as well as vendor-neutral testing and professional services through its RFID Solutions Center in Dayton, Ohio.

What you won't find in marketing slicks: Alien has the cheapest tags and the fastest order time on readers, and it is working on improving its customer service and support, which used to be its weakness. Alien will not sell you its readers or tags or provide support unless you go through its Alien Academy training (which is not cheap).

Datamax

Datamax

4501 Parkway Commerce Blvd., Orlando, FL 32808

Website: `www.datamaxcorp.com`

Phone: 1-407-578-8007

Datamax is a subsidiary of Dover Corporation and offers a range of products related to barcode and RFID labeling. Datamax produces thermal printers, labels, tickets, and other tags, as well as thermal transfer ribbons. Datamax offers printers that can come RFID enabled or they can be enabled later using RFID modules. Datamax offers HF, as well as UHF RFID modules that are capable of EPC as well as ISO reading and encoding.

FOX IV Technologies

FOX IV Technologies, Inc.

6011 Enterprise Drive, Export, PA 98203

Website: `www.foxiv.com`

Phone: 1-724-387-3500

Fox IV, which has been in business for over 20 years, provides print-and-apply systems specially designed to withstand tough environments. It was the first company providing print-and-apply solutions to pass EPCglobal's certification for Class 0 and 1 tags.

What you won't find in marketing slicks: Fox IV Technologies has been a leader in tough environments and situations; however, its products tend to be more expensive than the products of other print-and-apply vendors.

IBM

IBM Corporation

1133 Westchester Ave., White Plains, NY 10604

Website: `www.ibm.com`

Phone: 1-800-426-4968

IBM was in RFID back in the 1990s but devolved its practice when it sold much of its intellectual property to Intermec in the late 1990s. The recent EPC revolution has seen it reenter the market with an interesting approach. IBM envisions RFID as an additional data-capture technology that interoperates with its WebSphere platform. To support this, IBM has created interoperability with most of the leading RFID hardware vendors by using the WebSphere RFID Device Infrastructure (WRDI). This combined with the WebSphere premises server creates a solid middleware package that interoperates with the entire WebSphere suite. It's a great product line for companies that are an IBM shop.

Impinj

Impinj, Inc.

701 N. 34th St., Suite 300, Seattle, WA 98103

Website: www.impinj.com

Phone: 1-206-517-5300

Impinj is a highly inventive, venture-backed company that started as a chip manufacturer with innovative design. Impinj played a major role in EPC Generation 2 specifications development. Its chip self-calibrates over the life of the system, which keeps its performance unchanged despite aging and outside conditions. The chip is smaller and consumes less power than other chips, which makes it more effective. Impinj also produces its own inlays and came up with a near-field UHF tag with a great performance around difficult materials (as the result of near-field magnetic coupling, which also causes short read ranges). This tag actually reads while submerged in water, as I saw at one of the RFID shows. Impinj also produces inlays for long read ranges. Impinj recently introduced a mono-static interrogator, which was specifically built for the EPCglobal UHF Gen 2 standard; besides traditional features, it also offers tag-response mapping capabilities and other interesting functions.

What you won't find in marketing slicks: Impinj has a talented and focused team, with strong partnerships among antenna and label manufacturers. Although its innovations increase chip and tag performance, the question is whether its prices will be competitive and whether this small company can keep up with the production volume.

Intermec

Intermec Technologies Corporation

6001 36th Ave. West, Everett, WA 98203

Website: www.intermec.com

Phone: 1-425-348-2600

Intermec has been in the automatic identification and data capture (AIDC) technology business for decades. Intermec provides not only standard automated data-collection technologies using bar codes, but also Intellitag RFID solutions including hardware (readers, antennas, printers) and tag manufacturing. Intermec also offers mobile computing systems for companies worldwide. Intermec's readers are certified for operation in the United States at UHF and microwave frequency, in Europe at UHF, and in Japan at microwave frequency. It provides fixed readers and handhelds as well as vehicle-mount units.

What you won't find in marketing slicks: When IBM decided to leave the RFID technology business several years ago, Intermec purchased IBM's RFID intellectual property; therefore, Intermec now owns patents on everything from tag design to testing equipment. As the RFID market started to mature and RFID companies started to come up with their own products, Intermec began to promote its patents and required licensing via its Rapid Start RFID licensing program. Intermec royalty requirements were also partially responsible for slowing down the process of EPC protocol standard design. Because Intermec's main activities have been focused on lawsuits for patent infringements, it has not been concentrating too much on the competitiveness of its products and services. However, once it does, it has a great chance of leading the RFID market.

MARKEM

MARKEM Corporation

150 Congress St., Keene, NH 03431

Website: www.markem.com

Phone: 1-800-258-5356

For almost a century, MARKEM has been a company concentrating on marking and printing technologies. It develops inks and printing machines and provides laser, thermal transfer, ink-jet, and ink roll printing, as well as print-and-apply solutions for barcode and RFID labels. MARKEM offers solutions for conveyor tagging, as well as desktop solutions and tagging software.

ODIN Technologies

ODIN Technologies

22960 Shaw Road, Suite 600, Dulles, VA 20166

Website: www.odintechnologies.com

Phone: 1-866-652-3052 or 1-703-968-0000

ODIN Technologies is the leading provider of specialized software and services for the RFID infrastructure. ODIN has developed novel software to make the testing, deployment, and management of RFID networks highly successful. It was the first company to release software based on sound scientific methodologies for testing tag selection and placement. ODIN has also created a system, called EasyReader automated system design, to design full RFID systems, create bills of materials, and automate configuration, tuning, and testing.

Because ODIN has a background in the physics of RFID, it is uniquely qualified to understand how to manage, monitor, and keep RFID networks healthy. ODIN has the first monitoring and management system in the RFID industry; this system looks at tag read performance over time, using artificial intelligence, machine learning, and fuzzy logic in a patent-pending solution designed to keep RFID networks up and working properly 24/7 in even the most remote locations. The EasySuite of software tools has been proven and utilized at the most complex and largest RFID deployments in the world—for example, for the U.S. Department of Defense, where ODIN technologies was the prime contractor deploying 26 facilities worldwide in the largest RFID deployment in history.

ODIN's laboratories—in Dulles, Virginia, and Budapest, Hungary—are the only commercial labs producing head-to-head comparisons of RFID readers, handhelds, tags, and other components in their RFID Benchmark Series. This "Consumer Reports" for the RFID industry is well recognized for unbiased, scientific information.

What you won't find in marketing slicks: ODIN has worked with more of the Wal-Mart, Target, and Department of Defense clients than any other firm in the marketplace on infrastructure testing, deployment, and monitoring. ODIN was selected over a long list of vendors based on technical excellence to supply the U.S. DoD with passive RFID infrastructure. ODIN bases all of its products and solutions on physics and years of experience in the RFID industry. (Since I am from ODIN, I can brag a little bit, right?)

OMRON

OMRON Regional Management Center

1920 Thoreau Dr. Suite 165, Shaumburg, IL 60173

Website: `www.omronrfid.com`

Phone: 1-888-303-7343

OMRON (based in Japan) is a large electronics manufacturer that has been in RFID for over 20 years and offers a range of RFID products. Omron's products include the ONE DAY compliance package including reader, antenna, printer, light stack, middleware, accessories, and training; LF, HF, UHF, and microwave RFID inlays; and readers (fixed units as well as handhelds). OMRON also offers a global tag that is suitable for use across all global UHF frequency bands.

OMRON started its UHF reader design by licensing the firmware and basic design from ThingMagic, while using more-powerful and efficient versions of components. The result was an immediately optimized reader.

Paxar

Paxar Corporation

170 Monarch Lane, Miamisburg, OH 45342

Website: `www.paxar.com`

Phone: 1-888-44PAXAR (72927)

Paxar is a major provider of tickets, tags, and labels, as well as the related technology for retail product identification including printers and software control systems. Paxar has been in business for over 100 years. It provides stationary as well as portable RFID and barcode printers, print-and-apply systems, and barcode and RFID labels. Paxar supplies smart labels for major retailers and manufacturers such as Marks & Spencer, Del Monte Foods, Conair, VF Imagewear, and others. Paxar provides a smart label guarantee by refunding money for failed labels, and it is able to ship out large quantities of labels the same day.

Printronix

Printronix, Inc.

14600 Myford Road, Irvine, CA 92606

Website: `www.printronix.com`

Phone: 1-800-665-6210

Printronix started as a manufacturer of line matrix printers and continued as an innovator of thermal and continuous form laser printers with engineering, manufacturing, sales, and customer support centers worldwide. Printronix also provides thermal transfer RFID printers/encoders and barcode printers, print-and-apply units, RFID labels, network printer management software, and a wide range of industrial printing solutions and solutions for global enterprises.

SATO

SATO America

10350-A Nations Ford Road, Charlotte, NC 28273

Website: `www.satoamerica.com`

Phone: 1-704-644-1659

SATO is a large international company that has been in the AIDC industry for a long time. You can thank SATO for inventing the first electronic thermal transfer barcode printer. SATO offers the Data Collection System & Labeling concept, which is SATO's complete barcode and labeling solution providing printers, scanners/handheld terminals, label design software, and supplies.

SATO also offers rugged HF and UHF RFID printers/encoders, labeling software, and HF and UHF smart labels, as well as a full RFID services program including site surveys, technical consulting, tag testing and evaluation, installation, and ongoing site support.

Savi Technology

Savi Technology

615 Tasman Drive, Sunnyvale, CA 94089

Website: `www.savi.com`

Phone: 1-408-743-8000

Savi has been in business for over 15 years and since its beginnings, it has established itself as one of the leaders in active supply-chain solutions, mainly due to engagements with the U.S. Department of Defense. Savi was recently acquired by Lockheed Martin Corporation. Savi has designed and developed the SmartChain software suite including a unique enterprise software platform, Savi SmartChain Enterprise Platform, which is Savi's RFID, site software, and enterprise software applications that provide the foundation for Savi's supply-chain asset management, consignment management, transportation, and security management solutions. The applications are integrated with other AIDC technologies.

Savi's EchoPoint active RFID systems have been implemented in various harsh environments and offer a wide selection of active RFID tags, including tags with sensors. Savi is a main provider of technology for U.S. DoD RFID consignment monitoring networks including RFID, barcode, cellular, and communications systems.

What you won't find in marketing slicks: Many of today's experts in the RFID industry started at Savi. Some of them learned about Savi while being in the military; for others, it was a next step to get into RFID from barcode and other AIDC technologies.

Sirit

Sirit, Inc.

372 Bay Street, Suite 1100, Toronto, Ontario M5H 2W9 Canada

or 1321 Valwood Parkway, Suite 620, Carrollton, TX 75006

Website: `www.sirit.com`

Phone: 1-800-498-8760 or 1-866-338-9586

Sirit is a provider of RFID hardware and solutions. It has been focusing on automatic vehicle identification (AVI), which includes toll collection, parking, access to gated communities, and fleet management. Sirit is one of the four suppliers of current toll-collection infrastructure in the United States. Sirit also offers LF, HF, and UHF readers as well as INfinity OEM reader modules and battery-assisted passive tags and readers for its toll-collection solutions IDentity FleX and Title 21.

What you won't find in marketing slicks: Sirit recently acquired SAMSys Technologies and integrated its reader and OEM solutions into its offerings. Sirit has been concentrating on AVI solutions and hardware and it is not very strong in the services department, mainly on the side of RFID supply-chain solutions.

Symbol Technologies

Symbol Technologies, Inc.

1 Symbol Plaza, Holtsville, NY 11742-1300

Website: `www.symbol.com`

Phone: 1-866-416-8545

Symbol is a large provider of hardware and solutions including barcode scanners, payment systems, Micro Kiosks, mobile computers, wireless infrastructure, and OEM products as well as voice-optimized products (Enterprise Digital Assistants with voice-over-IP). In 2004, Symbol acquired Matrics, a manufacturer of RFID readers and tags, as well as an RFID systems integrator. Matrics started as an aggressive, venture-backed company with technology borne out of scientists from the National Security Agency (NSA). Matrics patented a PICA tag-assembling process, which allowed for fast and cheaper tag production. Symbol continues in RFID by providing UHF EPC-compliant solutions using fixed and handheld readers, antennas, RFID portals, and RFID tags. Matrics originally produced only Class 0 read-only tags; however, Symbol now offers read-only and read-write Gen 1 tags and Gen 2.

What you won't find in marketing slicks: Although Matrics/Symbol readers are some of the best readers on the market (same with their antennas), Symbol continues to have problems with filling large orders of these devices because of slow production. Matrics/Symbol tags are well designed and used to be relatively large. Symbol now offers their Gen 2 tags also in sizes 1″ × 1″ and 2″ × 4″ besides the traditional 4″ × 4″.

TAGSYS

TAGSYS

196 West Ashland St., Doylestown, PA 18901

Website: `www.tagsysrfid.com`

Phone: 1-877-550-7343

TAGSYS is a large provider of item-level RFID systems and tags. TAGSYS also designs, manufactures, and integrates end-to-end RFID solutions and item-level tracking systems mainly for specialized industries such as pharmaceutical, fashion apparel, libraries, and textile rental. TAGSYS manufactures HF and UHF tags in various forms such as nano-size tags, disk tags, small and large tags, thermo tags, encapsulated tags, AK Family of UHF Gen 2 tags, flexible RFID tags, CD tags, and RFID patron cards. TAGSYS also offers short-, medium-, and long-range HF RFID readers, 3D RFID tunnels, inventory stations, circulation stations, and fast tagging stations.

Texas Instruments (TI)

Texas Instruments, Inc.

6550 Chase Oaks Blvd., MS 8470, Plano, TX 75023

Website: `www.ti.com/rfid`

Phone: 1-888-937-6536

TI is a world leader in digital signal processing and analog technologies. TI's offerings include semiconductors (ASIC, amplifiers, clocks, data converters, microcontrollers, sensors, switches and multiplexers, and so forth), digital light processing (DLP) technology (TV, cinema, projectors, and so forth), educational technology and calculators, sensors and control devices, and last but not least RFID. TI has significant experience in LF and HF RFID (providing tags and readers) and also has started to offer UHF Gen 2 tags.

What you won't find in marketing slicks: Several members of the RFID group have been involved with various standards organizations. TI therefore understands the direction in which the standards are going and is ahead on chip design. It released its first foray into EPC in 2006 and is vying for a leadership position with Gen 2 tags. TI has the capacity to produce tags in large quantities in a short amount of time; therefore, it can meet high demand. However, it has to continue with innovation to make sure that it is able to fight off the competition in the RFID market.

ThingMagic

ThingMagic

1 Broadway, Cambridge, MA 02142

Website: www.thingmagic.com

Phone: 1-617-758-4136 or 1-866-833-4069

ThingMagic is a privately held company specializing in RFID readers, sensors, and other embedded and low-cost computing technologies. ThingMagic products are also available as OEM. ThingMagic was one of the first producers of an agile reader, and the first to use Intel architecture coupled with a Linux core. ThingMagic started through early involvement with the Auto-ID Center at MIT and claims that it was profitable from the first day of operation. ThingMagic has licensed its design to Tyco/ADT as well as OMRON.

What you won't find in marketing slicks (although with this one you might): ThingMagic recently introduced its Mercury V as an innovative Gen 2 reader with solid performance in dense reader environments due to "ignoring the interference" techniques. This reader also has something for the design fans—its sleek silvery case with blue stripes and logo is really something. The issues that are keeping big companies away are past production challenges and partnership conflicts.

UPM Raflatac

UPM Raflatac, Inc.

1060 Hanover Street, Hanover Industrial Estates, Hanover Township, PA 18706

Website: www.upmraflatac.com

Phone: 1-570-821-2883

UPM Raflatac (previously UPM Rafsec) is a company made up of the combined legacies of UPM Rafsec and Raflatac. UPM Rafsec was a manufacturer of RFID tags and inlays, while Raflatac was a major provider of pressure-sensitive labels for various applications. UPM Raflatac offers HF and UHF RFID tags/smart labels as well as injection molding tags that are suitable for embedding into crates or pallets. UPM Raflatac focuses on pharma e-pedigree, supply chain management, libraries and media management, parcel and post, garment, and baggage-tagging applications.

Zebra

Zebra Technologies Corporation

333 Corporate Woods Parkway, Vernon Hills, IL 60061-3109

Website: www.zebra.com

Phone: 1-866-230-9494

Zebra is a large provider of rugged and reliable printing solutions, including thermal barcode label and receipt printers and supplies, plastic card printers, RFID smart label printers/encoders, certified smart media, and digital photo printers. Zebra offers HF and mainly UHF RFID printers/encoders with the possibility of wireless access using wireless LAN or Bluetooth. Zebra supplies printers complying with U.S. and European regulations. Zebra also offers labeling design software, ZebraDesigner; printer management software, ZebraNet Bridge Enterprise; and other useful software tools.

What you won't find in marketing slicks: Zebra developed Zebra Programming Language (ZPL) for printer programming, which also has been used by its competitors because of its flexibility and comprehensiveness. Zebra is well known for its robust printers and great customer service.

RFID Links

The RFID industry is changing quickly. The web is the best place to find new information and updates on what's going on with various vendors and products, inventions and innovations, new standards and protocols, as well as to learn more about RFID and related technologies and solutions.

The following links are mainly to RFID magazines and sources of vendor-neutral information. I will also show you links that I use for reference or when doing research on various RFID topics.

RFID Journal Online

`www.rfidjournal.com`

The online version of *RFID Journal* offers original articles and case studies related to RFID and its applications. Most of the articles are accessible to everyone; some of the content, such as key feature articles, is for subscribers only. RFID Journal online is a trusted source for RFID news and unbiased opinions on RFID matters. At the website, you can also subscribe to a free weekly newsletter that will bring links with new articles to your mailbox (this is the good kind of junk mail!).

EPCglobal

`www.epcglobalinc.org`

The EPCglobal website provides information about the EPCglobal organization, its activities, standards, and EPCglobal Network. Some of the content is accessible only to EPCglobal members (subscription to EPCglobal costs from $2 to $200,000, depending on the size of the subscribing organization and its yearly revenues). EPCglobal provides its published standards on the website for free, which is quite a relief. (You will see what I mean if you try to find some of the international standards and view them for a hefty fee.)

RFid Gazette

`www.rfidgazette.org`

The RFid Gazette lacks a bit in web design and original content, but not in the number of articles related to the RFID industry. The articles are grouped related to industry verticals (airline, DoD, healthcare, libraries, and so forth); therefore, you can search the information by the area you are interested in. The articles are also archived by the month when they were published, which makes it easy to go back and read up on the history of a certain event to see the way it played out.

UsingRFID

`www.usingrfid.com`

The UsingRFID website is full of original content related to RFID technology and supplies, news, analysis, research studies, and other information. The website is trying a bit too hard to make you a member (although the membership is free, in exchange for your personal information that is promised to never be sold), but that may be because of the marketing background of its editors. The site also provides RFIDIQ tests that range from beginners to advanced RFID users. The tests are quite basic (... now I sound like a Mr. Know-It-All), but are a fun feature.

Auto-ID Labs

`www.autoidlabs.org`

This website is an information source about the Auto-ID Labs (you must have heard about Auto-ID Center), which is an independent network of seven academic research labs that are concentrating on developing new technologies that support and improve global commerce. My favorite part of this website is its Publications section, which includes all Auto-ID Labs white papers, academic publications, pilots, software packages, presentations at workshops, and other information, all of which is searchable by paper type, topic, title, author, year, and text. This website is a great source of information on early research behind the RFID EPC technology.

RFID Switchboard

`www.rfidsb.com`

RFID Switchboard is an interesting type of RFID website. It is not only an information tool consisting of RFID news, but also a tool for learning and creating useful connections that could help you implement the RFID technology. This website includes RFID Guides with an interactive index and the articles sorted related to specific topics; Buyers' Guides, which intend to provide you with information you need to know in order to successfully select products or services (the information is general and vendor-neutral); and discussion forums. You can also sign up for a free weekly newsletter with a witty column by RFID Switchboards's chief. So far, none of this is terribly unusual. That comes now. Through this website, you can anonymously request proposals and pricing information, which can help you compare and select the best provider of the requested products and services. The technology providers can participate by paying a $650 monthly fee to become partners, and in exchange receive qualified leads and use various advertising and marketing features.

RFID Update

`www.rfidupdate.com`

RFID Update hits my inbox every day with great news and views on the RFID market as they happen. It has been responsible for breaking some of the biggest stories in the industry. Launched in early 2004, RFID Update publishes a free editorial briefing every business day for executives deploying RFID. Each issue delivers breaking news and analysis pertinent to successful RFID implementations, helping readers understand global RFID developments as they happen.

Glossary

AB symmetry A technique in which after a tag is inventoried, it changes its state from A to B or from B to A.

Active tags Tags that are able to transmit radio frequency (RF) signals to the environment without being near an interrogation zone or without needing power of some sort from an outside source.

Air interface protocol A protocol that defines the rules of communication between tags and interrogators. The air interface protocol includes rules for encoding, modulation, and anticollision, as well as for reading and writing to a tag and other operations. The protocol usually does not define the tag architecture or encoding capacity of the tag.

ALOHA protocol Developed by the University of Hawaii, this protocol was originally intended to avoid data collision in early LANs. ALOHA mode is based on a node not transmitting and receiving data packets all at once, but instead switching these functions based on time. If a collision occurs, the node transmits the data packet after a random delay.

Anticollision A feature of smart readers that uses polls tags by using certain algorithms to prevent tag collisions (two or more tags responding at the exact same time).

Application-specific integrated circuit (ASIC) An integrated circuit (IC) customized for a particular use, rather than intended for general-purpose use.

Asynchronous algorithm Also known as a probabilistic algorithm, an anticollision method based on tags responding at randomly generated times. This method includes several specific protocols, including the ALOHA protocol.

Baseband-FM0 A method of encoding that has been used by tags under the ISO standards but is now supported by Generation 2 as well. This type of encoding is very fast but susceptible to interference; therefore, it is not usually used in the dense reader mode of operation.

Baseline A performance level that can be used to assess the impact of individual changes on performance and offer insight into the most effective test sequence.

Beaconing Broadcasting a tag's information to the environment at regular intervals.

Bi-static antenna An antenna composed of two separate antennas: one for transmitting the RF signal to the tag and one for receiving the signal from the tag.

Critical boundary The outer edge of the interrogation zone (IZ), where you do not want to read any tags. This is critical to determine, because you may have a forklift with tag items driving by, or a printer printing RFID tags, or something similar, and you wouldn't want to pick up those stray tags.

Data protocol A protocol that specifies the size and structure of the tag memory, tag data formatting and length, and the means of storing, accessing, and transferring information.

Dense reader mode A mode in which readers are able to operate in an environment with many other readers present and are able to avoid or reduce the risk of interference.

Deterministic algorithm See *synchronous algorithm.*

Differential time of arrival (DTOA) DTOA is a method where a tag sends a signal to the environment, and the tag's location is calculated based on the difference in time it takes the signal to travel from the tag to each access point.

Direct thermal A printing method that requires heat-sensitive RFID media and no printing ribbon. Information is printed as the printhead applies heat directly onto a heat-sensitive label.

DoD Construct An identifier defined by the U.S. Department of Defense (DoD) used to encode the 96-bit Class 1 tag that is being shipped to the U.S. DoD, if the supplier has a Commercial and Government Entity (CAGE) code.

Dwell time Also referred to as *time in beam*, dwell time ensures tags are read by the interrogation zone by considering the time when the tags are present in the zone.

Electronic product code (EPC) A family of coding schemes for Gen 2 tags. The EPC is designed to meet the needs of various industries, while guaranteeing uniqueness for all EPC-compliant tags.

Electrostatic discharge (ESD) The rapid release of a charge that has accumulated on a person or object. Most materials can be electrically charged by friction; the charge is highly dependent on the material, speed of contact and separation, and the environmental humidity.

Filter value Used for fast filtering and preselection of defined logistic types.

Frequency hopping A method of switching channels when operating in dense reader mode.

Frequency-division multiplexing The division of the frequency spectrum into multiple channels, so each reader can have its own channel to operate on.

General manager number A number that identifies the organizational entity or company. This number is assigned by EPCglobal and is unique for each entity.

Header Part of the EPC number that carries the information about the encoding scheme used; this determines the type, length, and structure of the EPC. The header is followed by the unique EPC identifier and a filter value. EPC supports several encoding schemes.

High frequency (HF) 13.56 MHz, the globally accepted and implemented frequency at which HF tags operate.

Inductive coupling A process where the tag knows it is going to be in the magnetic field of the reader and is ready to respond appropriately.

Light stack A single tube with red, green, and yellow lights in it. Light stacks are often used to indicate whether the tag applied to the product or packaging functions (green for a read, red for no-read). Light stacks are used with an interrogation zone, where the tag's function is verified and the appropriate light indicates the result. There are several ways to make this work.

Linearity A property of electromagnetic waves. Linear waves do not affect the passage of other waves as they intersect. Thus, the total of two linear waves at their intersection is simply the sum of the two waves as they would exist separately.

Listen-before-talk (LBT) A method of communication used with the frequency-division multiplexing scheme. The reader has to listen for any other reader transmitting on the chosen channel; only after it determines that the channel is available can it start using this channel for communication. If the channel is being used by another reader, the listening reader has to switch to another channel. This technique is mainly required in Europe by regulatory agencies.

Low frequency (LF) A frequency from 125 kHz to 134 kHz, which is the frequency at which LF tags operate.

Microwave frequency Frequencies around 2.45 GHz and sometimes 5.8 GHz. Because of the frequency properties, microwave tags have the highest data-transfer rates of all tags, but the worst performance around liquids and metals.

Miller subcarrier A method of encoding that is slower but less susceptible to interference because of an advanced filtering technique that helps separate the tag responses from the signal transmitted by the reader. This method fits the tag responses between the channels used by the readers. It also guards the readers to prevent them from crossing into the tag channels.

Mono-static antenna An antenna that fulfills both transmitting and receiving functions.

Multi-path interference Caused by reflections of an RF signal interfering with the antenna's field. When the reflected wave crosses the transmitted wave, it causes either null points with no signal, or spots with a high signal concentration.

near field The electrostatic field of an electric charge and the magnetostatic field of a current loop.

near-field region The distance found by applying the Complete Laws to magnetic dipoles by using the formula $r = \lambda/(2\pi)$.

Object class A part of the general identifier (GID) that identifies a type or class of the item. It has to be unique within the general manager number domain. An object class can be a stock-keeping unit (SKU) or a related code, and it is assigned by the company.

Partition Part of the serialized global trade item number (SGTIN) that indicates the point where the company prefix and the item reference are divided, because their length is not fixed.

Passive backscatter Communication based on an electric field, which is out past the magnetic field.

Passive tags Tags that are not able to transmit a signal by themselves, but need energy from the reader to do this.

Permeability A material property that describes the ease with which a magnetic flux is established within the material.

Pneumatic piston label applicator A label applicator that works as follows: As the item approaches the applicator, it passes a sensor that triggers a pneumatic piston. The applicator places the label on a vacuum plate, which is moved by the pneumatic piston to the product. The label is then pressed or blown on this item.

Probabilistic algorithm See *asynchronous algorithm.*

Programmable logic controller (PLC) A small computer used for automation of various functions in device control, manufacturing lines, and other processes.

Q factor Often used as a classification of the quality or efficiency of a resonant circuit, which also applies to RFID tags. "Q" in this case is for "quality."

Reader-talks-first (RTF) Occurs when an active tag waits for an interrogation signal from the reader.

Read-only Occurs when LF tags carry a pre-encoded tag ID, which is then matched to a database in order to retrieve information related to the tag.

Real-time location system (RTLS) A system used to locate RFID-tagged objects within a specific area with relatively high accuracy. RTLS uses active RFID technology.

Received signal strength identification (RSSI) A measurement of signal strength used in RTLS for locating a tagged object. The closer the tag is to the access point, the stronger the signal will be received by the interrogator. Because the location of the access points is known, the tagged object will be found according to the closest access point.

Reserved memory Memory that carries 32-bit Access and 32-bit Kill passwords.

Right-hand rule A way to determine the direction of the magnetic field generated by an electric current. If you grasp the electric current, carrying the wire in your right hand and having your thumb point in the direction of the current, then your fingers will circle the wire in the direction of the magnetic field.

Semi-passive tags See *passive tags.*

Serial number A part of the general identifier. It is a unique number identifying a single item. The number has to be unique within the object class, and it is assigned by the company.

Sessions A technique used by Generation 2 for tag management. Each tag has the capability to operate in four sessions. Each reader or group of readers interrogates tags in a separate session, and therefore does not interfere with other readers when interrogating tags. The session number is sent to a tag during the inventory round.

Slap-and-ship The process of using just a printer that allows you to quickly create RFID labels with an electronic product code (EPC) number encoded on them.

Synchronization The process of synchronizing the transmitting and receiving functions of readers in multiple reader environments in order to avoid interference.

Synchronous algorithm Also known as a deterministic algorithm, this anticollision method is used by Generation 1 tags and is based on a reader going through the tags according to their unique ID.

Tag identification (TID) memory Consists of information about the tag itself, such as tag ID.

Tag-talks-first (TTF) When an active tag sends out the signal first.

Thermal transfer A printing method that requires RFID labels and a printing ribbon. The ribbon is a wax- and/or resin-coated plastic strip that comes in rolls. The coating is transferred by a printhead onto a label, creating the printed information.

Time in beam See *dwell time.*

Time-division multiplexing A process based on readers sending signals on the same frequency in assigned time slots or operating for a certain time interval when other readers are turned off.

Ultra-high frequency (UHF) 860 MHz to 960 MHz, which is the frequency at which passive UHF tags operate. Active tags usually operate around 433 MHz.

User memory Provides a space for user-defined data.

Variable isolation approach The process of isolating a problem by effectively documenting the business process and recording the entire system, component by component.

Voltage standing wave ratio (VSWR) Allows you to tune an antenna properly for whatever resonant frequency you are looking to read across. You can also compare the performance across the antenna.

Wipe-on label applicator A label applicator that works as follows: As the item approaches the applicator, a sensor detects the item and triggers the applicator to issue a label. This label is then "wiped on" the item, and a foam roller helps to press down the label to ensure its hold.

Write-once read-many (WORM) A tag's data or number can be written by the user.

Index

Note to the Reader: Throughout this index **boldfaced** page numbers indicate primary discussions of a topic. *Italicized* page numbers indicate illustrations.

A

B

C

D

F

G

H

I

O

P

Q

R

S

T

U

V

W

X

Z

Wiley Publishing, Inc.
End-User License Agreement

READ THIS. You should carefully read these terms and conditions before opening the software packet(s) included with this book "Book". This is a license agreement "Agreement" between you and Wiley Publishing, Inc. "WPI". By opening the accompanying software packet(s), you acknowledge that you have read and accept the following terms and conditions. If you do not agree and do not want to be bound by such terms and conditions, promptly return the Book and the unopened software packet(s) to the place you obtained them for a full refund.

1.License Grant. WPI grants to you (either an individual or entity) a nonexclusive license to use one copy of the enclosed software program(s) (collectively, the "Software," solely for your own personal or business purposes on a single computer (whether a standard computer or a workstation component of a multi-user network). The Software is in use on a computer when it is loaded into temporary memory (RAM) or installed into permanent memory (hard disk, CD-ROM, or other storage device). WPI reserves all rights not expressly granted herein.

2.Ownership. WPI is the owner of all right, title, and interest, including copyright, in and to the compilation of the Software recorded on the physical packet included with this Book "Software Media". Copyright to the individual programs recorded on the Software Media is owned by the author or other authorized copyright owner of each program. Ownership of the Software and all proprietary rights relating thereto remain with WPI and its licensers.

3.Restrictions On Use and Transfer.

(a) You may only (i) make one copy of the Software for backup or archival purposes, or (ii) transfer the Software to a single hard disk, provided that you keep the original for backup or archival purposes. You may not (i) rent or lease the Software, (ii) copy or reproduce the Software through a LAN or other network system or through any computer subscriber system or bulletin-board system, or (iii) modify, adapt, or create derivative works based on the Software.

(b) You may not reverse engineer, decompile, or disassemble the Software. You may transfer the Software and user documentation on a permanent basis, provided that the transferee agrees to accept the terms and conditions of this Agreement and you retain no copies. If the Software is an update or has been updated, any transfer must include the most recent update and all prior versions.

4.Restrictions on Use of Individual Programs. You must follow the individual requirements and restrictions detailed for each individual program in the About the CD-ROM appendix of this Book or on the Software Media. These limitations are also contained in the individual license agreements recorded on the Software Media. These limitations may include a requirement that after using the program for a specified period of time, the user must pay a registration fee or discontinue use. By opening the Software packet(s), you will be agreeing to abide by the licenses and restrictions for these individual programs that are detailed in the About the CD-ROM appendix and/or on the Software Media. None of the material on this Software Media or listed in this Book may ever be redistributed, in original or modified form, for commercial purposes.

5.Limited Warranty.

(a)WPI warrants that the Software and Software Media are free from defects in materials and workmanship under normal use for a period of sixty (60) days from the date of purchase of this Book. If WPI receives notification within the warranty period of defects in materials or workmanship, WPI will replace the defective Software Media.

(b)WPI AND THE AUTHOR(S) OF THE BOOK DISCLAIM ALL OTHER WARRANTIES, EXPRESS OR IMPLIED, INCLUDING WITHOUT LIMITATION IMPLIED WARRANTIES OF MERCHANTABILITY AND FITNESS FOR A PARTICULAR PURPOSE, WITH RESPECT TO THE SOFTWARE, THE PROGRAMS, THE SOURCE CODE CONTAINED THEREIN, AND/OR THE TECHNIQUES DESCRIBED IN THIS BOOK. WPI DOES NOT WARRANT THAT THE FUNCTIONS CONTAINED IN THE SOFTWARE WILL MEET YOUR REQUIREMENTS OR THAT THE OPERATION OF THE SOFTWARE WILL BE ERROR FREE.

(c)This limited warranty gives you specific legal rights, and you may have other rights that vary from jurisdiction to jurisdiction.

6.Remedies.

(a)WPI's entire liability and your exclusive remedy for defects in materials and workmanship shall be limited to replacement of the Software Media, which may be returned to WPI with a copy of your receipt at the following address: Software Media Fulfillment Department, Attn.: CompTIA RFID+ Study Guide, Wiley Publishing, Inc., 10475 Crosspoint Blvd., Indianapolis, IN 46256, or call 1-800-762-2974. Please allow four to six weeks for delivery. This Limited Warranty is void if failure of the Software Media has resulted from accident, abuse, or misapplication. Any replacement Software Media will be warranted for the remainder of the original warranty period or thirty (30) days, whichever is longer.

(b) In no event shall WPI or the author be liable for any damages whatsoever (including without limitation damages for loss of business profits, business interruption, loss of business information, or any other pecuniary loss) arising from the use of or inability to use the Book or the Software, even if WPI has been advised of the possibility of such damages.

(c)Because some jurisdictions do not allow the exclusion or limitation of liability for consequential or incidental damages, the above limitation or exclusion may not apply to you.

7.U.S. Government Restricted Rights. Use, duplication, or disclosure of the Software for or on behalf of the United States of America, its agencies and/or instrumentalities "U.S. Government" is subject to restrictions as stated in paragraph (c)(1)(ii) of the Rights in Technical Data and Computer Software clause of DFARS 252.227-7013, or subparagraphs (c) (1) and (2) of the Commercial Computer Software - Restricted Rights clause at FAR 52.227-19, and in similar clauses in the NASA FAR supplement, as applicable.

8.General. This Agreement constitutes the entire understanding of the parties and revokes and supersedes all prior agreements, oral or written, between them and may not be modified or amended except in a writing signed by both parties hereto that specifically refers to this Agreement. This Agreement shall take precedence over any other documents that may be in conflict herewith. If any one or more provisions contained in this Agreement are held by any court or tribunal to be invalid, illegal, or otherwise unenforceable, each and every other provision shall remain in full force and effect.

The Absolute Best RFID+ Book/CD Package on the Market!

Get ready for CompTIA's RFID+ exam with the most comprehensive and challenging sample tests anywhere!

The Sybex Test Engine features

- All the review questions, as covered in each chapter of the book
- Challenging questions representative of those you'll find on the real exam
- Two full-length bonus exams available only on the CD
- An Assessment Test to narrow your focus to certain objective groups

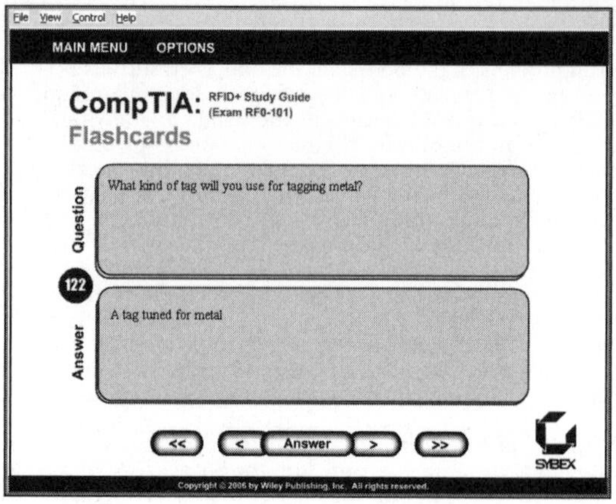

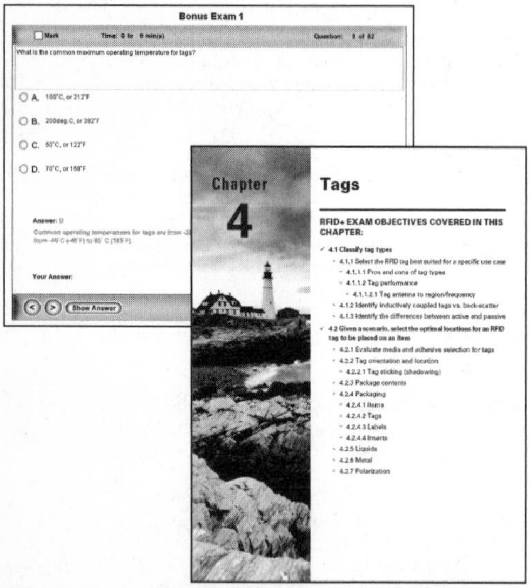

Use the Electronic Flashcards for PCs or Palm devices to jog your memory and prep last-minute for the exam!

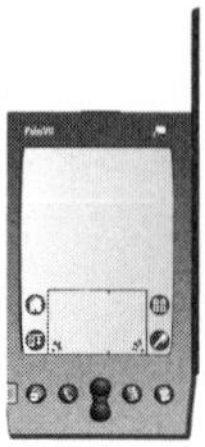

- Reinforce your understanding of key concepts with these hard-core flashcard-style questions.
- Download the flashcards to your Palm device and go on the road. Now you can study for the RFID+ exam anytime, anywhere.

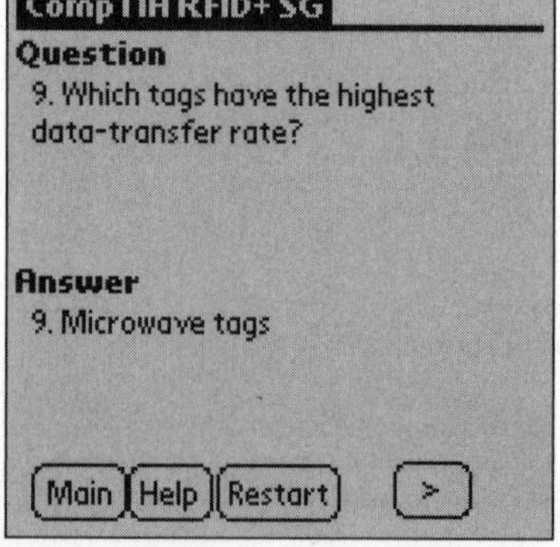

Search through the complete book in PDF!

- Access the entire *CompTIA RFID+ Study Guide*, complete with figures and tables, in electronic format.
- Search the *CompTIA RFID+ Study Guide* chapters to find information on any topic in seconds.